Programmer's Guide
to Internet Mail

Programmer's Guide
to Internet Mail

SMTP, POP, IMAP, and LDAP

John Rhoton

**Digital
Press**

Boston • Oxford • Auckland • Johannesburg • Melbourne • New Delhi

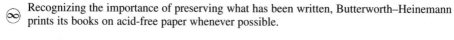

Butterworth–Heinemann supports the efforts of American Forests and the Global ReLeaf program in its campaign for the betterment of trees, forests, and our environment.

Library of Congress Cataloging-in-Publication Data
Rhoton, John.
    Programmer's guide to internet mail : SMTP, POP, IMAP, and LDAP /
    John Rhoton.
      p. cm.
    ISBN 1-55558-212-5
     1. Electronic mail systems.   2. Internet programming.   I. Title.
  TK5105.73.R48   2000
  005.7'1376—dc21   99-36739
                     CIP

British Library Cataloguing-in-Publication Data
A catalogue record for this book is available from the British Library.

The publisher offers special discounts on bulk orders of this book.
For information, please contact:
Manager of Special Sales
Butterworth–Heinemann
225 Wildwood Avenue
Woburn, MA 01801-2041
Tel: 781-904-2500
Fax: 781-904-2620

For information on all Digital Press publications available, contact our World Wide Web home page at: http://www.bh.com/digitalpress

10 9 8 7 6 5 4 3 2

Printed in the United States of America

Niddedikha lil
Għażiża Marti

Contents

Preface

I recently wrote a book called *X.400 and SMTP: Battle of the E-mail Protocols*. While I was researching the standards for SMTP (Simple Mail Transfer Protocol) I was forced to take a look at the Internet mail protocols. Until then I had been under the impression that these were complex interfaces that could only be used with extreme caution. Fortunately, I found that I was mistaken. Not only were they much easier than I had anticipated, but they were fun to play with. You may well think that I have a warped sense of fun, but I found it very satisfying—after working with different messaging systems for more than a dozen years—to observe how Internet mail protocols interoperate, as well as to try to exploit their functionality fully.

Internet mail has swept the computer industry. Products such as Lotus Notes/Domino and Microsoft Exchange Server are continually leapfrogging each other in their support of the newest protocols. There is no question that it has become the mail backbone of the decade.

When you have finished this book, I hope that you will agree that it is with good reason that the mail community has so wholeheartedly embraced these standards.

Audience

There are broadly two types of people who I feel would benefit from *Programmer's Guide to Internet Mail:*

- *Mail administrators, solution architects, product specialists, IT managers.* These people can benefit from a deeper understanding of how mail works. An understanding of how the interfaces work and what internal mechanisms they represent makes it much easier to predict and understand how these systems will behave.

- *Application developers, software engineers, engineering managers.* Most applications could benefit from being mail-enabled. In some cases it would be enough to send messages in response to certain events. Other applications may need to access user information stored in a directory, or may require a structured repository similar to a post office. Knowledge of the protocols is essential for making the right decisions regarding when to mail enable and how.

Code Examples

Rather than formulating abstract descriptions I have tried to implement a set of functions for each code. To illustrate I have provided examples written in Visual Basic 5.0. There is no reason my examples could not be adapted to other programming languages, such as C++ or Java. I have chosen Visual Basic (VB) since it is fairly simple (i.e., comprehensible even by developers who do not ordinarily program in Basic) and because there are a large number of VB programmers around. I would hazard a guess that C++ programmers will have fewer problems understanding VB than vice versa. At the same time, I would be very cautious about writing production software in VB, since it is neither the most efficient nor the most robust tool for the job.

The code in *Programmer's Guide to Internet Mail* is not intended for production. I would also add a few words of warning to anyone who makes use of the code that I have provided. I have deliberately omitted the bulk of error checking and recovery. I may have been partially motivated by laziness, but more importantly, my intent was to show how the protocols operate. I believe that fully robust programs would not be nearly as comprehensible as the simplified versions I have provided. They work, assuming that they are fed consistent and not completely marginal data. But don't expect meaningful responses to unconventional commands or a graceful recovery if you send corrupt data!

Structure

Programmer's Guide to Internet Mail begins with an overview of the Internet mail formats and protocols and how they interrelate. This first chapter is essentially a synopsis of the rest of the book. The second chapter gives some relevant information on the underlying networking protocols (with particular attention to Winsock). I begin the practical examples in the third chapter with some illustrations of how to use Winsock to build both clients and servers and how to use these tools to analyze Internet protocols.

The next set of chapters deals with each of the relevant protocols in sequence. I begin with those dealing with mail message formats (RFC822 and MIME) and continue on with message transfer (SMTP and DNS). There is a discussion of the post office protocols (POP and IMAP). Finally, there are the directory protocols (ASN and LDAP). The book concludes with a final chapter that ties everything together and gives a taste of what has been left untouched.

References

You may be interested in exploring some of the areas covered in this book in more detail, or you may wish to broaden your understanding of the background. Some of the topics you might consider include the following areas.

Books

GENERAL NETWORKING

Computer Networks by Andrew S. Tanenbaum (Prentice Hall, 1996). ISBN 0-13-349945-6.

TCP AND IP

TCP/IP Explained by Philip Miller (Digital Press, Butterworth–
Heinemann, 1997). ISBN 1-55558-166-8.

TCP/IP Illustrated by Gary R. Wright and W. Richard Stevens
(Addison Wesley, 1995). ISBN 0-201-63354-X.

TCP/IP and Related Protocols by Ulysses Black (McGraw-Hill,
1995). ISBN 0-07-113296-1.

WINSOCK

Networking Programming with Windows Sockets by Patrice Bonner
(Prentice Hall Computer Books, 1995). ISBN 0-13-230152-0.

Windows Sockets Network Programming by Bob Quinn and David K.
Shute (Addison-Wesley Publishing, 1995). ISBN 0-201-63372-8.

Winsock 2.0 by Lewis Napper (IDG Books Worldwide, 1997). ISBN
0-7645-8049-3.

CONCEPTUAL COMPARISON OF INTERNET MAIL AND X.400

X.400 and SMTP: Battle of the E-mail Protocols by John Rhoton
(Digital Press, Butterworth–Heinemann, 1997). ISBN 1-55558-
165-X.

VISUAL BASIC

Fortunately, there are many good books on Visual Basic and they are
readily available. Unfortunately, new versions of Visual Basic quickly
make the old books obsolete. Since I am sure you will have no trouble locating material on the language I will refrain from offering a specific recommendation and refer you to your local technical bookstore.

On the Web

If you need help understanding any particular facet of Internet mail,
the Web is your best friend. I suspect that you will be able to find

answers to almost any of your questions there, somewhere. To get you started in the right direction I have included a few URLs.

INTERNET MAIL CONSORTIUM

http://www.imc.org

Contains information on many of the (draft and approved) standards relating to Internet mail.

INTERNET MAIL STANDARDS

ftp://ds.internic.net/rfc/

This is the authoritative location for the current list of Internet Mail Standards, also known as Request for Comments (RFCs).

INTERNATIONAL TELECOMMUNICATIONS UNION-TELECOMMUNICATIONS STANDARDIZATION SECTOR (ITU-T)

http://www.itu.int/

The ITU-T (formerly known as CCITT) has developed a very large list of international standards that are largely incompatible with the Internet RFCs. There are, however, a few that do concern us. In particular, LDAP (a "lightweight" version of the ITU-T standard DAP) utilizes X.208 and X.209 to encapsulate data.

Questions and Feedback

If you have any questions on the contents of *Programmer's Guide to Internet Mail*, or want to let me know what you thought of it, please don't hesitate to send me mail. At the time of this writing, my ever-changing E-mail address was John.Rhoton@compaq.com. I would love to hear from you.

Acknowledgments

I would like to thank Olivier D'hose and Tony Redmond for their help in reviewing this book and providing valuable suggestions for improvement. I would also like to recognize Phil Sutherland and all the others at Digital Press who worked with me to edit and publish my manuscript. In particular, I am very grateful to Pam Chester for her considerable effort in ensuring my documents fit the submission guidelines.

Claudia, my wife, was not directly involved with the production of this book and yet, I would never have been able to complete it without her never-tiring support and understanding.

Chapter 1

Internet Mail

To most people, E-mail is a mysterious application that takes their message and magically ensures it is delivered to someone else they have chosen. The average user is not interested in what is happening behind the scenes as long as it works. But E-mail, like most systems, is composed of individual parts, such as the functions of a mail system:

1. Message submission and delivery to target system
2. Message retrieval from a central host
3. Directory lookup

As we shall see later on, it so happens that the Internet Mail standards fall in line with this division of functionality and provide interfaces for each.

Message System Topology

Another way of looking at a mail system is to identify the components that use these interfaces. You can see a typical mail topology in Figure 1.1. There are three components that roughly correspond to the interfaces above.

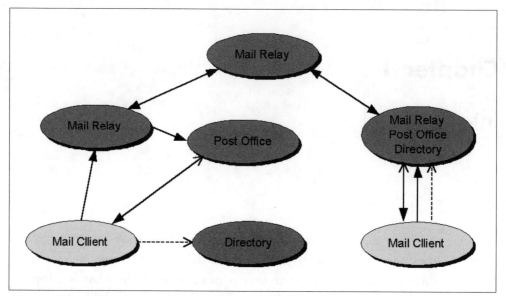

Figure 1.1 *Mail and directory topology*

Mail Relay

A mail relay takes mail from one component, which could be a mail client or another mail relay, and transfers the messages on to another component. This could likewise be another relay or it could be a post office.

Directory

A directory is a service that allows users to look up another person's E-mail address as well as other information. You might think of your personal address book as a directory, or you might have a central server in a larger company that contains every address. E-mail industry leaders suggested early on that we allow different companies to access each other's directories in order to create a global directory. Four11 Switchboard and other systems have since provided this type of functionality via a Web browser.[1] However, their applications are accessed via HTTP rather than the protocols described here.

---

[1] http://www.switchboard.com, http://www.four11.com, and http://www.bigfoot.com are a few of many Web sites providing people-search capability.

Post Office

The post office is primarily a repository of messages that a user may later retrieve. I classify host-based messaging systems as post offices too, although they do not typically use this terminology.

Before we begin to look at the protocols of mail relay, directory, and post office we must first understand the structure of the data (e.g., messages, directory requests, and responses) that they use to communicate.

Duality of Protocols

In Table 1.1 you can see which components implement which protocols. As you will notice, each protocol is implemented by two entities. This is not a coincidence. A standard data format is useless without two accompanying actions. Firstly, it must be encoded. Usually it is not the native format of an application, so you must convert your data to achieve the standard.

Of course, having data in a particular format is only interesting if you can also read it. Thus, secondly, it must be decoded. Someone must also write code to interpret the data structure and parse it into meaningful components.

It is not much different with protocols. It is hoped that someone will receive every piece of data sent across the network. And someone has presumably sent anything we receive. This means that every command must also be encoded and decoded.

Table 1.1 *Two Parts of Protocols*

Sending Client	Server	Receiving Client
SMTP	SMTP	
RFC 822		RFC 822
MIME		MIME
	POP	POP
	IMAP	IMAP
LDAP	LDAP	

Client and Server

While there are inherently two participants in any protocol session. The relationship between the participants is not typically symmetrical. One of them initiates the session and is called the client. The other waits for connections and is called the server. Note that there is no indication that a server holds the data. The only distinction is who requests the session. The role of composition/interpretation may change during the protocol session. Usually the client manages the connection (i.e., decides what will be done). It does so by sending requests, which trigger responses from the server.

RFC 822

Internet mail messages all adhere to the same standard format. Unfortunately, in contrast to most other standards, this one has no real name. RFC 822[2] is titled *Standard for the Format of ARPA Internet Text Messages*. This is clearly a bit long for everyday use so most people just refer to it as RFC 822.

In Figure 1.3 you can see an example of what a message in RFC 822 format (Figure 1.2) might look like if you viewed it using a Pegasus client.

```
Date: Fri, 31 Dec 99 23:00 -0000
From: "Prometheus" prometheus@know.it.all
To: "Phoebe" phoebe@looney
Subject: Science Exam Paper
The Earth makes one resolution every 24 hours.
We believe that the reptiles came from the amphibians by spontaneous
generation and study of rocks.
A triangle which has an angle of 135 degrees is called an obscene triangle.
Bar magnets have north and south poles, horseshoe magnets have east and
west poles.
When you smell an odorless gas, it is probably carbon monoxide.
```

Figure 1.2 *Example of RFC 822 message*

---

[2] RFC stands for Request for Comment. All Internet standards are initially proposed as RFCs and circulated within the Internet Engineering Task Force and other interested parties. Even after they are adopted as standards, they are still frequently referred to by their RFC number.

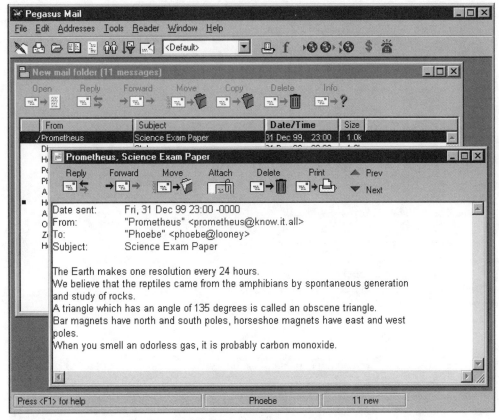

Figure 1.3 *Pegasus display of RFC 822 message*

MIME

Although RFC 822 is the standard Internet mail format, it does have some inadequacies that make it insufficient for today's use. For example, it does not permit 8-bit characters. This makes it difficult to send messages in many languages. (English is one of the very few languages that uses only 7-bit characters.) It also makes it impossible to send binary data such as executable programs.

RFC 822 has no facility for structuring multiple bodyparts. If I want to forward several files in one message, for instance, I can only concatenate them together and hope my recipient can figure out what to do with them.

To address these needs some additional RFCs have been written that extend RFC 822 without breaking existing mail readers. The

```
Date: Fri, 31 Dec 99 23:02 -0000
From: Hephaestus <Hephaestus@only.skindeep>
To: Themis <Themis@just.order>
Subject: College Entry Exam
MIME-Version: 1.0
Content-Type: multipart/mixed; boundary="—Boundary.2995219.5476435—"

—Boundary.2995219.5476435—

Time Limit: 1 year
Minimum to pass:  1 question answered correctly


—Boundary.2995219.5476435—
Content-Type: text/plain; name="exam.txt"
Content-Transfer-Encoding: 7bit

1. What language is spoken in France?
2. Would you ask William Shakespeare to
 (a) build a bridge
 (b) sail the ocean
 (c) lead an army or
 (d) WRITE A PLAY
3. What time is it when the big hand is on the 12 and the little hand
is on the 5?
4. Six kings of England have been called George, the last one being
George the Sixth. Name the previous five.
5. Can you explain Einstein's Theory of Relativity?
 (a) yes
 (b) no
6. Advanced math. If you have three apples how many apples do you have?

—Boundary.2995219.5476435—
Content-Type: application/octet-stream; name="short.exe"
Content-Transfer-Encoding: base64

VGhpcyBpcyBhIGR1bW15IGZpbGUA

—Boundary.2995219.5476435——
```

Figure 1.4 *Example of MIME message*

RFCs numbered 2045 to 2049 are known collectively as MIME (Multipurpose Internet Mail Extensions). As you can see in Figure 1.4, the format is a little less straightforward than RFC 822, but it

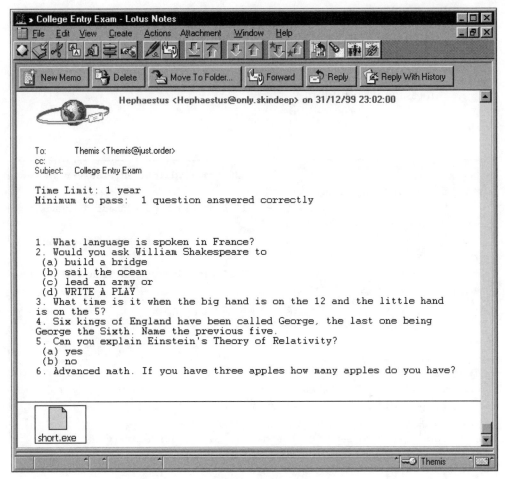

Figure 1.5 *Lotus Notes display of MIME message*

permits mail clients like Lotus Notes (Figure 1.5) to provide more functionality to the user.

SMTP

SMTP (Simple Mail Transfer Protocol) is the core protocol of Internet mail. It takes care of delivering mail from one system to another. Unlike directories and post offices, which are not absolutely critical to mail, the transfer of messages is the essence of a messaging system. In heterogeneous environments it is also the protocol that most needs a standard since it typically connects a large number of computer systems. Figure 1.6 shows a protocol session for delivering a very simple message.

In Figure 1.7 you can see what this might look like if you sent the message with Eudora.

```
                              220 oracle.delphi SMTP Server ready⇐
⇒mail from:<zeus@dont.stealmy.thunder>
                     250 OK - mail from <zeus@dont.stealmy.thunder>⇐
⇒rcpt to:<epimetheus@no.brainer>
                     250 OK - Recipient <epimetheus@no.brainer>⇐
⇒data
                     354 Send data.   End with CRLF.CRLF⇐
⇒Date: Fri, 31 Dec 99 23:04 -0000
⇒From: "Zeus" <zeus@dont.stealmy.thunder>
⇒To: "Epimetheus" <epimetheus@no.brainer>
⇒Subject: Letter to Son
⇒
⇒Dear Son,
⇒  I'm writing this slow 'cause I know you can't read fast. We don't live
⇒  where we did when you left. Your dad read in the paper where the most
⇒  accidents happened within twenty miles of home,...so we moved.
⇒  I wont be able to send you the address as the last family that lived
⇒  here took the numbers with them for their next house so they wouldn't
⇒  have to change their address, wish I would have thought of that.
⇒  About your sister, she had a baby this morning. I haven't found out
⇒  whether it is a boy or a girl. So I don't know if you are an aunt or
⇒  uncle.
⇒
⇒Love, Mom.
⇒
⇒P.S. I WAS GOING TO SEND YOU MONEY, but the envelope was already
⇒sealed.
⇒.
                                                      250 OK⇐
⇒quit
                              221 closing connection⇐
```

Figure 1.6 *Example of SMTP Protocol Session*

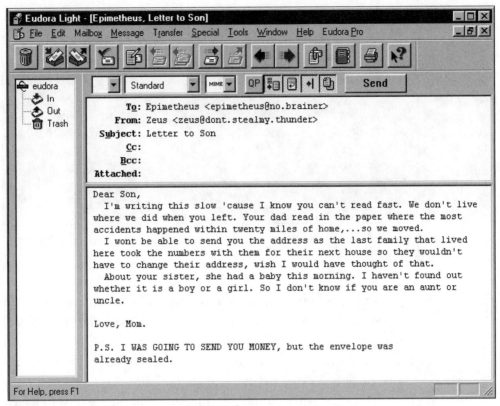

Figure 1.7 *Using Eudora to compose an SMTP message*

DNS

Domain Name System is a distributed database shared and used by millions of users worldwide. While it started out primarily as a mechanism for mapping Internet domains (e.g., www.compaq.com) to Internet addresses (e.g., 207.18.199.3), it has been extended to include several other types of resources. The DNS standard continues to evolve, in particular through Microsoft's promotion of Dynamic DNS in Windows 2000.

In order to contain this broad topic I have limited my discussion on DNS to its involvement with mail. The flow of Internet mail through a network is managed through so-called MX (Mail Exchange) records. Each Internet mail domain has one or more MX records in DNS. When

```
C:\WINNT\System32\command.com                              _ □ X
C:\>nslookup
Default Server:  oracle.delphi
Address:  10.1.1.1

> set type=mx
> chariotsof.fire
Server:  oracle.delphi
Address:  10.1.1.1

chariotsof.fire    MX preference = 10, mail exchanger = chariot1.fire
chariotsof.fire    MX preference = 10, mail exchanger = chariot2.fire
chariotsof.fire    nameserver = oracle.delphi
chariot1.fire      internet address = 10.1.2.1
chariot2.fire      internet address = 10.1.2.2
oracle.delphi      internet address = 10.1.1.1
> exit

C:\>_
```

Figure 1.8 *Lookup of MX record for "chariotsof.fire" using the NT command* nslookup

a mail router attempts to send mail to a particular domain, it looks up the records and attempts to send to the host with the lowest preference.

In the example given in Figure 1.8, a system attempting to deliver mail addressed to the fictitious[3] domain chariotsof.fire would find records with the same preference: chariot1.fire and chariot2.fire. Assuming that both were available, the system could then randomly choose the host to which to send the mail. This technique (two records with equal preference) is frequently used to load-balance incoming mail traffic.

POP

POP (Post Office Protocol) is the original Internet standard for retrieving mail messages from a server. If all computers were online all the time, then POP would not really be necessary or useful. Mail would just be delivered to the recipient's PC where it could be read

---

[3] The examples in this book refer mostly to fictitious domains. Present restrictions limit the top level (last element) of all public domain names to a small set including *com, gov, edu, mil,* and most of the two-letter ISO (International Organization for Standardization) country codes. There are no technical reasons for these restrictions, and there has been some debate on removing them. Within a private network there are no such restrictions.

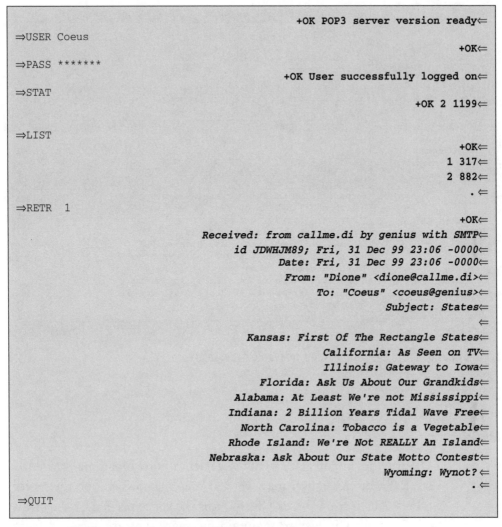

```
                                         +OK POP3 server version ready⇐
⇒USER Coeus
                                                                  +OK⇐
⇒PASS ******
                                   +OK User successfully logged on⇐
⇒STAT
                                                        +OK 2 1199⇐

⇒LIST
                                                               +OK⇐
                                                            1 317⇐
                                                            2 882⇐
                                                              . ⇐
⇒RETR  1
                                                               +OK⇐
                            Received: from callme.di by genius with SMTP⇐
                               id JDWHJM89; Fri, 31 Dec 99 23:06 -0000⇐
                                 Date: Fri, 31 Dec 99 23:06 -0000⇐
                                 From: "Dione" <dione@callme.di>⇐
                                  To: "Coeus" <coeus@genius>⇐
                                       Subject: States⇐
                                                       ⇐
                        Kansas: First Of The Rectangle States⇐
                              California: As Seen on TV⇐
                              Illinois: Gateway to Iowa⇐
                        Florida: Ask Us About Our Grandkids⇐
                        Alabama: At Least We're not Mississippi⇐
                        Indiana: 2 Billion Years Tidal Wave Free⇐
                        North Carolina: Tobacco is a Vegetable⇐
                        Rhode Island: We're Not REALLY An Island⇐
                        Nebraska: Ask About Our State Motto Contest⇐
                                    Wyoming: Wynot? ⇐
                                                 . ⇐
⇒QUIT
```

Figure 1.9 *Example of POP3 Protocol Session*

upon request. But since most people turn their PCs off regularly, it is useful to have a server hold any incoming messages until the user comes back online. POP defines the interaction between a client and the server holding the messages.

In Figure 1.9 you can see a simple transaction to list messages on the server. Figure 1.10 shows you what this might look like if you were using Microsoft Outlook to download the messages.

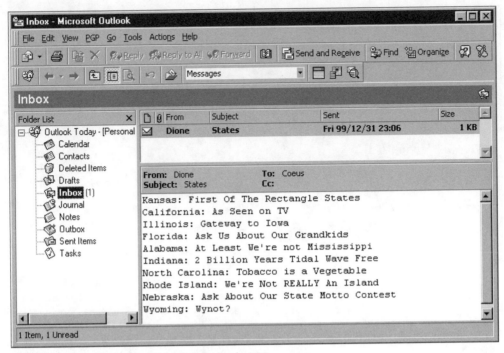

Figure 1.10 *Microsoft Outlook downloads POP messages*

IMAP

POP provides an interface to allow a client to download mail from the server. But often the user may want to keep the messages on the server and read them from there. This reduces the space needed by the client and also makes it easy to maintain messages that are accessed from different points. Thus, if a user needs to frequently visit other offices, she can still access mail by using someone else's PC.

IMAP (Interactive Mail Access Protocol) is much more extensive than POP. As you can see in Figure 1.11, the underlying protocol is not quite as intuitive as POP, but, to make up for that lack, it is more powerful. It provides many functions for a user to manage his mailbox, including the support of hierarchical folders (Figure 1.12).

```
                                    * OK IMAP4rev1 server version 5 ready⇐
⇒0009 CAPABILITY
                                              * CAPABILITY IMAP4⇐
                                    0009 OK CAPABILITY completed. ⇐
⇒000C LOGIN "OFFICESI\\Rhoton\\JohnR" "noubliezpas"
                                        000C OK LOGIN completed. ⇐
⇒000E LSUB "" "*"
                                        * LSUB () "/" INBOX⇐
                                        * LSUB () "/" Play⇐
                                    * LSUB () "/" Play/Games⇐
                                   * LSUB () "/" Play/Humour⇐
                                        * LSUB () "/" Work⇐
                                   * LSUB () "/" Work/Articles⇐
                                   * LSUB () "/" Work/Projects⇐
                           * LSUB () "/" Work/Projects/Completed⇐
                     * LSUB () "/" "Work/Projects/In Progress"⇐
                                       000E OK LSUB completed. ⇐
⇒000I SELECT " Play/Humour"
                                              * 252 EXISTS⇐
                                              * 0 RECENT⇐
                  * FLAGS (\Seen \Answered \Flagged \Deleted \Draft) ⇐
                  * OK [UNSEEN 2] Is the first unseen message⇐
                  * OK [UIDVALIDITY 422] UIDVALIDITY value. ⇐
                  000I OK [READ-WRITE] SELECT completed. ⇐
```

Figure 1.11 *Example of IMAP4 Protocol Session*

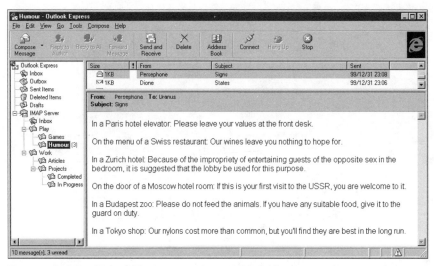

Figure 1.12 *Outlook Express accesses IMAP folders*

ASN.1

So far all of our protocols have been text-based. In other words, our commands and their parameters are sent over the network encoded in ASCII. There is an advantage to making the protocols easier for humans to understand, even though they are transparent to the end-users (human users). Someone has to troubleshoot the protocols or at least program them. Anything to make life easier for these people (who are us, by the way!) is generally appreciated.

Nonetheless, we now come to another protocol and it is not text-based. LDAP, as we shall see in this section, uses ASN.1 format for sending requests and responses. ASN.1 is not an Internet standard. It was designed by the ITU-T (formerly known as CCITT), the same people who have given us X.25, X.400, and, most importantly, (for LDAP later on) X.500.

You might wonder why anyone would use a terse binary format. While its advantages may not outweigh its disadvantages there are a couple of points in its favor:

1. It is more concise (needs less space).

2. It is easier to parse (in my opinion, anyhow).

```
Certificate                          ::=     SIGNED { SEQUENCE {
 version                    [0]      Version DEFAULT v1,
 serialNumber                        CertificateSerialNumber,
 signature                           AlgorithmIdentifier,
 issuer                              Name,
 validity                            Validity,
 subject                             Name,
 subjectPublicKeyInfo                SubjectPublicKeyInfo,
 issuerUniqueIdentifier     [1]      IMPLICIT UniqueIdentifier OPTIONAL,
 subjectUniqueIdentifier    [2]      IMPLICIT UniqueIdentifier OPTIONAL}
Validity                                     ::=     SEQUENCE {
      notBefore       UTCTime,
      notAfter        UTCTime }
SubjectPublicKeyInfo                         ::=     SEQUENCE {
      algorithm                      AlgorithmIdentifier,
      subjectPublicKey               BIT STRING }
```

Figure 1.13 *X.509 Certificate in ASN.1 format*[4]

---

[4] X.509 §8

```
ASN.1 Definition
LDAPResult ::=
      SEQUENCE {
          resultCode   ENUMERATED {
                            success                          (0),
                            operationsError                  (1),
                            protocolError                    (2),
                            timeLimitExceeded                (3),
                            sizeLimitExceeded                (4),
                            compareFalse                     (5),
                            compareTrue                      (6),
                            authMethodNotSupported           (7),
                            strongAuthRequired               (8),
                            noSuchAttribute                  (16),
                            undefinedAttributeType           (17),
                            inappropriateMatching            (18),
                            constraintViolation              (19),
                            attributeOrValueExists           (20),
                            invalidAttributeSyntax           (21),
                            noSuchObject                     (32),
                            aliasProblem                     (33),
                            invalidDNSyntax                  (34),
                            isLeaf                           (35),
                            aliasDereferencingProblem        (36),
                            inappropriateAuthentication      (48),
                            invalidCredentials               (49),
                            insufficientAccessRights         (50),
                            busy                             (51),
                            unavailable                      (52),
                            unwillingToPerform               (53),
                            loopDetect                       (54),
                            namingViolation                  (64),
                            objectClassViolation             (65),
                            notAllowedOnNonLeaf              (66),
                            notAllowedOnRDN                  (67),
                            entryAlreadyExists               (68),
                            objectClassModsProhibited        (69),
                            other                            (80)
                        },
          matchedDN      LDAPDN,
          errorMessage   LDAPString
      }

BindResponse ::= [APPLICATION 1] LDAPResult
```

```
ASN.1 Structure
[UNIVERSAL  16]  12
   [UNIVERSAL  2]  1 1
   [APPLICATION  1]  7
      [UNIVERSAL  10]  1 0
      [UNIVERSAL  4]  0 ><
      [UNIVERSAL  4]  0 ><
```

```
ASN.1 Data
48   12   2   1   1  97   7  10   1   0   4   0   4   0
```

Figure 1.14 *Example of ASN.1*

One ASN.1-encoded object that is currently becoming very popular is the X.509 Certificate (Figure 1.13) that is used to ensure the validity of public encryption keys. Within the scope of this book, the most important use of ASN.1 is for LDAP.

One of the LDAP objects is an LDAP result. In Figure 1.14 you can see its data *Definition*, as well as a sample encoding, both shown in the form of a *Structure* as well as the binary *Data*. You may find it a little difficult to correlate the three if you have never seen ASN.1 before, but I hope that by the time you finish this book, you will have no problem understanding their relationship.

LDAP

The name LDAP (Lightweight Directory Access Protocol) contains an indication that it is not an original protocol. In fact, it is a simplification of DAP (Directory Access Protocol) defined by the ITU-T in the X.500 recommendations. Some restrictions have been imposed to make implementation a little easier, but the biggest obstacle to many (ASN.1-encoded data) is still there.

Fortunately, the subset we will be looking at is not too difficult to follow, so you needn't be intimidated by the binary format. In Figure 1.15 you can see a subset of an LDAP transaction. If you are using Netscape Communicator, you might see the transaction in the course of a search that is similar to Figure 1.16.

```
⇒
  [UNIVERSAL  16]  12
   [UNIVERSAL  2]  1 1
   [APPLICATION  0]  7
    [UNIVERSAL  2]  1 3
    [UNIVERSAL  4]  0 ><
    [ 0]  0 −
                                                        [UNIVERSAL  16]  12    ⇐
                                                         [UNIVERSAL  2]  1 1
                                                         [APPLICATION  1]  7
                                                          [UNIVERSAL  10]  1 0
                                                          [UNIVERSAL  4]  0 ><
                                                          [UNIVERSAL  4]  0 ><
⇒
  [UNIVERSAL  16]  49
   [UNIVERSAL  2]  1 2
   [APPLICATION  3]  44
    [UNIVERSAL  4]  0 ><
    [UNIVERSAL  10]  1 2
    [UNIVERSAL  10]  1 3
    [UNIVERSAL  2]  1 10
    [UNIVERSAL  2]  1 30
    [UNIVERSAL  1]  1 −
    [ 4]  13
      [UNIVERSAL  4]  2 >cn<
      [UNIVERSAL  16]  7
       [ 0]  5 >demet<
     [UNIVERSAL  16]  10
      [UNIVERSAL  4]  2 >cn<
      [UNIVERSAL  4]  4 >mail<

                    [UNIVERSAL  16]  78                            ⇐
                     [UNIVERSAL  2]  1 2
                     [APPLICATION  4]  73
                      [UNIVERSAL  4]  20 >cn=Demeter,l=Olympus<
                      [UNIVERSAL  16]  49
                       [UNIVERSAL  16]  15
                       [UNIVERSAL  4]  2 >cn<
                       [UNIVERSAL  17]  9
                          [UNIVERSAL  4]  7 >Demeter<
                       [UNIVERSAL  16]  30
                        [UNIVERSAL  4]  4 >mail<
                        [UNIVERSAL  17]  22
                          [UNIVERSAL  4]  20 >demeter@the4.seasons<
⇒
  [UNIVERSAL  16]  12
   [UNIVERSAL  2]  1 2
   [APPLICATION  5]  7
    [UNIVERSAL  10]  1 0
    [UNIVERSAL  4]  0 ><
    [UNIVERSAL  4]  0 ><
```

Figure 1.15 *Example of LDAP*

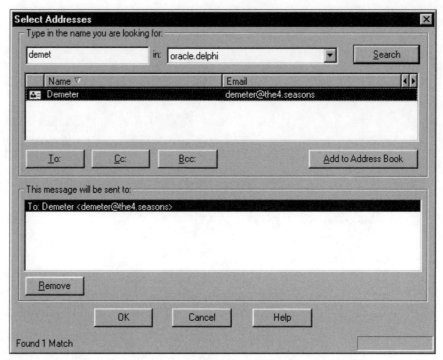

Figure 1.16 *Netscape Communicator lookup of LDAP addresses*

Protocols in Perspective

Now that we have gone through the protocols and formats one by one, I will try to put them into perspective for you by walking through some typical examples. See Figure 1.17 for reference.

Let's start with a user (*Oceanus*) running MailClient1. The user wants to send mail to another user (*Tethys*) running MailClient2. *Oceanus's* first action is to look up *Tethys's* E-mail address. His mail client sends an LDAP request of "Name=*Tethys*" to Directory1. The directory returns an LDAP response with her E-mail address (tethys@white.water).

After entering the rest of the message, *Oceanus* presses the Send key and his client creates a message in the RFC 822 (with or without MIME extensions) format and sends it via SMTP to MailRelay1. MailRelay1 makes a DNS lookup to see where to send the message. It

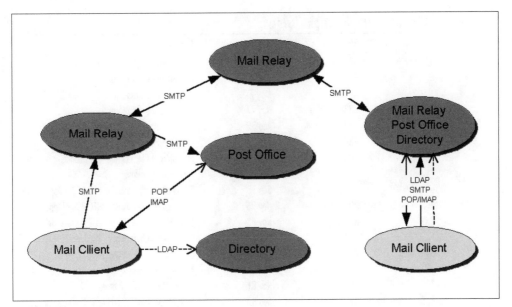

Figure 1.17 *Protocols in perspective*

finds both MailRelay2 and MailRelay3. So it sends the message via SMTP to MailRelay2. MailRelay2 does the same and passes the message on to MailRelay3.

MailRelay3 sees that *Tethys* is on its own post office (PostOffice2), so it stores her message there. Later in the day *Tethys* starts up MailClient2 and checks on PostOffice2 (with POP or IMAP) to see if any messages have arrived. She finds a message from *Oceanus*.

Revisions of Internet Mail Protocols

Standards are in a constant state of flux. Those that do not adapt usually find their way to obsolescence and disuse. A quick glance at Table 1.2 will reassure you that this is not the case with Internet mail. It will also give you a chronological view of the standards we will be using.

If you would like some historical background on the protocols, their specifications and their predecessors are a good place to start.

Table 1.2 *RFC Revision History*[5]

Protocol	RFC	Date	Changes
RFC 822	561	Sep 73	First Standardization of Mail Headers
	680	Apr 75	Addition of Mail Headers
	724	May 77	Support for Address Lists
	733	Nov 77	Formalization of Protocol
	822	Aug 82	Support Retransmission, Simplified Syntax
MIME	934	Jan 85	First Standard for Message Encapsulation
	1049	Mar 88	First Standard for Content-Type Headers
	1341-1342	Jun 92	First MIME Standard
	1521-1522	Sep 93	14 Small changes listed in RFC 1521, Appendix H
	2045-2049	Nov 96	32 Small changes listed in RFC 2049, Appendix B
DNS	882-883	Nov 83	Initial Standard for the Domain Name System
	1034-1035	Nov 87	MX records, other changes listed in RFC 973
SMTP	772	Sep 80	First draft of Mail Transfer Protocol, based on FTP
	780	May 81	Mail Transfer Protocol
	788	Nov 81	Simple Mail Transfer Protocol
	821	Aug 82	Inclusion of TURN, elaboration of some sections
POP	918	Oct 84	POP V1
	937	Feb 85	POP V2
	1081	Nov 88	POP V3
	1225	May 91	Republication
	1460	Jun 93	Removal of RPOP, addition of APOP
	1725	Nov 94	Removal of LAST, addition of TOP
	1939	May 96	Clarification and elaboration
IMAP	1064	Jul 88	IMAP V2
	1176	Aug 90	Minor changes
	1730	Dec 94	IMAP V4
	2060	Dec 96	IMAP V4rev1, changes listed in Appendix B
LDAP	1487	Jul 93	LDAP
	1777	Mar 95	LDAP V2
	2251-3	Dec 97	LDAP V3

---

[5] See ftp://ds.internic.net/rfc/

Chapter 2

Network Protocols

It is possible to write mail-enabled programs and manage E-mail networks with only a limited understanding of networks and their underlying protocols. Nevertheless, the more you know about the building blocks of your system the better you can understand why things work the way the do (or don't). This can only help you to do your job better.

I have tried to isolate some of the components of the Internet networking protocols that I think might be of value. Beyond these, you may wish to consult literature specifically targeted to networks.[1]

Networking protocols address a number of challenges at the same time:

1. How do we allow multiple applications to share a link using a single physical medium (wire, air, optical cable, etc)? (Multiplexing)

2. How do applications synchronize operation with their counterparts on the remote machines? (Flow Control)

3. When there are multiple hosts and network lines, how do we determine the path for communication to our remote correspondent? (Addressing, Routing)

4. How do we recover from errors in transmission? (Checksums, Retransmission)

---

[1] Two such books include *TCP/IP Illustrated* by Gary R. Wright and W. Richard Stevens (Addison Wesley, 1995, ISBN 0-201-63354-X), and *Computer Networks* by Andrew Tanenbaum (Prentice Hall, 1996, ISBN 0-13-329945-6).

Given the complexity of each of these issues, we obviously need to structure our networks to ensure that we are able to satisfactorily address all such needs.

Networks have been historically organized into layers as a way of decomposing and modularizing their functionality. Today the most accepted model for networks is called the OSI model. Virtually all networking architectures describe their components in terms of how they fit this model.

IP Stack

If you look at Figure 2.1 you will see that the Internet protocols do not match the model exactly. Most network designers today would acknowledge that the model is top-heavy. In other words, there are too many layers at the top and not enough at the bottom. Consequently, we will find that the protocols we'll be looking at in this book are comparatively simple, yet span several OSI (Open Systems Interconnect) layers. At the same time, the data-link layer (which we can take for granted) has to provide multiple complex functions. I guess we are just lucky!

Network Layer	Protocols				
Application					
Presentation	DNS	SMTP	POP	IMAP	LDAP
Session					
Transport	UDP	TCP			
Network	IP				
Data Link					
Physical					

Figure 2.1 *Relationship of TCP/IP Protocols to OSI model*

Internet Protocol

IP (Internet Protocol) is specified in RFC 791 and operates at the network layer. The primary purpose of this layer is to take packages of data and transfer them to their destination. If you look at Figure 2.2 you will notice the highlighted fields indicating the source and desti-

Version	IHL	Type of Service	Total Length	
Identification			Flags	Fragment Offset
Time to Live		Protocol	Header Checksum	
Source Address				
Destination Address				
Options				Padding
Transport Level Data				

Figure 2.2 *Internet Datagram*

nation addresses. The network module of each node looks at the destination address of each packet and then decides where to send the packet next by looking up the shortest path in its routing tables.

Most of the other fields are not of interest to us. IP also does some basic error checking and fragmentation to pass through dissimilar networks, but essentially IP takes no responsibility for delivering its datagrams or for notifying the sender if anything goes wrong. It is fun being an IP module. If you don't like the data you receive you can just ignore it!

The only other field we are interested in is the *protocol*. Since there are multiple transport-level protocols on most nodes, the receiving IP must know to whom to give each packet when it receives it. In our case, this will usually be TCP (Transmission Control Protocol). The value of the protocol field is 6 if the protocol is TCP, although in the real world you might also encounter a substantial amount of UDP (User Datagram Protocol) (value of 17).[2]

Transmission Control Protocol

Like IP, TCP also offers a few functions that need not overly concern us (Figure 2.3). It ensures that packets are given to the application in the order they were sent, as well as providing for flow control and more complete error-checking.

---

[2] You can find the entire list of assigned protocol numbers at: ftp://ftp.isi.edu/in-notes/iana/assignments/protocol-numbers.

Source Port							Destination Port	
Sequence Number								
Acknowledgment Number								
Data Offset	Reserved	U R G	A C K	P S H	R S T	S Y N	F I N	Window
Checksum							Urgent Pointer	
Options								Padding
Application Level Data								

Figure 2.3 *TCP packet*

Of interest to us is what RFC 793 calls *multiplexing*. Just as IP was able to transfer incoming packets to various transport layers (TCP or UDP) depending on the protocol number, so TCP also has a number of upper-layer applications to deal with. To accommodate all of them at once, each application must request a *port* from the TCP module. Any requests coming into the port are held by TCP and can be read by the application. Similarly, any outgoing messages are sent by the application to the port, and TCP takes the responsibility to send them on to the destination application.

In Table 2.1 you can see the ports that we will be dealing with in our testing. Note that there is no technical restriction on which port each protocol can use. However, both client and server must agree on the same port. Since virtually all clients and servers in the industry use these ports, you will want to keep to the standard to interoperate with them.

Table 2.1 *Internet Mail Port Numbers* [3]

Protocol	Port
SMTP	25
DNS	53
POP3	110
IMAP4	143
LDAP	389

---

[3] You can find the entire list of assigned port numbers at: ftp://ftp.isi.edu/in-notes/iana/assignments/port-numbers.

TCP also defines a *socket*, which may some times be confused with a port (Table 2.2). It is essentially a specific port on a specific node or the combination of IP address and port number.

Table 2.2 *TCP Socket Definition*

TCP Socket	
Address	Port
10.32.44.41	25

Another important term is the *connection*. A socket can have multiple connections from different nodes or even different ports on the same node. We call the association of two sockets with each other a connection.

Winsock

If you look at Figure 2.4, you will see the data structure you need to give your network interface in order to issue the SMTP command "HELO." Clearly, if you had to fill out these structures each time you wanted to send a command you would not be too pleased. This is the reason for compartmentalizing the network into modules. You can call the TCP module rather than having to replicate its functionality in your code.

Even so, every system and TCP implementation could conceivably have a different interface putting the burden back on you to develop versions of your program that work on every available protocol stack. The 4.2 version of BSD UNIX addressed this issue by defining a common programming interface for networking operations. It was loosely based on the UNIX approach to reading and writing files but addressed the needs of network users.

This API (Application Programming Interface) was called Berkeley Sockets and was eventually ported to many different operating systems. The name originated because its principal data structure was called a socket. Note that this socket is not simply a host-port combination as we discussed earlier. In this context, a socket is one end of a communications link. It holds all the information related to the link

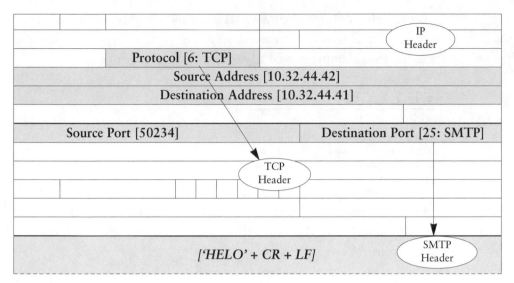

Figure 2.4 *IP datagram containing SMTP "HELO" command*

(including addresses, queues, and data buffers). Most socket-calls require a socket descriptor, also called a socket. The socket descriptor will be the usual meaning of the word socket in this book.[4]

Early Windows applications did not have a socket library available to them. Each application had to program to the API of the TCP/IP stack of the vendor, much like users of other operating systems before Berkeley Sockets. In 1993, Microsoft and others produced a specification called Winsock, which was closely based on Berkeley Sockets. There are some additional functions (starting with WSA [Windows Socket API]), but the rest closely match the Berkeley specifications, making it easy to write portable code.

In Table 2.3 and Table 2.4 you can see the set of functions defined by Sockets and Winsock respectively. On 32-bit Windows systems (e.g., Windows 95, Windows 98, Windows NT) they are stored in a library called wsock32.dll, usually found in the Windows path.[5]

---

[4] I will stop at three meanings, but the term socket is actually even more ambiguous. Wright and Stevens (*TCP/IP Illustrated*, Addison-Wesley, 1995) list six definitions of the word socket.

[5] While these routines can also be made to run on older versions of Windows, all references to wsock32.dll would need to be changed to winsock.dll.

Table 2.3 *Standard Socket Calls*

Basic Operation	Addressing	Socket Operations	Utility Functions
accept	Gethostbyaddr	getsockname	htons
bind	Gethostname	getsockopt	htonl
close	Getpeername	ioctlsocket	inet_addr
connect	Getprotobyname	setsockopt	inet_ntoa
listen	Getprotobynumber		ntohl
recv	Getservbyport		ntohs
recvfrom			
select			
send			
sendto			
shutdown			
socket			

Table 2.4 *Microsoft Windows Socket Calls*

WSAAsyncGetHostByAddr	WSACancelBlockingCall
WSAAsyncGetHostByName	WSACleanup
WSAAsyncGetProtoByName	WSAGetLastError
WSAAsyncGetProtoByNumber	WSAIsBlocking
WSAAsyncGetServByName	WSASetBlockingHook
WSAAsyncGetServByPort	WSASetLastError
WSAAsyncSelect	WSAStartup
WSACancelAsyncRequest	WSAUnhookBlockingHook

I will briefly discuss some of the Winsock calls that we will be using. You can find the full Winsock specifications at numerous locations on the Web.[6]

The examples in this book use the following declarations.

```
Declare Function WSAStartup Lib "wsock32.dll"
 (ByVal a As Integer,
  b As WSAdata_type) As Integer
Declare Function WSACleanup Lib "wsock32.dll" () As Integer
Declare Function WSAAsyncSelect Lib "wsock32.dll"
 (ByVal sock As Integer,
  ByVal hWnd As Integer,
  ByVal msg As Integer,
  ByVal event2 As Long) As Integer
Declare Function WSAGetLastError Lib "wsock32.dll" () As Integer
```

Figure 2.5 *WSA functions*

---

[6] For example, http://www.stardust.com/wsresource/winsock1/ws_c.html.

```
Declare Function gethostbyname Lib "wsock32.dll"
(ByVal HostName As String) As Long
Declare Function gethostbyaddr Lib "wsock32.dll"
(HostAddress As Long,
 ByVal lenaddress As Integer,
 ByVal pftype As Integer) As Long
Declare Function inet_ntoa Lib "wsock32.dll"
(ByVal iaddr As Long) As Long
Declare Function htons Lib "wsock32.dll"
(ByVal a As Integer) As Integer
```

Figure 2.6 *Host lookup functions*

```
Declare Function socket Lib "wsock32.dll"
(ByVal af As Integer,
 ByVal typesock As Integer,
 ByVal protocol As Integer) As Integer
Declare Function bind Lib "wsock32.dll"
(ByVal s As Integer,
 addr As sockaddr_in_type,
 ByVal namelen As Integer) As Integer
Declare Function connect Lib "wsock32.dll"
(ByVal sock As Integer,
 sockstruct As sockaddr_in_type,
 ByVal structlen As Integer) As Integer
Declare Function send Lib "wsock32.dll"
(ByVal sock As Integer,
 ByVal msg As String,
 ByVal msglen As Integer,
 ByVal flag As Integer) As Integer
Declare Function recv Lib "wsock32.dll"
(ByVal sock As Integer,
 ByVal msg As String,
 ByVal msglen As Integer,
 ByVal flag As Integer) As Integer
Declare Function closesocket Lib "wsock32.dll"
(ByVal sock As Integer) As Integer
Declare Function setsockopt Lib "wsock32.dll"
(ByVal sock As Integer,
 ByVal level As Integer,
 ByVal optname As Integer,
 optval As sockopt_bool_type,
 ByVal optlen As Integer) As Integer
Declare Function listen Lib "wsock32.dll"
(ByVal sn As Integer,
 ByVal blog As Integer) As Integer
Declare Function accept Lib "wsock32.dll"
(ByVal sn As Integer,
 saddr As sockaddr_out_type,
 namelen As Integer) As Integer
```

Figure 2.7 *Socket functions*

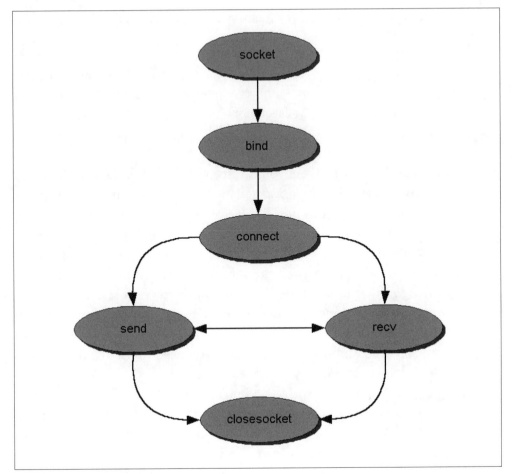

Figure 2.8 *Flow of client socket calls*

The sequence of Winsock calls for a client (module initiating a connection) is shown in Figure 2.8. First, a socket structure is created with a call to the *socket* function. It must then be *bound* to a local port so that it can receive incoming messages (responses from the server). Once our local side is set up, we can *connect* to the remote port. The connection is then established, and client and server can *send* and receive (*recv*) messages according to the specification of the higher-level protocol. After completion, the client calls *closesocket* to terminate the connection and release the port and socket.

Two features of servers distinguish them from clients:

1. They do not initiate connections. (In some cases, server processes may also need to act in client mode in order to connect to other servers. However, on the links where they are acting as servers they do not initiate any connections.)
2. They may have multiple connections to the same port.

Let's start with 1. As you can see in Figure 2.9, the client connect function is replaced by a *listen*. This effectively means: "I am accepting connections to this port." If we issue an *accept* the server will wait for an incoming client connection. These connections need not be immediate. In fact, there may never be an incoming request. In the meantime, the server is blocked from doing anything else. I hope we can agree that this is not the best use of the server's resources.

The *accept* function does something else that you may not have expected. It returns a new Windows socket. When you issue your subsequent send and receive commands, you need to use the new socket. Why does it do this?

This brings us to the second point above. Since we can have multiple client connections to the same port, it would be terribly confusing if they were all using the same socket. We would have to sort out from whom each request came and make sure we responded to the right client. At the same time, we need to watch out for any new connections. Instead, we let our initial socket wait for connections and each client connection is associated with a new socket.

Synchronous versus Asynchronous Operations

Network functions are different from your typical subroutines in an important way: They are quite unpredictable.

- They may complete immediately.
- They may complete after a prolonged wait.
- They may never complete.

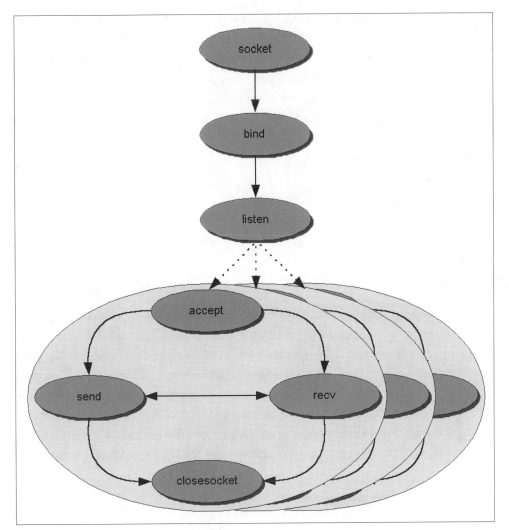

Figure 2.9 *Flow of server socket calls*

While such unpredictability is true, to some extent, of every program, it is particularly apparent and generally expected in the case of network calls.

This poses a problem for programmers. Most function calls are blocking. That is to say, when the main routine dispatches a subroutine it will not continue until the subroutine completes. The main routine can then continue knowing the operation it has requested is complete.

When making network calls this approach is not always a good idea. It can take a long time for the request to complete when you are relying on a different target system and a whole host of routing nodes. In the meantime, your program could be doing some useful work.

With this in mind, we must look for alternatives. There are four fundamental ways of dealing with this situation:

- Blocking calls
- Nonblocking calls
    Polling
    Notification

Blocking Calls

Listing 2.1 shows an example of a blocking call to receive data. You can see it is quite straightforward and succinct. The only advantage of this approach is its simplicity both in reading and writing. For the purposes of this book, I found this argument to be most compelling and thus have used this approach in most of my examples. However, this is not an endorsement of synchronous calls. On the contrary, as they can cause all processes on your system to grind to a halt, I would recommend that you remove all blocking calls from any *production* software.

```
Dim lngSocket As Long
Dim strSocketResponse As String
Dim intResponseLength As Integer

Status = recv (lngSocket, strSocketResponse, intResponseLength, 0)
```

Listing 2.1 *Blocking recv*

Nonblocking Calls

When you issue a nonblocking call your program receives control immediately. Your function may or may not (the more likely result, actually) have completed when you continue to the next instructions.

If any of your subsequent actions depend on completion of the network call, then it is your responsibility to synchronize. You have two basic ways to do this:

1. Keep checking until the action completes.
2. Request to be notified when it completes.

POLLING SOCKETS

"Polling" is the process of continually asking the socket if it is ready (e.g., has any incoming data). To do this we set the socket to non-blocking mode and try to receive data from it. We know that the error status WSAEWOULDBLOCK means that there is no data in the socket yet. So, as shown in Listing 2.2, we can write a small loop that continues to check until it completes or receives some other error.

```
Status = ioctlsocket(Socket, FIONBIO, 1)

Do
  Status = recv (lngSocket, strSocketResponse, intResponseLength, 0)
  DoEvents()
While Status = WSAEWOULDBLOCK
```

Listing 2.2 *Polling socket to receive data*

SOCKET NOTIFICATION

The last approach is known as notification and is what I have used for the server examples where blocking would be unacceptable. As with polling we need to prepare the socket. In this case, we call *WSAAsyncSelect,* which allows us to specify a control, an event to send to the control, and a socket event that should trigger the process.

Notification is best understood with an example. Figure 2.10 shows how we call the *WSAAsyncSelect* function passing a dummy textbox control, a Windows event (left button of mouse pressed down), and a Winsock trigger (data available for reading). When data comes in on the socket, our subroutine *txtDummyControl_MouseDown* will be

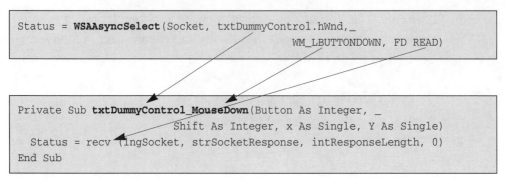

Figure 2.10 *Notfication for reading socket*

dispatched, and it can safely call a blocking *recv* knowing that there is data waiting.

The main disadvantage of socket notification is that its use is not particularly intuitive. We must register (*WSAAsyncSelect*) in one routine. When a particular event occurs, Winsock then dispatches another procedure (e.g., *txtDummyControl_MouseDown*). The lack of a visible sequence is difficult for a procedural mind to follow, but that is how client-server applications operate. Socket notification merely mirrors the network model.

Chapter 3

Generic Utilities

The best way to understand Winsock is to see it in operation. To get us started, I have written some small "generic" programs that demonstrate the client and server functionality available.

When writing and testing our code we obviously need to consult the standard. However, it is not always efficient to try to start with the standards. If we were the first implementation of a particular standard there would be nowhere else to go. Fortunately, however, many have gone before us, and, assuming we have access to some of their applications, we would be foolish not to make use of them. We can take advantage of the complementary operation of the protocols to decode what they have encoded and vice versa. If the results match our input then we have a good indication that we are on the right track.

Generic Client Example

The Generic Client is a short program that can attach to any port on any server. You can then transmit data to and receive data from the remote port. Most of what you see here is common to all my clients, so by dealing with it now I will be able to focus on the protocol-specific extensions later on.

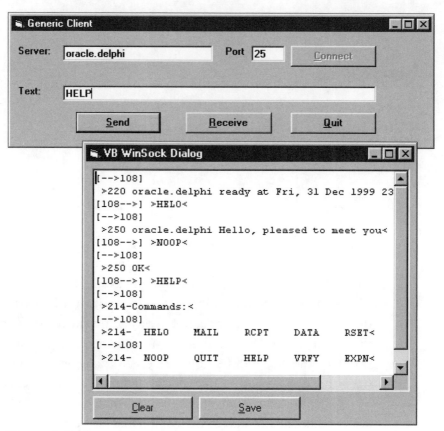

Figure 3.1 *Generic Client*

In Figure 3.1 you can see the associated Visual Basic forms. The user presses *Connect* after filling in the *Server* and *Port*. After this he or she can *send* any text or *receive* a response from the server. The entire conversation is logged in a separate form, so I have not included a separate response field.

Let's take a look behind the scenes. In Listing 3.1 I have started up Winsock during the loading of the form. I do this in all my Winsock applications. Similarly, I always call *WSACleanup* when the main form unloads. To avoid repetition, I haven't shown this throughout the book, but you can assume it is there in the other applications too.

```
Private Sub Form_Load()
  Status = StartWinSock()
End Sub

Private Sub Form_Unload()
  Status = WSACleanup()
End Sub
```

Listing 3.1 *Startup and Cleanup*

Listing 3.2 shows the code for the Connect button. The first function call converts the Servername (www.microsoft.com) to a server address (207.46.130.149). CreateSocket allocates a socket and associates it with the next available port (0). We then connect our socket to the remote server and port. That is all there is to setting up a connection.

```
Dim lngTransmitSocket As Long

Private Sub btnConnect_Click()

  Dim lngServerAddress As Long
  Dim strServerName As String

  Dim strSocketResponse As String
  Dim intRemotePort As Integer

  lngTransmitSocket = 0
  intRemotePort = val(txtPort.Text)
  strServerName = txtServer.Text

  Status = GetIPAddress(lngServerAddress, strServerName)
  Status = CreateSocket(lngTransmitSocket, 0)
  Status = ConnectSocket(lngTransmitSocket, lngServerAddress, _
      intRemotePort)

End Sub
```

Listing 3.2 *Establishing the connection*

With an established connection we can now *send* and receive (*recv*) at will. As you can see in Listing 3.3, the buttons simply call the functions *SendSocket* and *ReceiveSocket*.

```
Private Sub btnSend_Click()
  Dim strSendLine As String

  strSendLine = txtSendLine.Text
  lngStatus = SendSocket(lngTransmitSocket, SendLine)
End Sub

Private Sub btnReceive_Click()
  Dim strSocketResponse As String
  lngStatus = ReceiveSocket(lngTransmitSocket, strSocketResponse)

  txtSendLine.SetFocus
End Sub
```

Listing 3.3 *Sending and Receiving a line of text to/from the server*

To be tidy, we also have an orderly way for the user to terminate
(Listing 3.4). We release the socket so that it is available for other
applications.

```
Private Sub btnQuit_Click()

  lngStatus = ReleaseSocket(lngTransmitSocket)
  End

End Sub
```

Listing 3.4 *Cleaning up*

It would be possible to use the client to try out ad hoc commands on a server. However, if you just want to send straight text
without performing any manipulation of the data you are probably
better off just using the Internet terminal emulator *telnet*. You can
connect it to any port by specifying a second parameter in your
command line (e.g., telnet oracle.delphi 25). Make sure you have
the Local Echo option turned on, and you should see something
like Figure 3.2.

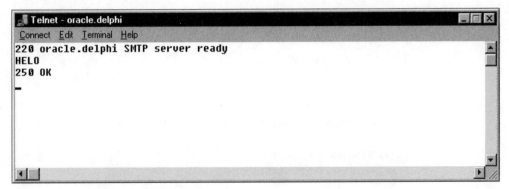

Figure 3.2 *Telnet session*

Generic Server Example

As we discussed earlier, servers follow a somewhat different paradigm than clients. We will now look at what this means in terms of implementation. Figure 3.3 shows the User Interface of the server counterpart to our previous example. In order to illustrate the function of listening and accepting I have started with a synchronous server.

The first button pushed should be the *Listen* (Listing 3.5). It calls *CreateSocket* to allocate a socket and bind to the port indicated on the form. Then we *listen* for the first incoming client connection to that port. The second parameter to the listen function (5) is the number of incoming requests that can be queued. If the number of unprocessed client requests exceeds this number, then further requests are rejected.

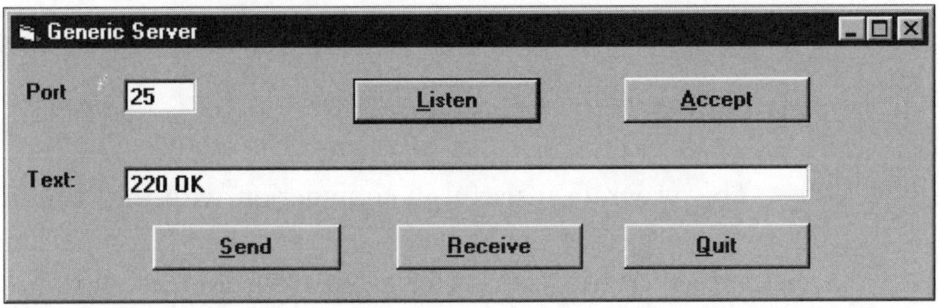

Figure 3.3 *Generic Blocking Server*

```
Dim lngListenSocket As Long
Private Sub btnListen_Click()

  Dim intListenPort As Integer

  intListenPort = val(txtPort.Text)

  Status = CreateSocket(lngListenSocket, intListenPort)

  If listen(lngListenSocket, 5) Then
    MsgBox "Could not listen"
    End
  End If

End Sub
```

Listing 3.5 *Listen for incoming connections*

Once the client requests connection we can press the *Accept* button. As seen in Listing 3.6, the *accept* function returns the new socket *lngTransmitSocket*. From then on we can exchange data with the client.

```
Dim lngTransmitSocket As Long
Private Sub btnAccept_Click()

  Dim sotTransmitSocketAddress As SocketOutputType
  Dim intTransmitSocketAddressSize As Integer

  intTransmitSocketAddressSize = 20

  lngTransmitSocket = accept(lngListenSocket, _
                        sotTransmitSocketAddress, _
                        intTransmitSocketAddressSize)

End Sub
```

Listing 3.6 *Accept the connection*

This program is useful in conjunction with the Generic Client to give you a feel for the sequence of events in a Winsock connection. It assumes you are working in a lab environment with direct control over the form. If you try them out, take care, as you can easily hang your applications by pressing the buttons out of order.

Generic Asynchronous Server

In order to write a full-fledged server we must address its distinguishing characteristics, those that were mentioned earlier.

- Multiple connections
- Asynchronous operation

In Figure 3.4 you see that the possibility of multiple connections means another control to indicate the current connection being displayed. We also need to be able to receive client data automatically whenever it arrives. It will be appended to the main text box on the form.

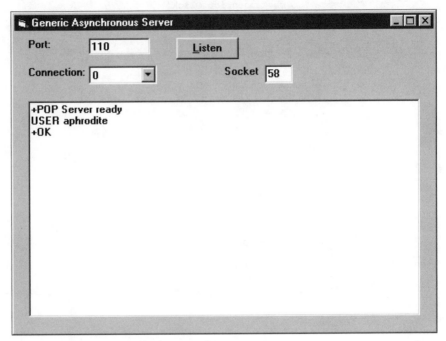

Figure 3.4 *Generic Asynchronous Server*

Since we may have multiple connections, we need to implement control arrays for any connection-specific controls. This would include the socket and dialog as well as the request socket we shall see in a moment.

```
Dim lngListenSocket As Long
Dim lngTransmitSocket As Long

Const WM_MBUTTONUP = &H208
Const WM_MBUTTONDBLCLK = &H209
Dim CRLF As String
```

Listing 3.7 *Server declarations*

For completeness of the User Interface, we allow the user to monitor the various connections by selecting from the combo-box. All the corresponding control array elements are then made visible on the form.

```
Dim intCurrentConnection As Integer
Private Sub cboConnection_Click()
  Dim intNewConnection As Integer

  intNewConnection = cboConnection.ListIndex

  If intNewConnection < 0 Or _
     intNewConnection >= cboConnection.ListCount Then
    intNewConnection = 0
  End If

  If intNewConnection = intCurrentConnection Then Exit Sub

  txtSocket(intCurrentConnection).Visible = False
  txtSocket(intNewConnection).Visible = True
  txtDialog(intCurrentConnection).Visible = False
  txtDialog(intNewConnection).Visible = True

  cboConnection.ListIndex = intNewConnection
  intCurrentConnection = intNewConnection

End Sub
```

Listing 3.8 *Display new connection*

The server begins when someone presses the *Listen* button (Listing 3.9). It *creates* a *socket* bound to the user-specified port. We then issue a *listen* to let Winsock know it can accept connection requests for us on the port. But we don't know when a client will try to connect to us. The *WSAAsyncSelect* function specifies that we wish to be notified when there is a request we can *accept* (a connection request). It should send the *middle-button-up* event to the *txtConnect* control.

```
Private Sub btnListen_Click()

    Dim sitListenSocketAddress As SocketInputType
    Dim intTCPPort As Integer

    intTCPPort = val(txtPort.Text)

    Status = CreateSocket(lngListenSocket, intTCPPort)

    If listen(lngListenSocket, 5) Then
        MsgBox "Could not listen on Port " + Str(intTCPPort)
        End
    End If

    If WSAAsyncSelect(lngListenSocket, txtConnect.hWnd, WM_MBUTTONUP, _
                    FD_ACCEPT) Then
        MsgBox "Unable to set Asynch mode"
    End If

End Sub
```

Listing 3.9 *Listen on Port*

This will cause the *txtConnect_MouseUp* subroutine to execute (Listing 3.10). It *accepts* the client connection creating a new socket (*lngTransmitSocket*) for this connection. The displayable controls are loaded for each connection as they are accepted.

```
Private Sub txtConnect_MouseUp(Button As Integer, Shift As Integer,
x As Single, Y As Single)

    Dim sotTransmitSocketAddress As SocketOutputType
    Dim intTransmitSocketAddressSize As Integer
    Dim intCurrentConnection As Integer

    intTransmitSocketAddressSize = LenB(sotTransmitSocketAddress)
    intTransmitSocketAddressSize = 20

    intCurrentConnection = cboConnection.ListCount
```

```
cboConnection.AddItem Trim(Str(intCurrentConnection))
Load txtSocket(intCurrentConnection)
Load txtRequest(intCurrentConnection)
Load txtDialog(intCurrentConnection)

lngTransmitSocket = accept(lngListenSocket, _
                          sotTransmitSocketAddress, _
                          intTransmitSocketAddressSize)

txtSocket(intCurrentConnection) = Trim(Str(lngTransmitSocket))

DisplayConnection intCurrentConnection

If WSAAsyncSelect(lngTransmitSocket, _
                  txtRequest(intCurrentConnection).hWnd, _
                  WM_MBUTTONDBLCLK, FD_READ) Then
    MsgBox "Unable to set Asynch mode"
End If

End Sub
```

Listing 3.10 *Accept Connection*

We are now ready to receive data sent by the client. Again, we
don't know when this might occur, so we need to be notified.
WSAAsyncSelect asks for any data ready to be received (*FDREAD*) to
trigger the middle button-double-click (*WM_MBUTTONDBLCLK*)
event on the *txtRequest* (*intCurrentConnection*) control.

```
Private Sub txtRequest_DblClick(Index As Integer)

Dim strClientRequest As String

lngTransmitSocket = val(txtSocket(Index).Text)
Status = ReceiveSocket(lngTransmitSocket, strClientRequest)
DisplayConnection Index
txtDialog(Index).Text = txtDialog(Index).Text + _
                        strClientRequest + CRLF
DialogLength(Index) = Len(txtDialog(Index).Text)

txtDialog(Index).SelStart = DialogLength(Index)
End Sub
```

Listing 3.11 *Process client request*

Whenever a client sends data Winsock will invoke the *txtRequest_DblClick* subroutine (Listing 3.11). We only need to receive the incoming data and append it to the dialog.

```
Dim DialogLength(20) As Integer
Private Sub txtDialog_KeyUp(Index As Integer, KeyCode As Integer, _
    Shift As Integer)
Dim strLastLine As String

  If KeyCode = 13 Then
    lngTransmitSocket = val(txtSocket(Index).Text)

    strLastLine = Mid(txtDialog(Index).Text, DialogLength(Index) + 1)
    Status = SendSocket(lngTransmitSocket, strLastLine)
    DialogLength(Index) = Len(txtDialog(Index).Text)
  End If

End Sub
```

Listing 3.12 *Send data to client*

In order to make the data exchange bi-directional we also allow the user to add lines to the dialog (Listing 3.12). Any time a key is released (*txtDialog_KeyUp*), we check to see if it is the end of a line (CarriageReturn is an ASCII 13). If so, we extract the last line and send it to the client.

Generic Interceptor

The process of debugging protocols reminds me of an old story of two master chess champions who were challenged by a young boy to simultaneous matches. While the boy knew that he could not beat them both, he guaranteed that neither could they both win.

The boy let one play white and the other black. After the first chess champion had moved the boy went to the other and made the same move. He waited there for the countermove before going back to the first where he, again, copied the move. He repeated this process for every move of the game. In effect, the masters were playing against each other with the boy in between. Either they would all draw, or one would beat the boy and the boy would beat the other.

The reason I have mentioned this story is that it closely parallels the approach I use in familiarizing myself with a protocol. I have already shown examples of both clients and servers, which we can use to probe our counterpart and try out different commands and responses. But sometimes this can be tedious and requires a substantial amount of user input.

To help with this, I have written another utility that imitates the boy's actions. It will let the masters play against each other and give us the opportunity simply to observe. The program that follows will listen for a client connection on a given port and will then establish another connection to the server (Figure 3.5). It then relays any incoming requests from the client to the server and vice versa. All we need to do is log the dialog; we can examine it later to understand how the protocol works.

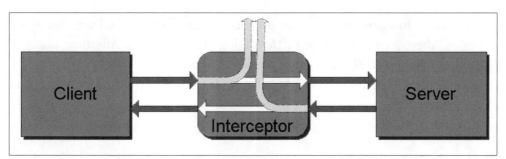

Figure 3.5 *Intercepting Client-Server dialog*

Using the Interceptor should be quite straightforward (Figure 3.6). We need to specify the port we are listening on as well as the server and port we are connecting to. In addition to this we can indicate where to log the protocol and whether the protocol is ASCII (e.g., SMTP, POP, and IMAP) or binary (e.g., DNS and LDAP).

When the fields are complete we press *Listen* and start a client application, pointing it to our Interceptor rather than its normal

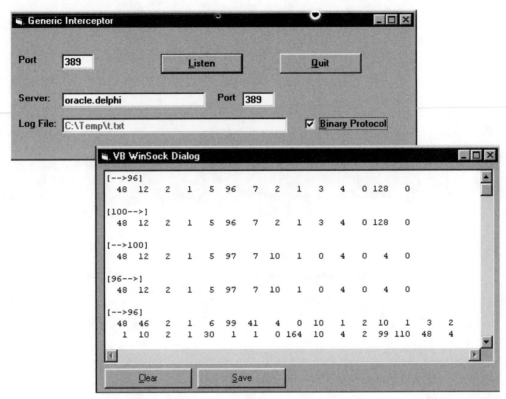

Figure 3.6 *Generic Interceptor*

server. When the client connects the interceptor connects to the server in the background. We can then perform some typical operations on the client, terminate both the client and interceptor, and look at the protocol in the log file.

To implement the interceptor we need to merge the code for the client and the (nonblocking) server. The program is both a client (to the server) and a server (for the client).

As you can see in Listing 3.13, listening for the connection is the same as for the nonblocking server. It is only once the connector has been set up and data begins to flow that our client function becomes active.

When the client attempts to *connect* (*FD_ACCEPT*) to our interceptor (*lngListenClientSocket*), we will be notified by a left-button-down

(*WM_LBUTTONDOWN*) sent to the *txtListenClient* control. Visual Basic will then invoke *txtListenClient_MouseDown*.

```
Private Sub btnListen_Click()

  Dim intListenPort As Integer

  ingListenPort = val(txtLocalPort.Text)

  Status = CreateSocket(lngListenClientSocket, intListenPort)

  If listen(lngListenClientSocket, 5) Then
    MsgBox "Could not listen"
    End
  End If

  If WSAAsyncSelect(lngListenClientSocket, txtListenClient.hWnd, _
                    WM_LBUTTONDOWN, FD_ACCEPT) Then
    MsgBox "Unable to set Asynch mode"
  End If

End Sub
```

Listing 3.13 *Listen for client connection*

```
Private Sub txtListenClient_MouseDown(Button As Integer, _
                                      Shift As Integer, _
                                      x As Single, Y As Single)

  Dim sotTransmitClientSocketAddress As SocketOutputType
  Dim intTransmitClientSocketAddressSize As Integer

  Dim lngServerAddress As Long
  Dim strServerName As String

  Dim strSocketResponse As String
  Dim intConnectPort As Integer

  intTransmitClientSocketAddressSize = 20
  lngTransmitClientSocket = accept(ListenClientSocket, _
                            TransmitClientSocketAddress, _
                            TransmitClientSocketAddressSize)

  lngTransmitServerSocket = 0
```

```
intConnectPort = val(txtintRemotePort.Text)

strServerName = txtServer.Text
Status = GetIPAddress(lngServerAddress, strServerName)
Status = CreateSocket(lngTransmitServerSocket, 0)
Status = ConnectSocket(lngTransmitServerSocket, lngServerAddress, _
                            intConnectPort)


If WSAAsyncSelect(lngTransmitClientSocket, txtReceiveClient.hWnd, _
                    WM_LBUTTONDOWN, FD_READ) Then
   MsgBox "Unable to set Asynch mode"
End If


If WSAAsyncSelect(lngTransmitServerSocket, txtReceiveServer.hWnd, _
                    WM_LBUTTONDOWN, FD_READ) Then
   MsgBox "Unable to set Asynch mode"
End If


End Sub
```

Listing 3.14 *Accept client connection*

When a connection request is received we *accept* the connection
(Listing 3.14). We immediately establish the relay connection to the
server (*GetIPAddress*, *CreateSocket*, *ConnectSocket*).

We then issue two notification (*WSAAsyncSelect*) requests. The
first is for any data received from the client. The second is for any data
received from the server.

If the client tries to *send* (*FD_READ*) to our interceptor
(*lngTransmitClientSocket*) Winsock will trigger a left-button-down
(*WM_LBUTTONDOWN*) event to the *txtReceiveClient* control.
Visual Basic will invoke the *txtReceiveClient_MouseDown* procedure.

Likewise, if the server tries to *send* (*FD_READ*) to our interceptor (*lngTransmitServerSocket*) Winsock will trigger a left-button-down (*WM_LBUTTONDOWN*) event to the *txtReceiveServer*
control. Visual Basic will invoke the *txtReceiveServer_MouseDown*
procedure.

At this point we have set everything up. All we can do is wait for
data to arrive either from the client or the server.

When we are notified that there is server data waiting we do nothing more than send it on to the client (Listing 3.15).

```
Private Sub txtReceiveServer_MouseDown(Button As Integer, Shift As _
    Integer,_ x As Single, Y As Single)
  Dim strSocketResponse As String

  Status = ReceiveSocketBinary(lngTransmitServerSocket, _
                      strSocketResponse)
  Status = SendSocketBinary(lngTransmitClientSocket, _
                      strSocketResponse)


End Sub
```

Listing 3.15 *Relay Server Data*

Similarly, in the opposite direction (Listing 3.16), when there is client data waiting we pass it on to the server.

```
Private Sub txtReceiveClient_MouseDown(Button As Integer, Shift As _
    Integer, x As Single, Y As Single)
  Dim strSocketResponse As String

  Status = ReceiveSocketBinary(lngTransmitClientSocket, _
                      strSocketResponse)
  Status = SendSocketBinary(lngTransmitServerSocket, _
                      strSocketResponse)


End Sub
```

Listing 3.16 *Relay Client data*

To summarize, there are three events we are responding to (Figure 3.7). The first is the client connection. In the *btnListen_Click* procedure we have registered a notification of *MouseUp* to the *txtConnect* control so WinSock will call the *txtConnect_MouseUp* procedure. Our procedure will *accept* the client connection and then *connect* to the server. This will occur once per client connection.

The second event (although not necessarily chronologically speaking) is when a client sends a request. This will invoke the *txtReceiveClient_MouseDown* procedure (notification was requested

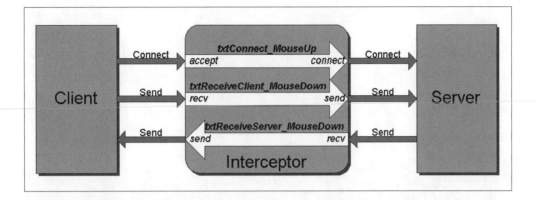

Description	Initiator	Action	Event	Response Action	Relay Action
Client requests a connection	Client	Connect	*txtConnect_ MouseUp*	*accept* from Client	*connect* to Server
Client sends data to server	Client	Send	*txtReceiveClient_ MouseDown*	*recv* from Client	*send* to Server
Server sends data to client	Server	Send	*txtReceiveServer_ MouseDown*	*recv* from Server	*send* to Client

Figure 3.7 *Interceptor events*

in the *txtConnect_MouseUp* procedure), which will receive (*recv*) the data from the client and relay (*send*) it to the server.

The last event is when a server sends a response. Our procedure *txtReceiveServer_MouseDown* will receive (*recv*) the data from the server and relay (*send*) it on to the client.

Chapter 4

RFC 822—Internet Text Messages

The most important objects we will encounter in E-mail are messages. Most protocols operate on them, so it seems like as good a place as any to start. A message is more than just the text it contains. It implies an author and readers as well as many other attributes that help us to identify it and understand its context.

We could liken a message to a postal letter in terms of its sender, recipient address, and content. But unlike postal letters, our electronic data must be packaged in a completely uniform and unambiguous format in order for computers and programs to be able to identify its components.

On the Internet, the standard format for encapsulating a message is RFC 822. In Figure 4.1, you can see an example of how it might look.

RFC 822 Structure

Most of the content of RFC 822 is probably self-explanatory. Still, we need to examine the structure systematically to make sure we have all the bases covered. At the highest level, as Figure 4.2 shows, a message consists of a header and a body separated by a blank line (two consecutive CRLFs).[1] Since no blank lines are allowed in the header, the

---

[1] CRLF is used throughout the book to denote the Carriage-Return Line-Feed combination encoded in ASCII as a binary 13 followed by a binary 10.

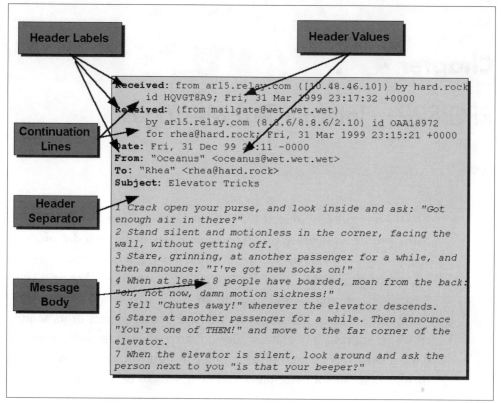

Figure 4.1 *RFC 822 message*

first blank line clearly marks the end of the header section and the subsequent beginning of the body (which may, of course, contain any number of blank lines).

Header Section

We can decompose the header section into a number of headers. As you can see in Figure 4.3, each header-field consists of a label (or name), terminated by a colon and a value (or body).

In most cases, the complete header will fit on one line. However, if the header is long (usually more than 72 to 76 characters) it would become difficult to read unless we insert some line breaks. RFC 822 calls this *folding*. As you will notice in the example, every continuation line must be prefixed with some white space (spaces or tabs). We

Header Section	Received: from arl5.relay.com ([10.48.46.10]) by hard.rock
	   id HQVGT8A9; Fri, 31 Mar 1999 23:17:32 +0000
	Received: (from mailgate@wet.wet.wet)
	   by arl5.relay.com (8.8.6/8.8.6/2.10) id OAA18972
	   for rhea@hard.rock; Fri, 31 Mar 1999 23:15:21 +0000
	Date: Fri, 31 Dec 99 23:11 –0000
	From: "Oceanus" <oceanus@wet.wet.wet>
	To: "Rhea" <rhea@hard.rock>
	Subject: Elevator Tricks

Body	1 Crack open your purse, and look inside and ask: "Got enough air in there?" 2 Stand silent and motionless in the corner, facing the wall, without getting off. 3 Stare, grinning, at another passenger for a while, and then announce: "I've got new socks on!" 4 When at least 8 people have boarded, moan from the back: "Oh, not now, damn motion sickness!" 5 Yell "Chutes away!" whenever the elevator descends. 6 Stare at another passenger for a while. Then announce "You're one of THEM!" and move to the far corner of the elevator. 7 When the elevator is silent, look around and ask the person next to you "is that your beeper?"

Figure 4.2 *Message Structure*

Header	Field Name	Field Body

Received: from arl5.relay.com ([10.48.46.10]) by hard.rock
  id HQVGT8A9; Fri, 31 Mar 1999
   23:17:32 +0000
	Received	from arl5.relay.com ([10.48.46.10]) by hard.rock id HQVGT8A9; Fri, 31 Mar 1999 23:17:32 +000 0

Received: (from mailgate@wet.wet.wet)
  by arl5.relay.com (8.8.6/8.8.6/2.10) id OAA18972
   for rhea@hard.rock; Fri, 31 Mar 1999
   23:15:21 +0000
	Received	(from mailgate@wet.wet.wet) by arl5.relay.com (8.8.6/8.8.6/2.10) id OAA18972 for rhea@hard.r ock; Fri, 31 Mar 1999 23:15:21 +0000

Date: Fri, 31 Dec 99 23:11 –0000	Date	Fri, 31 Dec 99 23:11 –0000
From: "Oceanus" <oceanus@wet.wet.wet>	From	"Oceanus" <oceanus@wet.wet.wet>
To: "Rhea" <rhea@hard.rock>	To:	"Rhea" <rhea@hard.rock>
Subject: Elevator Tricks	Subject	Elevator Tricks

Figure 4.3 *Header Section Structure*

can easily differentiate them from initial header lines (immediately beginning with a label) and concatenate them to the value.

The set of message headers is not fixed. While a number are defined in RFC 822 (Table 4.1) only three (*From*, *Date*, and one of *To/Cc/Bcc*) are mandatory.

Table 4.1 *RFC 822 Header Labels*[2]

Header Label	Description
Bcc	Secondary recipients not visible to other recipients
Cc	Secondary recipients
Comments	Text comments not affecting message contents
Date	Date the message was composed
Encrypted	Software used to encrypt the message
From	Identity of person on whose behalf message was sent (usually the sender)
In-Reply-To	Identifies previous correspondence answered by this message
Keywords	Comma-separated keywords or phrases
Message-ID	Globally unique machine-readable identifier of the message
Received	Trace information added by each mail relay
References	Identifies previous correspondence referenced by this message
Reply-to	Mailbox to which responses should be sent
Resent-bcc	Same as Bcc but applying to forwarded message
Resent-cc	Same as Cc but applying to forwarded message
Resent-Date	Same as Date but applying to forwarded message
Resent-From	Same as From but applying to forwarded message
Resent-Message-ID	Same as Message-ID but applying to forwarded message
Resent-Reply-to	Same as Reply-To but applying to forwarded message
Resent-Sender	Same as Sender but applying to forwarded message
Return-Path	Address and route back to message originator
Sender	Address of user who sent the message (e.g., secretary)
Subject	Sender specified summary of message contents
To	Primary recipients of the message

The list is also far from exhaustive. In other words, you can add your own headers at will (typically in the framework of another standard such as MIME). As long as both sender and recipient agree on the meaning associated with the label you should have no problem. Nonetheless, to prevent conflict between proprietary use and future

---

[2] RFC 822 §4.1

standards you are encouraged to use labels beginning with "X-" (e.g., X-Mailer or X-Loop).

Header Syntax

The syntax of each of the standard headers is defined in RFC 822 using Backus-Naur Form. If the header doesn't look familiar don't worry. The syntax of several of the fields (*Subject, Comments, Keywords*) is free form. You can use most almost any common 7-bit characters, including alphabetic and numeric values, and most punctuation marks. Other fields are used rarely or are simple to understand. Dates and addresses are probably the most likely to cause you problems so let's take a closer look at them.

Dates

The full date syntax is specified in RFC 822 Section 2.1. While many variations are possible, most of them can be summarized with:

> *[weekday ","] day month year hours ":" minutes [":" seconds] zone*

as in,

> *Fri, 31 Dec 99 23:04:11 –0000*

Most of the items should be evident from the example, but some require a little elaboration.

WEEKDAY

Weekday is composed of the first three letters of the weekdays in English (Mon, Tue, Wed, Thu, Fri, Sat, Sun), regardless of the language of the users.

MONTH

Month is the first three letters of the month in English (Jan, Feb, Mar, Apr, May, Jun, Jul, Aug, Sep, Oct, Nov, Dec), again, regardless of the language being used in the message.

Year

Obviously, RFC 822 predates interest in Y2K. The original specification (since updated in RFC 1123) only allows a two-digit year. Fortunately, there should be no cause for ambiguity until around the year 2082.

Hour

Hour is self-explanatory. However, take note that it should be specified using a twenty-four-hour clock.

Zone

The time zone can be one of a list of hard-coded zones (UT, GMT, EST, EDT, CST, CDT, MST, MDT, PST, PDT), or preferably, it can be the four-digit (two-digit hour plus two-digit minute) time offset from Greenwich Mean Time (GMT). For example, Central European Summer Time (CEST) can be specified as "+0200" since it is two hours ahead of GMT. Bombay would have a zone of "+0530" since it is five and a half hours ahead of GMT.

Writing a date using this format is a trivial concatenation of the various fields. It is more challenging to read the format. Fortunately, it is easily readable by humans, so many simple applications will not require you to parse the field. There are, however, some situations where you cannot simply pass the date on to the user:

- If your applications require you to sort messages according to date you will need to be able to determine the date programmatically.

- If your users, or other applications, require a specific date format (e.g., 1999-12-31 23:59), then you will need to extract the particular fields and reformat them.

- If your application caters to international users then, in addition to supporting various date formats, you will need to be able to translate the weekdays and months into the target language.

Visual Basic offers a number of string functions that can facilitate parsing these fields, but due to the number of variations possible, you would probably be best off to write a finite state machine to perform the complete lexical analysis if you are intent on writing production-quality code.

Addresses

Addresses can be specified in both simple and expanded form. A simple address uses the typical E-mail format:

local-mailbox@ fully-qualified-domain-name

For example,

John.Rhoton@compaq.com

Most people receiving a message from the above address will have no trouble deducing my name. On the other hand, only the highly imaginative would be able to guess the identity of g23w5l@hotmail.com. Often older mail applications such as IBM mainframe E-mail systems provide a maximum of eight characters to identify a mailbox. While some people use cryptic E-mail addresses to remain anonymous or keep a low profile, this is clearly not the norm. Rather than requiring everyone to rename his or her mailboxes, we have the option of adding a user-friendly description to the address in the expanded form:

friendly-name <simple address>

For example,

John Rhoton <John.Rhoton@compaq.com>

As with dates, you may be able to get away without parsing these fields for many applications. Some reasons to parse include:

- If the application offers the ability to reply to sender, then it will be necessary to identify the sender's address.
- If the application needs to be able to present the addresses in a custom format (for example, only showing the friendly-name), then it will be necessary to extract the relevant items.

If you do need to fully parse an address field, then you can and should refer to RFC 822 Section 6 for the full address specification.

Body

Compared to the headers, the body of the message is extremely simple. Once we reach the first blank line, the header is terminated and we know that everything else is the body. It has no standard structure and can be formatted as the user chooses. Its only restrictions are that the lines should not extend beyond 80 characters and that the text should consist of only 7-bit U.S. ASCII characters.

Object Declaration

While it is not strictly necessary to create class modules to read and write RFC 822 messages, they are very convenient, especially since they can then be used by some of the other protocols (SMTP, POP, IMAP) in a very modular way. I also find the notation (object.property) simple and more intuitive than subroutine calls.

RFC 822 Message Class

Since a message consists of a set of lines it is convenient to define a collection of strings called *Lines* that contains the entire message without any structure. At the same time, the message can be analyzed and divided into body and header. The body is then a collection of strings or *BodyLines*, whereas the Header Section is a collection *Headers*, as defined below.

```
Public Lines As New Collection
Public Headers As New Collection
Public BodyLines As New Collection
```

Listing 4.1 *RFC822Message class members*

If you think this looks redundant (since the lines could be derived from the Headers and the BodyLines, or vice versa), you are absolutely right! However, I have found it simpler to use two parallel data structures with dual mapping functions (*Compose*, *Parse*) rather than to try to economize on memory. This should become clearer as we look at the code in the rest of the chapter.

RFC 822 Header Class

The Headers mentioned form their own class called RFC822Header.

```
Public Label As String
Public Value As String
```

Listing 4.2 *RFC822 Header class members*

For our purposes, each header consists of a *Label* (the field name) and a *Value* (the field body, including all continuation lines). Both of these strings are opaque. In other words, we don't perform any further syntax checking at this level.

Encoding RFC 822

To encode RFC 822 we need to

- Identify which headers we will support (at least From, Date and To, CC or BCC)
- Set the values for each header-field (folding them if necessary)
- Set the body
- Compose the message

Code Example

This example allows a user to enter some of the primary fields of a message. After completing these, he or she selects an output file and presses the Save button. The code then constructs an RFC 822 message and writes it to the file.

The only important routine in the form is the code for the Save button.

As you can see in Listing 4.3, the routine declares a (New) instance of a message. It adds the headers *Date*, *From*, *To*, (optionally) *CC* and *Subject* and then the body. These are all copied from the appropriate fields on the form.

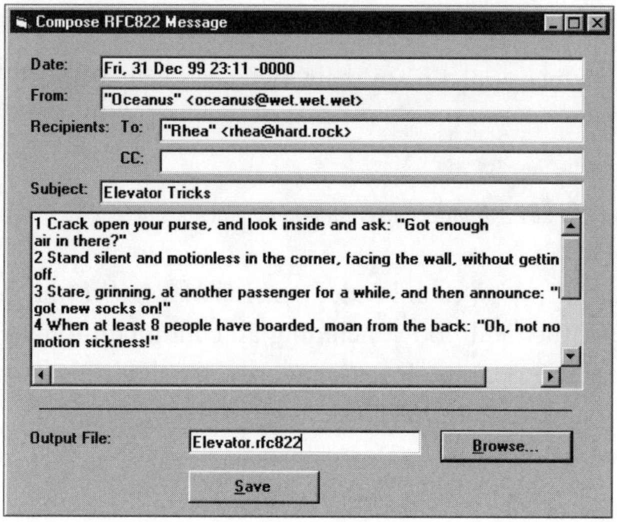

Figure 4.4 *RFC 822 Message Composer*

```
Private Sub btnSave_Click()

    Dim intOutputFileNumber As Integer
    Dim rmsgCurrentMessage As New RFC822Message
    Dim strCurrentLine

    rmsgCurrentMessage.AddHeader "Date", txtDate.Text
    rmsgCurrentMessage.AddHeader "From", txtFrom.Text
    rmsgCurrentMessage.AddHeader "To", txtToRecipient.Text
    If txtCCRecipient.Text <> "" Then
        rmsgCurrentMessage.AddHeader "CC", txtCCRecipient.Text
    End If
    rmsgCurrentMessage.AddHeader "Subject", txtSubject.Text

    rmsgCurrentMessage.BodyLines.Add txtContent.Text

    rmsgCurrentMessage.Compose

    intOutputFileNumber = FreeFile
    Open txtOutputFile.Text For Output As #intOutputFileNumber
    For Each strCurrentLine In rmsgCurrentMessage.Lines
        Print #intOutputFileNumber, CStr(strCurrentLine)
    Next
    Close #intOutputFileNumber

End Sub
```

Listing 4.3 *Save an RFC message to a file*

We then call *Compose* to create the message, loading the *Lines* collection in the message from the *Headers* and *BodyLines* collections. All that is left is to loop through the *Lines* and print them to our output file.

There are two routines related to writing a message:

- *AddHeader* allows us to add header to the message.
- *Compose* converts the components of the message into its final form.

Note that we don't need to write functions for adding *Lines* or *BodyLines* as we can use the in-built *Add* method (for collections).

```
Public Sub AddHeader(HeaderLabel As String, HeaderValue)
Dim rhdrCurrentHeader As New RFC822HeaderLine

   rhdrCurrentHeader.Label = HeaderLabel
   rhdrCurrentHeader.Value = HeaderValue
   Headers.Add rhdrCurrentHeader

End Sub
```

Listing 4.4 *Add a header line to the current message*

To add a *Header* we declare a new instance. We then set the *Label* and *Value* from the supplied parameters and add the newly created header to the *Headers* collection of this message.

```
Public Sub Compose()

   Dim rhdrCurrentHeader
   Dim strCurrentLine

   For Each rhdrCurrentHeader In Headers
     Lines.Add CStr(rhdrCurrentHeader.Label) + ":" + _
             CStr(rhdrCurrentHeader.Value)
   Next

   Lines.Add ""

   For Each strCurrentLine In BodyLines
     Lines.Add CStr(strCurrentLine)
   Next

End Sub
```

Listing 4.5 *Construct the RFC 822 Message from its components*

Message composition is the translation from its internal form (all its components) to its external form (the way it is transmitted). To do this we loop through all the headers, adding them to *Lines*. To terminate the Header Section we add the mandatory blank line. Then we loop though all the bodylines.

Decoding RFC 822

To decode RFC 822 will usually take a form similar to:

- Read in the file.
- Loop through the headers, concatenating any continuation lines.
- Trap for the blank line.
- Read in the body.
- Display all fields to the user.

Code Example

The example reads in an RFC 822 format file and displays both the source message file as well as the typical message components, as shown in Figure 4.5.

In a manner similar to the RFC 822 composer, the reader also contains the two class modules and its own form. But we have also added a startup module to the project. While not indispensable, it modularizes the Read form for use in other projects.

```
Public Sub Main()

    Dim strRFC822File As String
    Dim intInputFileNumber As Integer
    Dim strCurrentLine As String

    strRFC822File = Command()

    If strRFC822File = "" Then strRFC822File = Dir("*.RFC822")
    Do While Dir(strRFC822File) = ""
```

```
strRFC822File = InputBox("File name to open: ", _
                         "RFC822 Reader", "Test.RFC822")
Loop

Load frmReadRFC822Messages

intInputFileNumber = FreeFile
Open strRFC822File For Input As #intInputFileNumber
Do While Not EOF(intInputFileNumber)
  Line Input #intInputFileNumber, strCurrentLine
  frmReadRFC822Messages.DisplayMessage.Lines.Add strCurrentLine
Loop
Close #intInputFileNumber

frmReadRFC822Messages.Show

End Sub
```

Listing 4.6 *Module to invoke and display RFC 822 Message Reader*

When this project is started the *Main* routine takes control. After
identifying which file to open it loads the form, opens the file, and

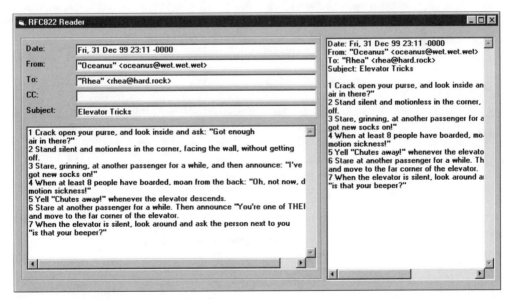

Figure 4.5 *RFC 822 Message Reader*

loads all the lines in the file into the form's *DisplayMessage* object.
Now the form should have everything it needs, so we make it visible
to the user and let the form take it from there.

```
Public DisplayMessage As New RFC822Message

Private Sub Form_Activate()
  LoadSource
  LoadComponents
End Sub

Private Sub LoadSource()
  Dim CurrentLine

  txtSource.Text = ""
  For Each CurrentLine In DisplayMessage.Lines
    txtSource.Text = txtSource.Text + CRLF + CurrentLine
  Next
End Sub

Private Sub LoadComponents()
  Dim HeaderLine
  Dim BodyLine

  DisplayMessage.Parse

  For Each HeaderLine In DisplayMessage.Headers
    Select Case LCase(HeaderLine.Label)
      Case "from":
        txtFrom.Text = HeaderLine.Value
      Case "to":
        txtTo.Text = HeaderLine.Value
      Case "subject":
        txtSubject.Text = HeaderLine.Value
      Case "date":
        txtDate.Text = HeaderLine.Value
    End Select
  Next

  For Each BodyLine In DisplayMessage.BodyLines
    txtContent.Text = txtContent.Text + CRLF + BodyLine
  Next

End Sub
```

Listing 4.7 *Load message from file into form*

When the form is activated it loads all of the fields of the form. The source is a single concatenation of all the Lines in the message.

To determine the fields of the form we first need to parse the message. We can then loop through all the headers, watching out for any that we need to display. We then loop through the BodyLines and concatenate them for viewing.

```
Public Sub Parse()

  Dim strBoundary As String
  Dim strCurrentLine As String
  Dim rhdrCurrentHeader As RFC822HeaderLine

  strBoundary = ""

    ' Headers
  Do While Not bolEndOfMessage And NextLine <> ""

    strCurrentLine = GetLine
    Do While SpaceBegin(NextLine)
      strCurrentLine = strCurrentLine + GetLine
    Loop

    Set rhdrCurrentHeader = New RFC822HeaderLine
    rhdrCurrentHeader.Parse (strCurrentLine)
    Headers.Add rhdrCurrentHeader

  Loop

    ' Blank Lines
  Do While NextLine = ""
    strCurrentLine = GetLine:      If bolEndOfMessage Then Exit Sub
  Loop

    ' Body
  Do While Not bolEndOfMessage
    strCurrentLine = GetLine
    BodyLines.Add strCurrentLine
  Loop
End Sub
```

Listing 4.8 *Parse RFC 822 Message into its component*

The only public function of *RFC 822Message* is *Parse*. It first loops through the Header Section. For each header it concatenates all continuation lines. Then it parses the *Header* and adds it to the collection of headers.

We then skip through the divider (one or more blank lines) and add the rest of the lines to the collection of *BodyLines*.

```
Private Function SpaceBegin(HeaderLine As String) As Boolean

    Select Case Left$(HeaderLine, 1)
        Case " ", Chr$(9)
            SpaceBegin = True
        Case Else
            SpaceBegin = False
    End Select

End Function

Private Function GetLine() As String

  intLineIndex = intLineIndex + 1
  GetLine = Lines(intLineIndex)
  If intLineIndex >= Lines.Count Then bolEndOfMessage = True

End Function

Private Function NextLine() As String

  If intLineIndex < Lines.Count Then
    NextLine = Lines(intLineIndex + 1)
  Else
    NextLine = ""
  End If

End Function
```

Listing 4.9 *Miscellaneous Line parsing functions*

In order to assist the parsing above you will have noticed three custom functions used above:

- *SpaceBegin* returns whether or not the Header begins with white space.
- *GetLine* advances our internal line index and returns the string at that position.
- *NextLine* also returns the next line, but it does so without advancing the index. This allows us to peek ahead at the next line before we complete processing our current line.

```
Public Sub Parse(strHeaderLine As String)

  Dim intTokenPosition As Integer
  intTokenPosition = InStr(strHeaderLine, ":")

  If intTokenPosition = 0 Then
    Exit Sub
  End If

  Label = Trim(Left(strHeaderLine, intTokenPosition - 1))
  Value = Trim(Mid(strHeaderLine, intTokenPosition + 1))

End Sub
```

Listing 4.10 *Parse a header into its label and value*

As part of parsing the message we need to parse the individual headers. The Header class therefore has its own *Parse* routine (Listing 4.10). The key point in the line is the first colon. Everything before it is the *Label*, or Field Name. Everything thereafter is the *Value*, or Field Body.

Wrapping Up

The applications in this chapter illustrate how to read and write RFC 822 messages. The goal is to give you an idea of what is involved in working with RFC 822. If you want to develop applications more suitable for production, there are a few areas to consider expanding.

- *Support for the additional headers*—A number of other RFC headers (e.g., all the Resent-headers for forwarding) are defined.
- *Complete parse of the headers*—We have performed an approximate parse of some of the headers (e.g., dates and addresses). While the routines serve the purposes of illustration, you may well find formats that would be incorrectly interpreted. The most typical approach to parsing is the use of finite-state-automata (FSA). A discussion of lexical analysis is beyond the scope of this book, but you can find descriptions in many books, particularly those concerned with compiler construction.

Chapter 5

MIME—Multipurpose Internet Mail Extensions

From its beginning, RFC 822 was charged with two deficiencies:

1. Lack of support for binary data and 8-bit (not to mention multi-octet) character sets.
2. Lack of structure for multiple bodyparts.

These two omissions did not do much to hamper the adoption rate of RFC 822, but they did make its use much more cumbersome. The MIME contributors, in addition to creating a message format without these restrictions, tried to accommodate several other considerations:

- Maintain backward compatibility with RFC 822.
- Ensure maximum human readability.
- Provide extensible and intuitive bodypart definitions.

There is also an effort to keep the structure concise, but this takes a lower priority than the above considerations.

MIME is implemented as an extension of RFC 822. Rather than using an entirely new format it uses RFC 822 with a couple of enhancements:

- It defines additional headers using RFC 822 standard syntax. These will be ignored by any non-MIME readers.
- It defines a structure for the body of the message. While non-MIME readers will not be able to parse the new body, it is represented as best as possible in text format. Therefore, the user has a good chance of still being able to interpret parts of the message.

Binary Support

Since RFC 822 only permits 7-bit characters, MIME has introduced two types of encoding formats that will convert 8-bata data to 7-bit characters:

1. Base64
2. QuotedPrintable

We will examine these in more detail later, but you may already wonder why the authors of the standards would offer two types of encoding when one would suffice. True, of course, but different encodings are suitable, and more efficient, for different data. Base64 encoding is more appropriate for true binary data with a medium or high proportion of 8-bit values. QuotedPrintable is typically more useful for text that is primarily 7-bit with occasional 8-bit characters.

Structure

Storing several objects in one file is not difficult. Simple concatenation would do the trick. However, in order to distinguish the bodyparts, we must know when each component ends and the next begins. To do this, MIME uses a special string termed the *boundary* to demarcate attachments in a message.

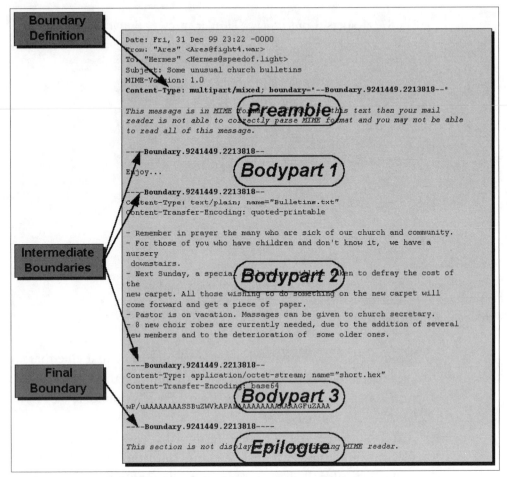

Figure 5.1 *MIME message*

These concepts are most easily understood by looking at an actual MIME message. In Figure 5.1, we have an example with two attachments (bulletins.txt and short.hex). One is encoded with Base64 and the other with QuotedPrintable.

Block Structure of Format

As you analyze the components in the example you will see that its structure can be summarized generically, as shown in Figure 5.2.

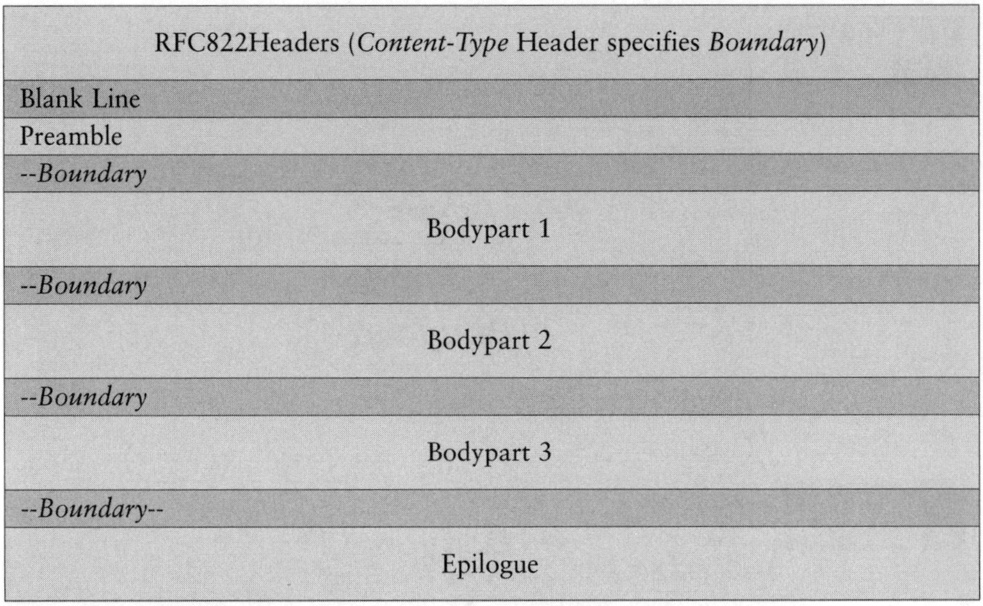

RFC822Headers (*Content-Type* Header specifies *Boundary*)
Blank Line
Preamble
--*Boundary*
Bodypart 1
--*Boundary*
Bodypart 2
--*Boundary*
Bodypart 3
--*Boundary--*
Epilogue

Figure 5.2 *MIME structure*

As in RFC 822, we have the header section. The first clue that we are dealing with MIME is the presence of additional headers. One of them, *Content-Type,* specifies the *Boundary* ("--Boundary.9241449. 2213818--", in this case).

After our blank line we come to the RFC 822 body. MIME subdivides this body into different sections. Until the first boundary we have the *Preamble.* This section is ironically only used to communicate to non-MIME users (those who do not have a MIME-compatible reader).

- MIME readers do not display this part. So MIME users never see the preamble!

- Non-MIME readers do not know to skip the section, and since it is at the beginning of the message it is the first part shown to non-MIME users.

To take advantage of this, MIME programs often place a warning in the preamble to warn non-MIME users that the message they are reading is not supported by their software and may not be completely legible.

After each boundary we have an *Attachment* (actual boundaries are preceded by two leading dashes). This continues until the final boundary (boundary preceded and followed by two dashes), which indicates the beginning of an optional *Epilogue*, also ignored by MIME readers and generally empty.

List of Header Fields

As mentioned earlier, MIME makes use of some additional headers. In Table 5.1 you can see the five labels specified by MIME.

Table 5.1 *RFC 822 Header Fields for MIME[1]*

Label	Typical Format	Description
MIME-Version	Number.Number	
Content-ID	Message ID	
Content-Description	Free Text	
Content-Type	Type/subtype; parameters	
Content-Transfer-Encoding	Mechanism	

Looking at Table 5.1 you can see that Content-Type, Content-Transfer-Encoding, and Content-Description appear not only in the header section of the message but also at the beginning of each attachment. Each attachment can have its own type, since it might represent different data and need different encoding.

The *MIME-version* is fairly straightforward, with a value of "1.0" being typical at present. The *Content-Id* and *Content-Description* are self-explanatory and only optional. For the purposes of writing a simple MIME program it is safe to ignore them and focus on the last two labels, which are the substance of MIME.

Content-Type and Content-Transfer-Encoding provide the features of MIME mentioned earlier. Content-Type allows us to structure our message by stating that it is of a particular type, or alternatively,

---

[1] For the full specification of the MIME header fields, please see RFC 2045 §3–§8.

that it is composed of multiple parts. The Content-Transfer-Encoding permits us to encode 8-bit data into 7-bit, or to leave it as it is (if it is already 7-bit text).

Content-Type

The *Content-Type* takes a value of the form *Type/Subtype*. In Table 5.2 you can see the defined types and subtypes. Note that the most common are:

- *Text/plain*—for ASCII text
- *Application/octet-stream*—for non-ASCII data
- *Multipart/mixed*—composite or multiple attachments

We will limit our discussion to these, since they will provide the functionality we need.

Table 5.2 *MIME Media Types[2]*

Category	Top-Level Media Type	Subtype
Discrete	Text	Plain
	Image	
	Audio	
	Video	
	Application	Octet-Stream
		PostScript
Composite	Multipart	Mixed
		Alternative
		Digest
		Parallel
	Message	RFC822
		Partial
		External-Body

The idea of media types is for the recipient's mail reader to know what kind of data you are sending so that it can associate it with the

---

[2] For the full specification of the MIME header fields, please see RFC 2046.

right application. While this concept has the potential of being very useful in principle, it is often neglected by Windows applications.

Windows has a history of application association based on File Extensions. Since the Content-Type also has a parameter specifying the filename, it is more convenient to use it rather than trying to spend much time on the other header fields. Other Windows MIME readers typically use this technique, which might not be portable to other platforms but is consistent with other Windows applications. Ultimately, the loss is not that great, since most Windows data formats are inaccessible for other platforms in any case.

Content-Transfer-Encoding

Content-Transfer-Encoding describes what mechanism is used to convert 8-bit data to 7-bit format for transfer across the network. Depending on our data we have three recommended solutions (see Table 5.3).

Table 5.3 *Transfer-Encoding Options*

Proportion of 8-bit characters	Preferred Encoding	Overhead of Encoding
None	None	0%
Usually Low	QuotedPrintable	200% for 8-bit characters 0% for 7-bit characters
Usually Medium or High	Base64	33%

If you are certain that your text has no 8-bit characters (e.g., English text), there is no reason to encode at all. Typically, any text using a small proportion of 8-bit characters (e.g., text in most Western European languages) would use QuotedPrintable encoding. Any other data (e.g., binary files and many Asian languages) would be encoded using Base64.

Base64

Base64 is so called because it only uses 64 characters (10 decimal digits, 26 uppercase characters, 26 lowercase characters, '+', '/'). The reason for reducing the character set to 64 (rather than the full 128 possible with 7 bits) is that the set selected is all printable characters, making it possible for humans to read the message. Even if a particular section is incomprehensible, at least it does not interfere with the rest of the text.

The encoding is a two-step process:

- Convert 8-bit characters to 6 bits.
- Map the 6-bit values to the Base64 character set.

Table 5.4 *Base64-Bit Mapping*

Binary Bytes	1								2								3							
Data Bits	1	2	3	4	5	6	7	8	9	10	11	12	13	14	15	16	17	18	19	20	21	22	23	24
Base64 Characters		1				2					3						4							

Figure 5.3 shows how the bit reduction works. We take advantage of the fact that 24 is both 3x8 bits and 4x6 bits. In other words, three 8-bit values can be transformed into four 6-bit values and vice versa. With this in mind, we subdivide the entire input stream into groups of three characters and transform each triple using the same procedure.

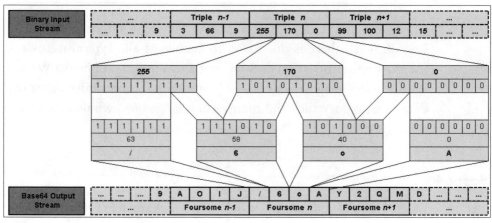

Figure 5.3 *Base64 Encoding*

In the example, our input triple is (255, 170, 0). We allocate four new variables for output. The first receives the first 6 bits of the first byte; the second receives the last 2 bits of the first byte and the first 4 of the second byte, and so on. We now have the four variables (63, 58, 40, 0).

The next step is to look up the values in the Base64 Encoding Table (Table 5.5). There we find the encoded characters ('/', '6', 'o', 'A'). We concatenate these ('/6oA'), add them to the output file, and continue with the next input triple.

Table 5.5 *Base64 Encoding Table*

Value	Encoding	Value	Encoding	Value	Encoding	Value	Encoding
0	A	16	Q	32	g	48	w
1	B	17	R	33	h	49	x
2	C	18	S	34	i	50	y
3	D	19	T	35	j	51	z
4	E	20	U	36	k	52	0
5	F	21	V	37	l	53	1
6	G	22	W	38	m	54	2
7	H	23	X	39	n	55	3
8	I	24	Y	40	o	56	4
9	J	25	Z	41	p	57	5
10	K	26	a	42	q	58	6
11	L	27	b	43	r	59	7
12	M	28	c	44	s	60	8
13	N	29	d	45	t	61	9
14	O	30	e	46	u	62	+
15	P	31	f	47	v	63	/

If the byte size of the file is exactly divisible by three, then this is all there is to it. Otherwise, we end up with an incomplete triple (one or two bytes) at the end of the file. We can add trailing zeros easily enough so that we can complete our algorithm, but we have to have some way to identify these or the recipient won't know if they are real zeros or only used for padding.

The proper solution for this is to use a 65th character "=" representing the artificial zeros added in the encoding. The "=" can only ever appear at the very end of a Base64 stream and can be either the last or the last two characters.

- If the input stream contains *two* remaining characters, then we add *one* zero, encode the triple, and replace the final output character with *one* "=."

- If the input stream contains *one* remaining character, then we add *two* zeros, encode the triple, and replace the final two output characters with "==."

To illustrate, the single byte 255 would be padded to (255, 0, 0). This would be reduced to (63, 48, 0, 0). This would map to ('/', 'w', 'A', 'A'), but would be appended to the output stream as ('/w=='). The same exercise with the two bytes (255, 255) leads to (255, 255, 0) →(63, 63, 60, 0)→('/'. '/', '8', 'A')→('//8=').

QuotedPrintable

Table 5.6 *QuotedPrintable Encoding*

Plain 8-Bit Text
Chat vit rôt. Rôt plut à chat.
Chat mit patte à rôt. Rôt brûla patte à chat.
Wir Wiener Wäscherweiber würden weiße Wäsche waschen,
wenn wir wüßten wo warmes Wasser wäre.
Con este puCal y aquél te descorazonaré.
¿Quién te descorazonará con este pu al y aquél?
Fem flade flødeboller på et fladt flødebollefad.
Paulo Pereira Pinto Peixoto, pobre pintor português
pinta perfeitamente portas, paredes e pias,
por pouco preço, patrão.

QuotedPrintable 7-Bit Text
Chat vit r=F4t. R=F4t plut =E0 chat.
Chat mit patte =E0 r=F4t. R=F4t br=FBla patte =E0 chat.
Wir Wiener W=E4scherweiber w=FCrden wei=DFe W=E4sche waschen,
wenn wir w=FC=DFten wo warmes Wasser w=E4re.
Con este pu=F1al y aqu=E9l te descorazonar=E9.
=BFQui=E9n te descorazonar=E1 con este pu=F1al y aqu=E9l?
Fem flade fl=F8deboller p=E5 et fladt fl=F8debollefad.
Paulo Pereira Pinto Peixoto, pobre pintor portugu=EAs
pinta perfeitamente portas, paredes e pias,
por pouco pre=E7o, patr=E3o.

QuotedPrintable works on the premise that the majority of a text uses 7-bit characters (Table 5.6). To avoid the overhead of encoding, as well as to maintain legibility, these are left as they are.

The 8-bit characters are encoded as follows:

- Obtain the index from the ASCII table (Table 5.7).
- Code the value as hexadecimal.
- Prefix the code with a "=."

Table 5.7 *ASCII Character Set*

0	<NUL>	32	<SP>	64	@	96	`	128	·	160	<SP>	192	À	224	à
1	<STX>	33	!	65	A	97	a	129	·	161	¡	193	Á	225	á
2	<SOT>	34	"	66	B	98	b	130	·	162	¢	194	Â	226	â
3	<ETX>	35	#	67	C	99	c	131	·	163	£	195	Ã	227	ã
4	<EOT>	36	$	68	D	100	d	132	·	164	¤	196	Ä	228	ä
5	<ENQ>	37	%	69	E	101	e	133	·	165	¥	197	Å	229	å
6	<ACK>	38	&	70	F	102	f	134	·	166	¦	198	Æ	230	æ
7	<BEL>	39	'	71	G	103	g	135	·	167	§	199	Ç	231	ç
8	<BS>	40	(	72	H	104	h	136	·	168	¨	200	È	232	è
9	<TB>	41	)	73	I	105	i	137	·	169	©	201	É	233	é
10	<LF>	42	*	74	J	106	j	138	·	170	ª	202	Ê	234	ê
11	<VT>	43	+	75	K	107	k	139	·	171	«	203	Ë	235	ë
12	<FF>	44	,	76	L	108	l	140	·	172	¬	204	Ì	236	ì
13	<CR>	45	-	77	M	109	m	141	·	173	–	205	Í	237	í
14	<SO>	46	.	78	N	110	n	142	·	174	®	206	Î	238	î
15	<SI>	47	/	79	O	111	o	143	·	175	—	207	Ï	239	ï
16	<DLE>	48	0	80	P	112	p	144	·	176	°	208	Ð	240	∂
17	<DC1>	49	1	81	Q	113	q	145	'	177	±	209	Ñ	241	ñ
18	<DC2>	50	2	82	R	114	r	146	'	178	²	210	Ò	242	ò
19	<DC3>	51	3	83	S	115	s	147	·	179	³	211	Ó	243	ó
20	<DC4>	52	4	84	T	116	t	148	·	180	´	212	Ô	244	ô
21	<NAK>	53	5	85	U	117	u	149	·	181	µ	213	Õ	245	õ
22	<SYN>	54	6	86	V	118	v	150	·	182	¶	214	Ö	246	ö
23	<ETB>	55	7	87	W	119	w	151	·	183	·	215	×	247	÷
24	<CAN>	56	8	88	X	120	x	152	·	184	¸	216	Ø	248	ø
25	<EM>	57	9	89	Y	121	y	153	·	185	¹	217	Ù	249	ù
26	<SUB>	58	:	90	Z	122	z	154	·	186	º	218	Ú	250	ú
27	<ESC>	59	;	91	[	123	{	155	·	187	»	219	Û	251	û
28	<FS>	60	<	92	\	124			156	·	188	¼	220	Ü	252	ü
29	<GS>	61	=	93	]	125	}	157	·	189	½	221	Ý	253	ý
30	<RS>	62	>	94	^	126	~	158	·	190	¾	222	P	254	ρ
31	<US>	63	?	95	_	127	<DEL>	159	·	191	¿	223	ß	255	Ÿ

So, for example, the letter "ß" is character 223 in the ASCII chart. The hexadecimal equivalent of decimal 223 is DF. We therefore encode "ß" as "=DF," and "weiße" as "wei=DFe." At the other end, the reader detects the 8-bit character by the "=" and translates the subsequent DF into its ASCII equivalent.

This may appear to be complete, but there is still one problem. What if I really want to send the string "wei=DFe" in a message? How do I ensure that the reader does not inadvertently substitute a "ß" where I didn't want one?

The solution is that, in addition to the 8-bit characters the "=" is itself encoded the same way. It is a decimal 61, or hex 3D, so it is encoded as "=3D."

This means that "wei=DFe" would be encoded as "we=3DDFe." The reader would know to decode the "=3D" but would leave the DF alone as it is not immediately prefixed by an "=."

Object Declaration

As with RFC 822 it is useful to package all the features of the message into class modules. For MIME there are three entities we can work with:

- Messages
- Headers
- Attachments

While we could reuse the RFC822Message, there are some significant additions for MIME, and Visual Basic is not necessarily ideal for trying to implement object inheritance. Rather than making things difficult, I have created a similar module called MIMEMessage.

We can continue to use RFCHeaders since, although we have additional headers, they have the same syntax. We now have a new object called MIMEAttachment, since MIME, in contrast to simple RFC 822, supports multiple bodyparts.

MIMEMessage Class

At the simplest level, MIME messages consist of a collection of *Lines*. We can divide these into *Headers* and *BodyLines*. Then we can go another step and parse the BodyLines into *Attachments*, *PreambleLines,* and *EpilogueLines*.

```
Public Lines As New Collection
Public Headers As New Collection
Public BodyLines As New Collection
Public Attachments As New Collection
Public PreambleLines As New Collection
Public EpilogueLines As New Collection
```

Listing 5.1 *MIMEMessage class member*

MIMEAttachment Class

The Attachments need to specify the type of *Encoding* used. In addition, we can store the content of each attachment either in a *File* or a collection of *Lines* (not to be confused with the Lines of the message).

```
Public Filename As String
Public Encoding As String
Public Lines As New Collection
```

Listing 5.2 *MIMEAttachment class members*

Encoding MIME

In addition to ensuring that we take care of the attachments, you will see that encoding MIME is very similar to encoding RFC 822.

Code Example

In Figure 5.4 you can see the form for the sample MIME Composer. It is primitive in the sense that it only allows two attachments. However, the concepts are the same regardless of the number of

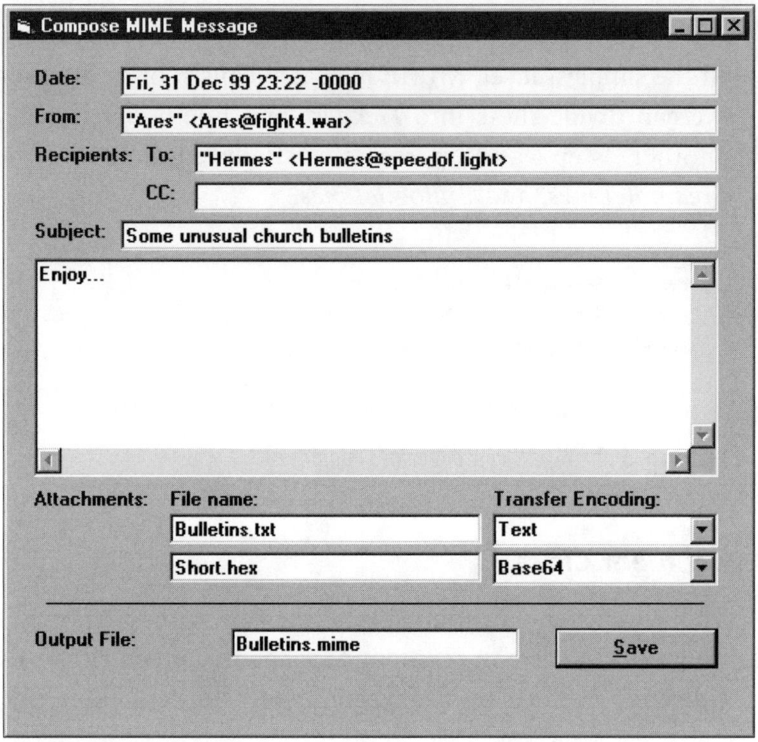

Figure 5.4 *MIME Message Composer*

attachments. Your main challenge with adding multiple files in an elegant manner will be the user interface.

Note in Listing 5.3 that when saving the message we need to add the two attachments with the encodings requested on the form.

```
Private Sub btnSave_Click()

    Dim intOutputFileNumber As Integer
    Dim mmsgCurrentMessage As New MIMEMessage
    Dim strCurrentLine

    mmsgCurrentMessage.AddHeader "Date", txtDate.Text
    mmsgCurrentMessage.AddHeader "From", txtFrom.Text
    mmsgCurrentMessage.AddHeader "To", txtToRecipient.Text
    If txtCCRecipient.Text <> "" Then
       mmsgCurrentMessage.AddHeader "CC", txtCCRecipient.Text
    End If
```

```
mmsgCurrentMessage.AddHeader "Subject", txtSubject.Text

mmsgCurrentMessage.BodyLines.Add txtContent.Text

If txtAttachment1.Text <> "" And _
   Dir(txtAttachment1.Text) <> "" Then
  mmsgCurrentMessage.AddAttachment txtAttachment1.Text, _
                                   cmbTransferEncoding1.Text
End If

If txtAttachment2.Text <> "" And _
   Dir(txtAttachment2.Text) <> "" Then
  mmsgCurrentMessage.AddAttachment txtAttachment2.Text, _
                                   cmbTransferEncoding2.Text
End If

mmsgCurrentMessage.Compose

intOutputFileNumber = FreeFile
Open txtOutputFile.Text For Output As #intOutputFileNumber
For Each strCurrentLine In mmsgCurrentMessage.Lines
   Print #intOutputFileNumber, CStr(strCurrentLine)
Next
Close #intOutputFileNumber

End Sub
```

Listing 5.3 *Save a MIME message to a file*

```
Public Sub AddAttachment(FilePath As String, Encoding As String)
  Dim mattCurrentAttachment As MIMEAttachment

  Set mattCurrentAttachment = New MIMEAttachment
  mattCurrentAttachment.Encoding = Encoding
  mattCurrentAttachment.Filename = FilePath
  mattCurrentAttachment.ReadFile FilePath, Encoding
  Attachments.Add mattCurrentAttachment

End Sub
```

Listing 5.4 *Add attachment to the current message*

The message class has a public method to add an attachment to it (Listing 5.4). In order to add an attachment to a message we first create a new *MIMEAttachment* object. We set its *Encoding* and *Filename* properties and then read the corresponding file into the object. To tie the attachment to the message we add it to the message's *Attachments* collection.

```
Public Sub Compose()

    Dim strAttachmentBoundary As String
    Dim mhdrCurrentHeader
    Dim mattCurrentAttachment

    Randomize
    strAttachmentBoundary = "--Boundary" + Trim(Str(Rnd)) + _
                            Trim(Str(Rnd)) + "--"

    For Each mhdrCurrentHeader In Headers
        Lines.Add CStr(mhdrCurrentHeader.Label) + ": " + _
                CStr(mhdrCurrentHeader.Value)
    Next

    Lines.Add "MIME-Version: 1.0"
    Lines.Add "Content-Type: multipart/mixed; " _
            + "boundary=""" + strAttachmentBoundary + """"
    Lines.Add ""

    Lines.Add "--" + strAttachmentBoundary
    Lines.Add ""
    Dim CurrentLine
    For Each CurrentLine In BodyLines
        Lines.Add CStr(CurrentLine)
    Next
    Lines.Add ""


    For Each mattCurrentAttachment In Attachments
        Lines.Add "--" + strAttachmentBoundary
        If mattCurrentAttachment.Encoding = "base64" Then
            Lines.Add "Content-Type: application/octet-stream; name=""" + _
                    Dir(mattCurrentAttachment.Filename) + """"
            Lines.Add "Content-Transfer-Encoding: base64"
        ElseIf mattCurrentAttachment.Encoding = "quoted-printable" Then
            Lines.Add "Content-Type: text/plain; name=""" + _
                    Dir(mattCurrentAttachment.Filename) + """"
            Lines.Add "Content-Transfer-Encoding: quoted-printable"
```

```
      Else
         Lines.Add "Content-Type: text/plain; name=""" + _
                  Dir(mattCurrentAttachment.Filename) + """"
         Lines.Add "Content-Transfer-Encoding: 7bit"
      End If
      Lines.Add ""
      For Each CurrentLine In mattCurrentAttachment.Lines
         Lines.Add CStr(CurrentLine)
      Next
      Lines.Add ""
   Next


   Lines.Add "--" + strAttachmentBoundary + "--"



End Sub
```

Listing 5.5 *Composing a MIME message*

The *Compose* function takes the headers and bodyparts of the current message and uses them to generate the *Lines* needed for the message.

It starts by creating a random *Boundary*. We do this to reduce the likelihood of the boundary being contained in the message. If we always used the same boundary it would cause confusion when forwarding messages, since it would be impossible to distinguish between boundaries in the forwarded and forwarding messages.

We then add the MIME specific headers (*MIME-Version* and *Content-Type*). The subsequent blank line signals the end of the header section. We start with the main bodypart signaled by our first boundary. Then we loop through our attachments, adding each. They start with a boundary followed by a Content-Type and Content-Encoding. The Attachment headers depend on the encoding specified by the user.

After we finish all attachments, we add the final boundary signaling the end of the message.

ReadFile (Listing 5.6) is a trivial dispatch function. Depending on the Encoding specified in the parameter, it calls the appropriate subfunction to read (and optionally encode) the input file.

```
Public Sub ReadFile(FilePath As String, Encoding As String)

    Select Case LCase(Encoding)
      Case "base64":
        EncodeFileBase64 (FilePath)
      Case "quoted-printable":
        EncodeFileQuotedPrintable (FilePath)
      Case Else
        ReadFilePlainText (FilePath)
    End Select

End Sub
```

Listing 5.6 *Reading an attachment file*

Reading a plain text file (Listing 5.7) requires no special skills. We just *Input* all the lines from the file and add them to the *Lines* collection.

```
Public Sub ReadFilePlainText(FilePath As String)
    Dim intFileNumber As Integer
    Dim strTextLine As String

    intFileNumber = FreeFile
    Open FilePath For Input As #intFileNumber

    Do While Not EOF(intFileNumber)
      Line Input #intFileNumber, strTextLine
      Lines.Add strTextLine
    Loop

    Close #intFileNumber

End Sub
```

Listing 5.7 *Reading a plain text attachment file*

Encoding a file as QuotedPrintable (Listing 5.8) is only marginally more difficult than reading plain text. We still read all the Lines and add them to the collection, but this time we scan them first and substitute each 8-bit character (ASCII value > 127) as well as the Equal-sign (ASCII value = 61) with the QuotedPrintable equivalent. This means converting it to Hexadecimal (adding a leading zero to single digits) and prefixing it with an equal sign.

```
Public Sub EncodeFileQuotedPrintable(FilePath As String)
  Dim intFileNumber As Integer
  Dim strInputLine As String
  Dim strOutputLine As String
  Dim intScanIndex As Integer
  Dim strScanValue As String
  Dim strHexString As String

  intFileNumber = FreeFile
  Open FilePath For Input As #intFileNumber

  Do While Not EOF(intFileNumber)
    Line Input #intFileNumber, strInputLine
    strOutputLine = ""
    For intScanIndex = 1 To Len(strInputLine)
      strScanValue = Asc(Mid(strInputLine, intScanIndex, 1))
      If strScanValue > 127 Or strScanValue = 61 Then
        strHexString = Hex(strScanValue)
        If Len(strHexString) = 1 Then _
                        strHexString = "0" + strHexString
        strOutputLine = strOutputLine + "=" + strHexString
      Else
        strOutputLine = strOutputLine + Chr(strScanValue)
      End If
    Next

    Lines.Add strOutputLine
  Loop

  Close #intFileNumber

End Sub
```

Listing 5.8 *Encoding an attachment file as QuotedPrintable*

Base64 is the most fun part of MIME (Listing 5.9). We first need to determine how many triplets there are by dividing the file size by three. Then we loop through all the triplets, encode each to a foursome, and add the result to the output line. If the line is over 72 characters wide, we add a carriage-return to make it easier to read.

```vb
Public Sub EncodeFileBase64(FilePath As String)
  Dim intInputFileNumber As Integer

  Dim bytInput1 As Byte
  Dim bytInput2 As Byte
  Dim bytInput3 As Byte
  Dim strFoursome As String * 4
  Dim strBase64Line As String
  Dim intTripletsCount As Integer
  Dim intRestBytes As Integer


  intInputFileNumber = FreeFile
  Open FilePath For Binary Access Read As #intInputFileNumber

  intTripletsCount = LOF(intInputFileNumber) / 3
  intRestBytes = LOF(intInputFileNumber) - Int(intTripletsCount) * 3
  bytInput1 = 0
  bytInput2 = 0
  bytInput3 = 0

  strBase64Line = ""

  Dim Counter
  For Counter = 1 To intTripletsCount
    Get #intInputFileNumber, , bytInput1
    Get #intInputFileNumber, , bytInput2
    Get #intInputFileNumber, , bytInput3
    strFoursome = Base64Encode(bytInput1, bytInput2, bytInput3)
    strBase64Line = strBase64Line + strFoursome
    If Len(strBase64Line) > 72 Then
      Lines.Add strBase64Line
      strBase64Line = ""
    End If
  Next

  If intRestBytes = 1 Then
    Get #intInputFileNumber, , bytInput1
    strFoursome = Base64Encode(bytInput1, 0, 0)
    strBase64Line = strBase64Line + Left$(strFoursome, 2) + "=="
  ElseIf intRestBytes = 2 Then
    Get #intInputFileNumber, , bytInput1
    Get #intInputFileNumber, , bytInput2
    strFoursome = Base64Encode(bytInput1, bytInput2, 0)
```

```
        strBase64Line = strBase64Line + Left$(strFoursome, 3) + "="
    End If


    Close #intInputFileNumber

    If Len(strBase64Line) > 0 Then
      Lines.Add strBase64Line
      strBase64Line = ""
    End If


End Sub
```

Listing 5.9 *Encoding an attachment file as Base64*

At the end of the file we need to check whether padding is required. Depending on the remaining bytes, we pad with either one or two zeros, and denote these in the encoded results by equal signs.

```
Private Function Base64Encode(InputByte1 As Byte, _
                              InputByte2 As Byte, _
                              InputByte3 As Byte) As String



    Dim bytBits01to06 As Byte
    Dim bytBits07to08 As Byte
    Dim bytBits09to12 As Byte
    Dim bytBits13to16 As Byte
    Dim bytBits17to18 As Byte
    Dim bytBits19to24 As Byte

    Dim bytIndex1 As Byte
    Dim bytIndex2 As Byte
    Dim bytIndex3 As Byte
    Dim bytIndex4 As Byte

    bytBits01to06 = Int(InputByte1 / 4)
    bytIndex1 = bytBits01to06

    bytBits07to08 = InputByte1 And 3
    bytBits09to12 = Int(InputByte2 / 16)
    bytIndex2 = bytBits07to08 * 16 + bytBits09to12

    bytBits13to16 = InputByte2 And 15
    bytBits17to18 = Int(InputByte3 / 64)
```

```
bytIndex3 = bytBits13to16 * 4 + bytBits17to18

bytBits19to24 = InputByte3 And 63
bytIndex4 = bytBits19to24

Base64Encode = Base64Table(bytIndex1) + _
               Base64Table(bytIndex2) + _
               Base64Table(bytIndex3) + _
               Base64Table(bytIndex4)


End Function
```

Listing 5.10 *Encoding a triplet as Base64*

The Base64Encode function (Listing 5.10) will be a piece of cake for anyone with assembly language programming experience. Others may need to resort to a pen and paper or just accept that it works. For reference, I have included a table of values (Table 5.8) needed to rotate and mask bits in a numeric value (e.g., a byte). To illustrate, if you want to shift the bits 3 to the right, you would divide by 8; to shift them 3 to the left, you would multiply by 8; and to use only the low-order 3 bits, you would perform a Boolean *AND* with 7 on the value.

Table 5.8 *Values for Bit Operations*

Number of Bits	Rotation Value	Mask Value
1	2	1
2	4	3
3	8	7
4	16	15
5	32	31
6	64	63
7	128	127

To encode a triplet with Base64, we need to first separate the bits. Using the functions described above, we subdivide the bytes as required. You may wish to refer back to Table 5.4 to see how the bits are mapped in the binary bytes and the Base64 characters, respectively. For the first character, we need the first 6 bits of the first byte. That is accomplished easily enough by rotating the bits 2 to the right. This means dividing by 4. To get bits 7 through 12, we need to get bits 7 and 8 from the first byte and bits 9 through 12 from the second byte. Bits 7 and 8 are the low-order 2 bits from the first byte. Bits 9-12 are the first nibble of the second byte and must be shifted 4 bits to the right. We then shift 7 or 8 4-bits to the left and add 9-12. Using similar operations, we also construct the third and fourth values.

We now have four 6-bit values, which need to be substituted with the corresponding Base64 characters and concatenated.

```
Private Function Base64Table(Index As Byte) As String

   Base64Table = Mid(Base64Sequence, Index + 1, 1)

End Function
```

Listing 5.11 *Encoding 6-bit value with Base64*

To find the Base64 character (Listing 5.11) for *n* we look up the *n*th value in the Base64 character sequence.

Decoding MIME

To decode MIME we need to read in the entire message. We can then parse it into recognizable components and display these to the user.

Code Example

The MIME reader used in this example looks like the one used in Figure 5.5. Note that there is a list of attached files at the bottom of the form. Since you will be familiar with the other parts, we will focus in on these attachments. The user can call them up by double-clicking on the filename.

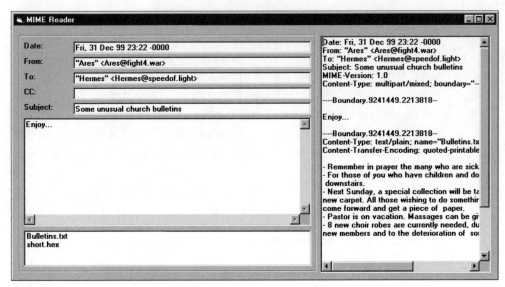

Figure 5.5 *Encoding MIME*

```
Private Sub LoadMessage()
  Dim strCurrentLine
  Dim mhdrHeaderLine
  Dim mattAttachment
  Dim strBodyLine

  txtSource.Text = ""
  For Each strCurrentLine In DisplayMessage.Lines
    txtSource.Text = txtSource.Text + CRLF + strCurrentLine
  Next

  DisplayMessage.Parse

  For Each mhdrHeaderLine In DisplayMessage.Headers
    Select Case LCase(mhdrHeaderLine.Label)
      Case "from":
        txtFrom.Text = mhdrHeaderLine.Value
      Case "to":
        txtTo.Text = mhdrHeaderLine.Value
      Case "cc":
        txtCC.Text = mhdrHeaderLine.Value
      Case "subject":
        txtSubject.Text = mhdrHeaderLine.Value
      Case "date":
```

```
                    txtDate.Text = mhdrHeaderLine.Value
            End Select
        Next

        For Each strBodyLine In DisplayMessage.BodyLines
            txtContent.Text = txtContent.Text + CRLF + strBodyLine
        Next

        For Each mattAttachment In DisplayMessage.Attachments
            lstAttachmentList.AddItem mattAttachment.Filename
        Next

    End Sub
```

Listing 5.12 *Load the message into the form*

When loading the form (Listing 5.12) we need to loop through all the attachments of the message and add the filenames to the list on the form.

```
    Private Sub lstAttachmentList_DblClick()
        DisplayMessage.Attachments(lstAttachmentList.ListIndex + _
                            1).CallAttachment
    End Sub
```

Listing 5.13 *Call double-clicked attachment*

We also add the subroutine (Listing 5.13) for the double-click event on the attachment list.

```
    Public Sub Parse()

      Dim strBoundary As String
      Dim strCurrentLine As String
      Dim rhdrCurrentHeader As RFC822HeaderLine
      Dim mattCurrentAttachment As MIMEAttachment

      strBoundary = ""

          Headers
      Do While Not EndOfMessage And NextLine <> ""
        strCurrentLine = GetLine
        Do While SpaceBegin(NextLine)
          strCurrentLine = strCurrentLine + GetLine
```

```
      Loop

      Set rhdrCurrentHeader = New RFC822HeaderLine
      rhdrCurrentHeader.Parse (strCurrentLine)
      Headers.Add rhdrCurrentHeader

      If LCase(rhdrCurrentHeader.Label) = "content-type" Then
         strBoundary = rhdrCurrentHeader.HeaderParameter("Boundary")
      End If
   Loop

   ' Blank Lines
   Do While NextLine = ""
      strCurrentLine = GetLine:        If EndOfMessage Then Exit Sub
   Loop

   ' Preamble
   Do While InStr(NextLine, strBoundary) = 0
      strCurrentLine = GetLine:        If EndOfMessage Then Exit Sub
      PreambleLines.Add strCurrentLine
   Loop


   ' Attachments
   Do While InStr(NextLine, strBoundary + "--") = 0

      strCurrentLine = GetLine:        If EndOfMessage Then Exit Sub

      Set mattCurrentAttachment = New MIMEAttachment

        ' Attachment Headers
      Do While NextLine <> ""
         ' Add wrapped lines
        strCurrentLine = GetLine:    If EndOfMessage Then Exit Sub
        Do While SpaceBegin(NextLine)
           strCurrentLine = strCurrentLine + GetLine
        Loop

        rhdrCurrentHeader.Parse (strCurrentLine)
        If LCase(rhdrCurrentHeader.Label) = "content-type" Then
          mattCurrentAttachment.Filename = _
                        rhdrCurrentHeader.HeaderParameter("name")
        End If

        If LCase(rhdrCurrentHeader.Label) = _
```

```
                                       "content-transfer-encoding" Then
            mattCurrentAttachment.Encoding = rhdrCurrentHeader.Value
         End If
      Loop

         ' Blank Lines
      Do While NextLine = ""
         strCurrentLine = GetLine:        If EndOfMessage Then Exit Sub
      Loop

      If mattCurrentAttachment.Filename = "" Then
            ' Message Body
         Set mattCurrentAttachment = Nothing
         Do While InStr(NextLine, strBoundary) = 0
            strCurrentLine = GetLine:     If EndOfMessage Then Exit Sub
            BodyLines.Add strCurrentLine
         Loop
      Else
            ' Attachment body
         Do While InStr(NextLine, strBoundary) = 0
            strCurrentLine = GetLine:     If EndOfMessage Then Exit Sub
            mattCurrentAttachment.Lines.Add strCurrentLine
         Loop
         Attachments.Add mattCurrentAttachment
      End If
   Loop

      ' Epilogue
   Do While Not EndOfMessage
      strCurrentLine = GetLine
      EpilogueLines.Add strCurrentLine
   Loop
End Sub
```

Listing 5.14 *Parse Message*

The most important function (Listing 5.14) of the MIMEMessage module is *Parse*. As we loop through the headers we need to check for a label of "content-type." When we see it we take note of its parameter called "Boundary," as we will need to use it for identifying the bodyparts. Until the first boundary, we add all the lines to the preamble. Once we hit the first Boundary, we loop on each attachment until we reach the final boundary (denoted by trailing dashes).

Each attachment implies a sequence of steps:

Define a new attachment object.

Loop through the attachment headers.

    Get *Filename* from the content-type header.

    Get *Encoding* from the content-transfer-encoding header.

If there is no filename, we add the lines to the main message.

    Otherwise we add the lines to the current attachment and add the attachment to the current message.

After the final boundary we can add any remaining lines to the Epilogue.

```
Public Sub CallAttachment()

  Dim strExecutablePath As String
  Dim intScanPosition As Integer
  Dim intStatus As Integer

  SaveFile

  strExecutablePath = Space$(255)
  intStatus = FindExecutable(Filename, WorkDirectory, _
                      strExecutablePath)

  For intScanPosition = 1 To Len(strExecutablePath)
      If Mid$(strExecutablePath, intScanPosition, 1) = Chr$(0) Then
          strExecutablePath = Left$(strExecutablePath, _
                                intScanPosition - 1) + _
                          " " + Mid$(strExecutablePath, _
                                intScanPosition + 1)
      End If
  Next

  strExecutablePath = Trim(strExecutablePath)

  Shell strExecutablePath, vbNormalFocus

End Sub
```

Listing 5.15 *Invoke attachment association*

The attachment object has a routine (*CallAttachment*) to invoke the executable program associated with the attachment file (Listing 5.15). This is to support the user double-clicking on the attachment list. We use the Windows API function *FindExecutable* to determine the associated application. The result is a list of zero-delimited parameters. We replace the zeroes with spaces and use the *Shell* function to invoke the command line.

SaveFile opens the output file and loops through the lines in the attachment, writing each to the file. Depending on the encoding of the attachment there are three differences that should be noted: the File Open Mode, the File Write function, and the Encoding function. Table 5.9 summarizes these differences, as you can verify in Listing 5.16.

Table 5.9 *Encoding-Dependent Differences in Saving Attachments*

Encoding	File Open Mode	File Write Function	Encoding Function
Base64	Binary	Put	DecodeBase64
QuotedPrintable	Output	Print	**DecodeQuotedPrintable**
Other	Output	Print	*None*

```
Public Sub SaveFile()

    Dim intOutputFileNumber As Integer
    Dim strCurrentLine

    intOutputFileNumber = FreeFile

    Select Case LCase(Encoding)

      Case "base64":
        Open WorkDirectory + Filename For Binary As #intOutputFileNumber
        For Each strCurrentLine In Lines
        Put #intOutputFileNumber, , DecodeBase64(CStr(strCurrentLine))
        Next
        Close #intOutputFileNumber
      Case "quoted-printable":
        Open WorkDirectory + Filename For Output As #intOutputFileNumber
        For Each strCurrentLine In Lines
        Print #intOutputFileNumber, _
```

```
              DecodeQuotedPrintable(CStr(strCurrentLine))
       Next
       Close #intOutputFileNumber
     Case Else
       Open WorkDirectory + Filename For Output As #intOutputFileNumber
       For Each strCurrentLine In Lines
         Print #intOutputFileNumber, CStr(strCurrentLine)
       Next
       Close #intOutputFileNumber
   End Select

End Sub
```

Listing 5.16 *Save Attachment to a File*

DecodeBase64 (Listing 5.17) accepts the current Base64-encoded
line and returns a string containing the decoded value. It loops for
every foursome (four-character-set) in the line. Each one is decoded
into a triple (3-byte set). We check whether this foursome was padded
(with one or two trailing equal signs), and only add the appropriate
number of real bytes to the result.

```
Private Function DecodeBase64(ContentLine As String) As String

   Dim intFoursomePosition As Integer
   Dim strWorkBuffer As String
   Dim strFoursome As String
   Dim bytWork1 As Byte
   Dim bytWork2 As Byte
   Dim bytWork3 As Byte
   Dim bytWork4 As Byte


   For intFoursomePosition = 0 To Len(ContentLine) / 4 - 1

     strFoursome = Mid$(ContentLine, (intFoursomePosition * 4 + 1), 4)
     Base64DecodeFoursome strFoursome, _
                     bytWork1, bytWork2, bytWork3

     If Mid$(strFoursome, 3, 2) = "==" Then
       strWorkBuffer = strWorkBuffer + Chr$(bytWork1)
```

```
    ElseIf Mid$(strFoursome, 4, 1) = "=" Then
        strWorkBuffer = strWorkBuffer + Chr$(bytWork1) + _
            Chr$(bytWork2)
    Else
        strWorkBuffer = strWorkBuffer + Chr$(bytWork1) + _
            Chr$(bytWork2) + Chr$(bytWork3)
    End If

Next

DecodeBase64 = strWorkBuffer

End Function
```

Listing 5.17 *Decode a line of Base64 data*

It shouldn't be a surprise that decoding Base64 is similar to encoding but backwards (Listing 5.18). We determine the Base64 index of each character. This should give us four 6-bit values. We then divide these up into bit fields and put them together again as three 8-bit values, which are returned as output parameters.

```
Private Sub Base64DecodeFoursome(InputString As String, _
                      ByRef OutputByte1 As Byte, _
                      ByRef OutputByte2 As Byte, _
                      ByRef OutputByte3 As Byte)


    Dim bytBits01to06 As Byte
    Dim bytBits07to08 As Byte
    Dim bytBits09to12 As Byte
    Dim bytBits13to16 As Byte
    Dim bytBits17to18 As Byte
    Dim bytBits19to24 As Byte

    Dim bytIndex1 As Byte
    Dim bytIndex2 As Byte
    Dim bytIndex3 As Byte
    Dim bytIndex4 As Byte

    bytIndex1 = Base64Index(Mid$(InputString, 1, 1))
```

```
bytIndex2 = Base64Index(Mid$(InputString, 2, 1))
bytIndex3 = Base64Index(Mid$(InputString, 3, 1))
bytIndex4 = Base64Index(Mid$(InputString, 4, 1))

bytBits01to06 = bytIndex1
bytBits07to08 = Int(bytIndex2 / 16)
bytBits09to12 = bytIndex2 And 15
bytBits13to16 = Int(bytIndex3 / 4)
bytBits17to18 = bytIndex3 And 3
bytBits19to24 = bytIndex4

OutputByte1 = bytBits01to06 * 4 + bytBits07to08
OutputByte2 = bytBits09to12 * 16 + bytBits13to16
OutputByte3 = bytBits17to18 * 64 + bytBits19to24

End Sub
```

Listing 5.18 *Decode four Base64 characters into 3 bytes*

To look up the index of a Base64 character (Listing 5.19), we use the *InStr* function to find its position in the Base64Sequence. This will work for all characters except the padding character ("="). We therefore check for it separately and set the index to zero for trailing equal signs.

```
Private Function Base64Index(EntryString As String) As Byte

  Base64Index = InStr(EntryString, Base64Sequence, vbBinaryCompare) - 1
  If EntryString = "=" Then Base64Index = 0

End Function
```

Listing 5.19 *Lookup index of Base64 character*

To decode a line of QuotedPrintable text (Listing 5.20) we scan through each character in the line and see if it is an equal sign. If so, we extract the next two characters and determine the decimal equivalent to the hexadecimal value (e.g., "&H10" would return 16), and advance past the three characters. If the current character is not an equal sign, then we just continue to the next character.

```
Private Function DecodeQuotedPrintable(ContentLine As String) As String

   Dim strWorkLine As String
   Dim intScanPosition As Integer
   Dim bytSpecialCharacter As Byte

   intScanPosition = 1
   Do While intScanPosition <= Len(ContentLine)
     If Mid$(ContentLine, intScanPosition, 1) = "=" Then
       bytSpecialCharacter = Val("&H" + _
                      Mid$(ContentLine, intScanPosition + 1, 2))
       strWorkLine = strWorkLine + Chr$(bytSpecialCharacter)
       intScanPosition = intScanPosition + 3
     Else
       strWorkLine = strWorkLine + Mid$(ContentLine, intScanPosition, 1)
       intScanPosition = intScanPosition + 1
     End If
   Loop

   DecodeQuotedPrintable = strWorkLine

End Function
```

Listing 5.20 *Decode line of QuotedPrintable text*

In order to determine the boundary of the message we need to parse the content-type header. Listing 5.21 shows a generic function to parse headers with this syntax. We search for the parameter name in the value of the header. We then assume everything from the subsequent "=" to the following ";" is the value. If there is no following ";" we take the rest of the line.

```
Public Function HeaderParameter(ParameterName As String) As String

   Dim intBeginPosition As Integer
   Dim intEndPosition As Integer
   Dim intParameterLength As Integer
   Dim strWorkValue As String

   intBeginPosition = InStr(1, Value, ParameterName, 1)

   If intBeginPosition = 0 Then
```

```
      GetHeaderParameter = ""
      Exit Function
   End If

   intBeginPosition = InStr(intBeginPosition, Value, "=") + 1
   intEndPosition = InStr(intBeginPosition, Value, ";")
   intParameterLength = intEndPosition - intBeginPosition

   If intParameterLength > 0 Then
      strWorkValue = Mid$(Value, intBeginPosition, intParameterLength)
   Else
      strWorkValue = Mid$(Value, intBeginPosition)
   End If

   strWorkValue = Trim(strWorkValue)

   If Left$(strWorkValue, 1) = """" Then
      strWorkValue = Mid$(strWorkValue, 2, Len(strWorkValue) - 2)
   End If

   HeaderParameter = strWorkValue

End Function
```

Listing 5.21 *Find parameter in a header*

Wrapping Up

That completes our examples. We have touched on all the aspects you need to think about when working with MIME. Some of the areas we did not explore in detail are:

- *Other content-types*—The vast majority of MIME messages only use the small subset we have covered. Yet it is possible to encounter the others as well. In particular, embedded messages can be a challenge to parse and work with.

- *Multiple attachments*—We have limited the number of attachments to two. This is not so much due to any inherent difficulty with more than two MIME attachments. The challenge becomes one of creating the supporting User Interface for a variable number of embedded attachments. Most production MIME readers will display an icon for each attachment. You might find it easier (although not quite as user-friendly) to use a list box.

- *Better memory management*—Although it is very convenient to cache the entire message in various collections and arrays, it is not the most efficient or reliable way of processing messages (particularly large ones). You may run into limits with Visual Basic if you try to process messages with multi-megabyte attachments. There are several ways to avoid the problem (e.g., storing the attachments in temporary files rather than holding them in memory). But every application will have its unique requirements, so it is difficult to develop a general purpose solution to satisfy all needs.

- *Embedded separators*—We have generated random separators and have then assumed that they do not occur in the text. While it is statistically improbable that we would ever clash, there is no guarantee unless we scan each line and trap any separator.

Chapter 6

SMTP—Simple Mail Transfer Protocol

You might have guessed it from the name: SMTP is responsible for transferring messages from one user to another. As there may be no direct connection possible between the users the path is often broken up into hops (Figure 6.1). Each protocol session carries the message one hop further along the path to the recipient's post office.

The message is initially composed by the sender and typically sent to a mail relay that sends it on to a number of intermediate relays until it arrives at its destination, usually a post office. The selection of mail relays involves DNS (Domain Name System), which is not covered until the next chapter, so we will postpone discussion of multi-hop paths until then.

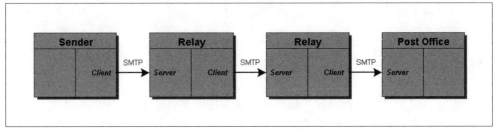

Figure 6.1 *Typical Message Flow*

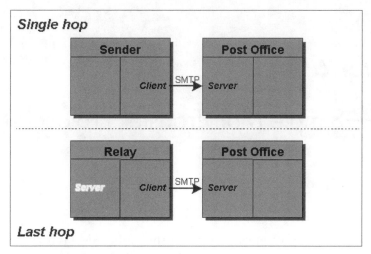

Figure 6.2 *Simple Message Flow*

Instead, this chapter will focus on the protocol of each session. To do this we reduce the model to its simplest form (Figure 6.2). This is the delivery of the message to the post office, either directly from the sender or else from the last relay in the path.

Figure 6.3 shows a typical SMTP session. The server begins the conversation by announcing its identity. This confirms to the client that the link is in order and that there is indeed an SMTP server at the other end. The client then specifies the sender and the recipient of the message followed by the (RFC 822) message itself. After successfully transmitting the message it closes the session.

Overview

Although there are more than a dozen SMTP commands (Table 6.1), you probably won't find much use for most of them other than to help you debug problems. We will focus on the commands in the example: MAIL, RCPT, DATA, and QUIT.

```
                                                    220 SMTP server here⇐
⇒mail from:<artemis@silver.arrow>
                                                                250 OK⇐
⇒rcpt to:athena@olive.tree
                                                                250 OK⇐
⇒data
                                                    354 Start sending... ⇐
⇒Date: Fri, 31 Dec 99 23:33 -0000
⇒From: "Artemis" <artemis@silver.arrow>
⇒To: "Athena" <athena@olive.tree>
⇒Subject: History of the world
⇒
⇒The pyramids are a range of mountains between France and Spain.
⇒The Egyptians built the pyramids in the shape of a huge triangular
⇒cube.
⇒
⇒The government of Athens was democratic because people took the
⇒law into their own hands.
⇒
⇒When they fought with the Persians, the Greeks were outnumbered
⇒because the Persians had more men.
⇒
⇒In midevil times, people were alliterate. The greatest writer
⇒of the futile ages was Chaucer. During this time, people put on
⇒morality plays about ghosts, goblins, virgins and other mythical
⇒creatures.
⇒
⇒Abraham Lincoln became America's greatest Precedent. Lincoln's
⇒mother died in infancy, and he was born in a log cabin he built
⇒with his own hands. Lincoln wrote the Gettysburg Address while
⇒traveling from Washington to Gettysburg on the back of an
⇒envelope. He also freed the slaves by signing the Emasculation
⇒Proclamation. On the night of April 14, 1865, Lincoln went to
⇒the theater and got shot in his seat by one of the actors in
⇒a moving picture show. The believed assinator was John Wilkes
⇒Booth, a supposingly insane actor. This ruined Booth's career.
⇒.
                                                                250 OK⇐
⇒quit
                                                                250 OK⇐
```

Figure 6.3 *Sample SMTP session*

Table 6.1 *SMTP Commands*[1]

Command	Parameters	Description
DATA		Signals transmission of RFC 822 message in subsequent lines
EXPN	distribution-list	Expand distribution list
HELO	domain	Identify sender-MTA to receiver-MTA
HELP	command	Send "helpful" information (e.g., list of commands supported)
MAIL	FROM: address	Initiate mail transaction destined for mailbox
NOOP		No action—return positive reply code
QUIT		Close transmission channel
RCPT	TO: address	Identify individual recipient of message
RSET		Abort current mail transaction
SAML	FROM: address	Initiate mail transaction destined for terminal and mailbox
SEND	FROM: address	Initiate mail transaction destined for terminal
SOML	FROM: address	Initiate mail transaction destined for terminal or mailbox
TURN		Reverse sender and receiver roles
VRFY	address	Verify existence of user

Typical Command Flow

The command flow is shown more abstractly in Figure 6.4. It is very logical if you keep in mind the three items required by the MTA:

1. The recipient list, so that it knows to whom to send the messages.

2. The message body, so that it knows what to send to these recipients.

3. The sender's identity, so that any subsequent delivery failures can be communicated back.

The client initiates the mail transaction (*MAIL FROM*) and indicates the sender of the message. It then proceeds by specifying all recipients individually with as many *RCPT TO* commands as necessary. Following these comes the RFC 822 formatted *DATA*.

This completes the first message. If there are additional messages, we repeat the process starting with the sender. Once we have sent all messages we *QUIT* the session.

---

[1] See RFC821 §4.1 for a full specification of these commands.

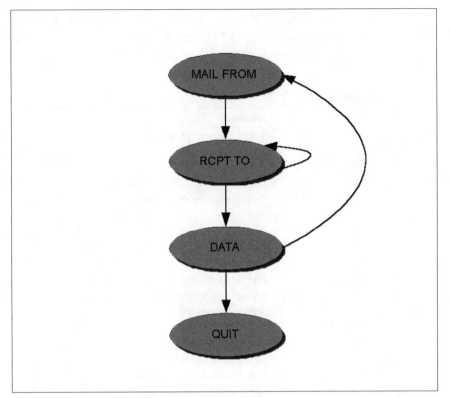

Figure 6.4 *Typical command flow*

Reply Codes

Table 6.2 lists all the reply codes supported by SMTP. Only a subset of these is meaningful for any given SMTP command. You can find the correlation of supported responses in RFC 821 §4.3, but in many cases you needn't know the full meaning of the reply code. Rather than choosing a completely random set of codes, the SMTP architects tried to make the individual digits as meaningful as possible.

The first digit is the primary indication of the success of the command. Generally you want to see reply codes beginning with a "2" and you want to avoid "4" and "5." A response beginning with "3," namely "354" (which happens to be the only code beginning with

"3"), is expected (and only ever occurs) when you transmit the DATA of the message. The "1" shows the good intentions of the architects but has not yet found its use in SMTP.

Table 6.2 *SMTP Reply Codes[2]*

Code	Description
211	System status, or system help reply
214	Help message
220	<domain> Service ready
221	<domain> Service closing transmission channel
250	Requested mail action okay, completed
251	User not local; will forward to <forward-path>
354	Start mail input; end with <CRLF>.<CRLF>
421	<domain> Service not available, closing transmission channel
450	Requested mail action not taken: mailbox unavailable
451	Requested action aborted: local error in processing
452	Requested action not taken: insufficient system storage
500	Syntax error, command unrecognized
501	Syntax error in parameters or arguments
502	Command not implemented
503	Bad sequence of commands
504	Command parameter not implemented
550	Requested action not taken: mailbox unavailable
551	User not local; please try <forward-path>
552	Requested mail action aborted: exceeded storage allocation
553	Requested action not taken: mailbox name not allowed
554	Transaction failed

Table 6.3 *Primary Reply Categories—First Digit of Reply Code*

Value	Reply Type	Description
1	Positive Preliminary	Command held pending confirmation
2	Positive Completion	Command successfully completed
3	Positive Intermediate	Command held awaiting further information
4	Transient Negative	Command failed due to temporary condition
5	Permanent Negative	Command failed

The second digit is far less useful than the first. Nonetheless, it can help to categorize some of the reply codes since it tells you where the

---

[2] See RFC 821 §4.2.2 for more details on the reply codes.

problem could lie. Again, the architects graciously allowed "3" and "4" to be reserved for future extensions.

Table 6.4 *Secondary Reply Categories—Second Digit of Reply Code*

Value	Reply Subtype
0	Syntax
1	Information
2	Connection
3	*not specified*
4	*not specified*
5	Mail System

The last digit of the reply serves only to distinguish between multiple replies in the same primary and secondary categories (e.g., 500-504 are all Permanent Negative Syntax errors; 550-554 are all Permanent Negative Mail System errors).

SMTP Client

The steps of a simple SMTP client are:

- Collect the message information from the user (or system).
    - Sender's mail address
    - List of recipients
    - Body of message
    - Date of message
    - Subject of message
- Establish connection with the server.
- Identify the sender.
- Identify the recipient.
- Transfer the RFC 822 message.
- Terminate with a period.
- Close the connection.

Code Example

I have two examples of SMTP clients. The first assumes that you
already have an RFC 822 encoded message stored in a file. This is the
simpler scenario since it only involves transferring the message via
SMTP. The second is more typical in that it allows a user to compose
the message on line, encapsulates the message in MIME, and then
calls the same SMTP commands as the first example.

In Figure 6.5 you can see the form needed to send an RFC 822
encoded file via SMTP. We need to specify the SMTP server as well as
all the data the server needs. As mentioned earlier in the chapter this is:

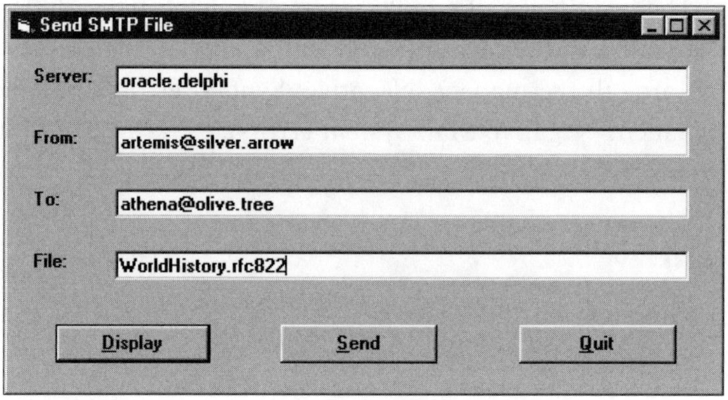

Figure 6.5 *Sending an RFC 822 file with SMTP*

1. Who it is *From* (for delivery notifications)
2. Who it is *To*
3. What should be sent (the *File*)

In addition to the *Send*, we have a *Display* button on the form just
in case the user wants to verify the contents before sending. We can
send one or multiple messages and then *Quit* when we are done.

The *Send* button (Figure 6.6) connects to the server and sends the
commands (*mail from, rcpt to*) corresponding to the (*from, to*) fields
on the form. To send the file, the *Send* command opens it and inputs
one line at a time sending each to the server. It concludes the *data* with
a period and then *quits* the session.

```
Private Sub btnSend_Click()
  Dim lngSMTPSocket As Long
  Dim lngServerAddress As Long
  Dim strServerName As String

  Dim strServerResponse As String
  Dim strInputFile As String
  Dim intInputFileNumber As Integer
  Dim strInputLine As String

  lngSMTPSocket = 0

  strServerName = txtServer.Text
  intStatus = GetIPAddress(lngServerAddress, strServerName)
  intStatus = CreateSocket(lngSMTPSocket, 0)
  intStatus = ConnectSocket(lngSMTPSocket, lngServerAddress, SMTPPort)

  intStatus = ReceiveSocket(lngSMTPSocket, strServerResponse)
  intStatus = SendSocket(lngSMTPSocket, "mail from:<" + txtFrom.Text + ">")

  intStatus = ReceiveSocket(lngSMTPSocket, strServerResponse)
  intStatus = SendSocket(lngSMTPSocket, "rcpt to:<" + txtToRecipient.Text + ">")
  intStatus = ReceiveSocket(lngSMTPSocket, strServerResponse)
  intStatus = SendSocket(lngSMTPSocket, "data")
  intStatus = ReceiveSocket(lngSMTPSocket, strServerResponse)

  intInputFileNumber = FreeFile
  Open txtFilename.Text For Input As #intInputFileNumber      ⎫
  Do While Not EOF(intInputFileNumber)                       ⎬ RFC822
    Line Input #intInputFileNumber, strInputLine             ⎪ Message
    intStatus = SendSocket(lngSMTPSocket, strInputLine)      ⎭
  Loop
  Close #intInputFileNumber

  intStatus = SendSocket(lngSMTPSocket, ".")
  intStatus = ReceiveSocket(lngSMTPSocket, strServerResponse)
  intStatus = SendSocket(lngSMTPSocket, "quit")
  intStatus = ReceiveSocket(lngSMTPSocket, strServerResponse)
  intStatus = ReleaseSocket(lngSMTPSocket)

End Sub
```

Figure 6.6 *Sending a file with SMTP*

The full SMTP client (Figure 6.7) looks much like the MIME form we saw earlier in the book. The main difference is that we now have to specify a server to which we wish to send the message. Note that we will use the *From* and *To* fields both for the RFC 822 message composition and the SMTP commands. Although there is no obligation to do so, it simplifies the User Interface.

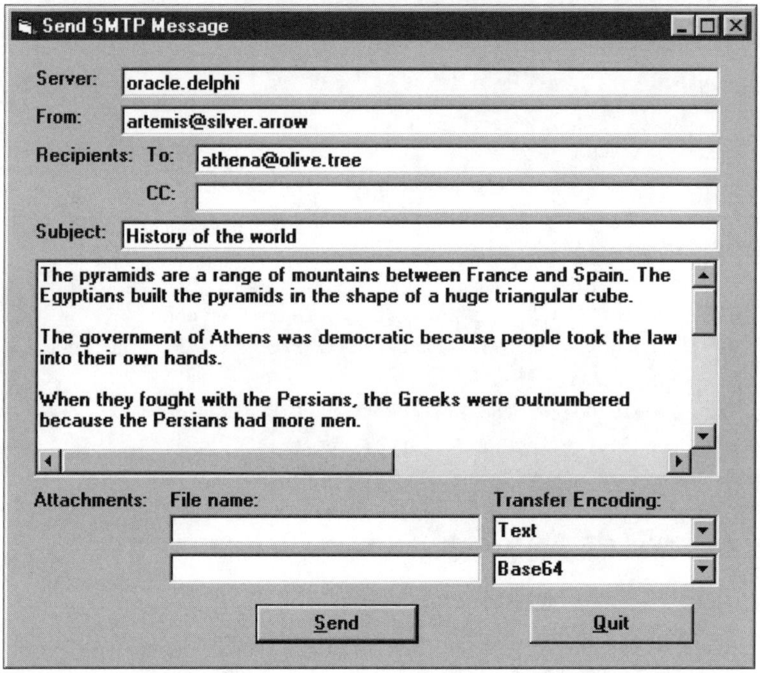

Figure 6.7 *SMTP Client*

The code in Listing 6.1 is similar to our previous example with some portions from the MIME composer. You will notice that up until the *data* command, it is the same as the earlier version, as is the portion beginning with the final period.

The part where we read from a file now constructs a MIME message on the fly. It adds the *From, To,* and *Subject* headers, the *Body Lines,* and both *Attachments.* Then it *composes* the message and sends each line to the SMTP server.

```
Private Sub btnSend_Click()
  Dim lngSMTPSocket As Long
  Dim lngServerAddress As Long
  Dim strServerName As String

  Dim strServerResponse As String

  Dim mmsgCurrentMessage As New MIMEMessage
  Dim strCurrentLine

  lngSMTPSocket = 0

  strServerName = txtServer.Text
  intStatus = GetIPAddress(lngServerAddress, strServerName)
  intStatus = CreateSocket(lngSMTPSocket, 0)
  intStatus = ConnectSocket(lngSMTPSocket, lngServerAddress, SMTPPort)

  intStatus = ReceiveSocket(lngSMTPSocket, strServerResponse)
  intStatus = SendSocket(lngSMTPSocket, "mail from:<" + txtFrom.Text _
      + ">")

  intStatus = ReceiveSocket(lngSMTPSocket, strServerResponse)
  intStatus = SendSocket(lngSMTPSocket, "rcpt to:<" + _
      txtToRecipient.Text + ">")
  intStatus = ReceiveSocket(lngSMTPSocket, strServerResponse)
  intStatus = SendSocket(lngSMTPSocket, "data")
  intStatus = ReceiveSocket(lngSMTPSocket, strServerResponse)

  mmsgCurrentMessage.AddHeader "From", txtFrom.Text
  mmsgCurrentMessage.AddHeader "To", txtToRecipient.Text
  mmsgCurrentMessage.AddHeader "Subject", txtSubject.Text

  mmsgCurrentMessage.BodyLines.Add txtContent.Text

  If txtAttachment1.Text <> "" And Dir(txtAttachment1.Text) <> "" Then
    mmsgCurrentMessage.AddAttachment txtAttachment1.Text, _
        cmbTransferEncoding1.Text
  End If

  If txtAttachment2.Text <> "" And Dir(txtAttachment2.Text) <> "" Then
    mmsgCurrentMessage.AddAttachment txtAttachment2.Text, _
        cmbTransferEncoding2.Text
  End If
```

```
mmsgCurrentMessage.Compose

For Each strCurrentLine In mmsgCurrentMessage.Lines
  intStatus = SendSocket(lngSMTPSocket, CStr(strCurrentLine))
Next

intStatus = SendSocket(lngSMTPSocket, ".")
intStatus = ReceiveSocket(lngSMTPSocket, strServerResponse)
intStatus = SendSocket(lngSMTPSocket, "quit")
intStatus = ReceiveSocket(lngSMTPSocket, strServerResponse)
intStatus = ReleaseSocket(lngSMTPSocket)

End Sub
```

Listing 6.1 *Sending a message with SMTP*

SMTP Server

An SMTP server accepts requests for mail delivery. A fully functional server would then determine whether any of the recipients are local and, if so, store the messages in the local post office. These can then be retrieved with a message retrieval protocol (e.g., POP or IMAP). Any mail to nonlocal recipients would need to be relayed on either to the final destination, or at least to the next hop. This chapter develops the first task and assumes all recipients are local. The second task will be continued in the next chapter.

Server Example

The form of the server (Figure 6.8) shows the data used by this server. The *From* field will not be used in the example but would be necessary to support delivery notification and failures.

We will use the *To* field to determine the mailbox of the recipient. For simplicity this will be the string prior to the "@." Typically, post offices will have a directory that matches the mail address to specific mailboxes, but this implementation is not required by the standard.

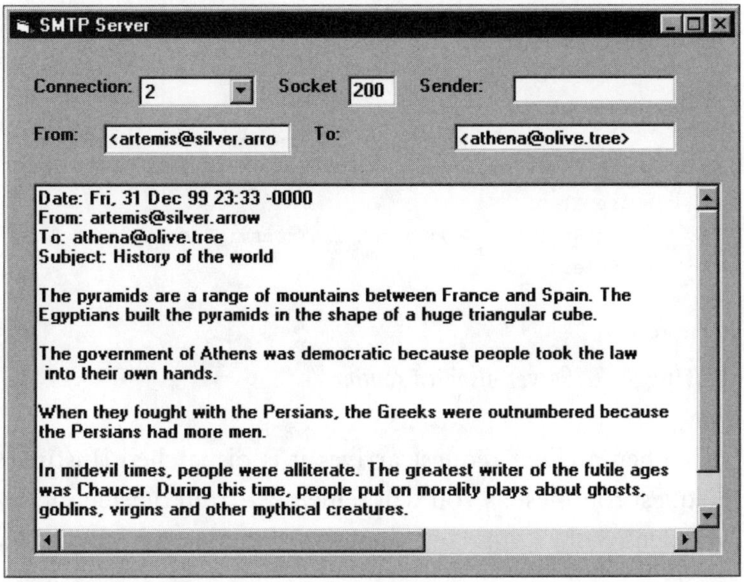

Figure 6.8 *SMTP Server*

Finally, we have the RFC 822 message that is to be delivered to the user. In our case, delivery will mean storage in a directory with the name of the user. It can then be retrieved by our retrieval protocols, as we shall see in later chapters.

```
Private Sub txtRequest_DblClick(Index As Integer)
  Dim strClientRequest As String

  intStatus = ReceiveSocket(lngTransmitSocket, strClientRequest)
  DisplayConnection Index
  txtRequest(Index).Text = strClientRequest

  strClientRequest = Trim(strClientRequest)
  Select Case Trim(UCase(Left$(strClientRequest, 4)))
    Case "HELO"
      txtSender(Index).Text = Trim(Mid$(strClientRequest, 5))
      intStatus = SendSocket(lngTransmitSocket, "250 olive.tree")
    Case "MAIL"
      txtFrom(Index).Text = Trim(Mid$(strClientRequest, 11))
      intStatus = SendSocket(lngTransmitSocket, "250 OK")
    Case "RCPT"
      txtTo(Index).Text = Trim(Mid$(strClientRequest, 9))
```

```
        intStatus = SendSocket(lngTransmitSocket, "250 OK")
     Case "DATA"
        ReceiveMessage Index
     Case "QUIT"
        intStatus = SendSocket(lngTransmitSocket, "250 OK")
        intStatus = ReleaseSocket(lngTransmitSocket)
     Case Else
        intStatus = SendSocket(lngTransmitSocket, "250 OK")
   End Select

 End Sub
```

Listing 6.2 *Server dispatch routine*

When a client request arrives it is dispatched (Listing 6.2) to the Request routines, as you will remember from the generic server. There we identify the command (first four letters) and process accordingly:

- *HELO*—Send back a successful status. If we don't support this command it will confuse some clients, and it is not overly difficult to implement.
- *MAIL FROM*—Extract the sender to the form. This data will not be used in this example but would be required if you chose to extend it to support delivery failure notifications.
- *RCPT TO*—Extract the recipient to the form. We will need this to know into which mailbox (Windows directory) to store the message.
- *DATA*—Extract the message to a file in the user's mailbox (Windows directory).
- *QUIT*—Release the socket.

To receive the message (Listing 6.3) we need to identify the user from the recipient string. We concatenate it with the Post Office string to determine our output directory. We can then generate a unique filename and open the output file.

The message is already waiting for us. All we need to do is loop through all the lines until we reach the final period. That marks the end of the message so we close the file.

```
Const PostOfficeDirectory = "C:\Post Office\"
Private Sub ReceiveMessage(Index As Integer)
  Dim strClientRequest As String
  Dim strFileName As String
  Dim intFileNumber As Integer
  Dim strUserName As String

  txtMessage(Index).Text = ""

  strUserName = Left(txtTo(Index).Text, _
                InStr(1, txtTo(Index).Text, "@") - 1)
  strUserName = Mid(strUserName, 2)

  intFileNumber = FreeFile
  strFileName = PostOfficeDirectory + strUserName + "\" + _
                RandomName + ".MIME"
  Open strFileName For Output As #intFileNumber

  intStatus = SendSocket(lngTransmitSocket, "354 Start sending...")
  Do
    intStatus = ReceiveSocket(lngTransmitSocket, strClientRequest)
    If intStatus Then
      If strClientRequest = "." Then Exit Do
      txtMessage(Index).Text = txtMessage(Index).Text + _
                          strClientRequest + CRLF
      Print #intFileNumber, strClientRequest
    End If
  Loop

  Close #intFileNumber
  intStatus = SendSocket(lngTransmitSocket, "250 OK")

End Sub
```

Listing 6.3 *Accept message for local post office*

Wrapping Up

We have a good start on the SMTP programs but, as always, there is
still room for improvement.

- *Embedded period*—It is possible for a message to contain a line with only a period. The client should trap for the period and pad the line with an initial period. Otherwise the server will interpret it as the end of the message. Likewise, the server should look for padded lines (lines beginning with a period, but not consisting solely of the single period) and remove the padding (the first character).

- *Typical commands*—We have only implemented the most typical SMTP commands. The client probably won't need to use any others. However, there are some commands (like TURN) that can be very useful for server-to-server communication.

- *SMPT host*—We have only implemented the server as an SMTP host, not as a relay. As we shall see in the next chapter, most SMTP servers do more than only accepting messages for local users. They are also able to accept messages for nonlocal recipients and relay them on to their destination.

- *Error processing*—We saw the rich set of reply codes that SMTP provides but did not implement these. Functional servers should send the correct reply codes for all failures. And clients should have error processing that is able to cater **to** all the error codes.

Chapter 7

DNS—Domain Name System

If you recall the discussion on networking protocols in Chapter 2, each IP datagram (and thus all network traffic) is sent to a destination based on a 4-byte address. This would correspond to an IP address of the format 204.152.190.72. However, users generally prefer to enter the mnemonic domain name (www.altavista.com) rather than the numeric address. This means that at some stage the domain name must be translated to its IP address.

We might hope that Winsock would translate the name for us. But alas, it doesn't. Most Winsock routines expect the numeric value. The onus is therefore on us to perform the translation. Fortunately, Winsock does give us a few functions to help make the job easier.

Host Lookup

In the UNIX world networked computers are called hosts, and this translation is known as a host lookup. With that in mind, the purpose of the function *gethostbyname* is fairly self-explanatory. In Listing 7.1 you can see its declaration.

```
Declare Function gethostbyname Lib "wsock32.dll"
                              (ByVal HostName As String) As Long
```

Listing 7.1 *Call to obtain IP address*

Its parameter *HostName* is the mnemonic domain name (also known as fully-qualified domain name or FQDN). A little less straightforward is the return value. Called a host-entry, it is a record describing the host and its address.

```
Dim ServerAddress As Long
Dim ServerName As String
Status = GetIPAddress(ServerAddress, ServerName)
```

Listing 7.2 *Example of GetIPAddress*

For C programmers extracting the address is a simple task. C can handle multiple levels of pointer indirection with relative ease. This is not the case with VB (Visual Basic). We need to use temporary variables to unravel each level. Rather than doing this with each call I have provided a wrapper function that will return the *ServerAddress* as a Long variable (Listing 7.2).

To understand how it works we need to look first at the host-entry structure used by Winsock.

The actual host entry (Figure 7.1) is simple to understand and implement.

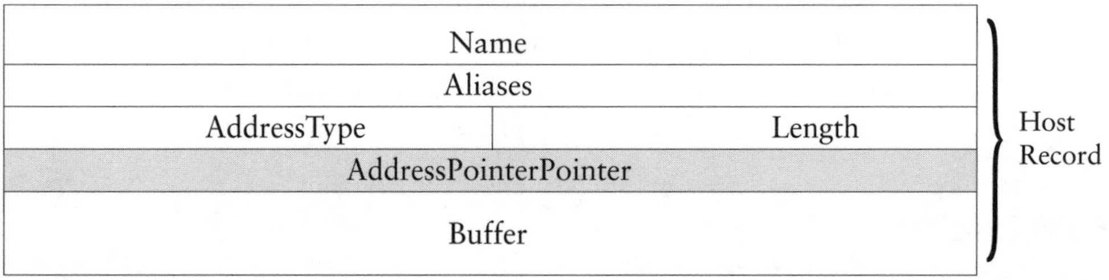

Name	
Aliases	
AddressType	Length
AddressPointerPointer	
Buffer	

Host Record

Figure 7.1 *Host-entry structure*

We are only really interested in the Name (the fully qualified domain name) and the Address, but to be complete we define all the fields in our declaration (Listing 7.3).

When it comes to actually using the host entries, we discover that it is not quite as simple as we might have thought (Figure 7.2). The return value (*HostRecordPointer*) from our function is not the host-

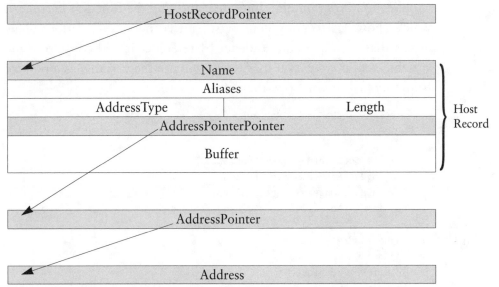

Figure 7.2 *Host-entry references*

entry but a pointer to the host-entry. We follow the link only to see
that, rather than putting the resolved IP address right in the record we
only have a pointer (*AddressPointerPonter*) there. We follow the
pointer and expect to find the IP address there. But again we have a
pointer (*AddressPointer*). Fortunately, we only have to look once
more, as this pointer does indeed lead us to the IP address (*Address*).

```
Type NameHostEntry
 Name As Long
 Aliases As Long
 AddressType As Integer
 Length As Integer
 AddressPointerPointer As Long
 Buffer As String * 100
End Type
```

Listing 7.3 *Host-entry declaration*

A seasoned C programmer wouldn't see the multiple levels of indirection as a problem. Yet in Visual Basic there is no elegant way to use
pointers. Rather than giving up we refer to the Windows API

(Application Programming Interface) and find the function *hmemcpy*, which allows us to copy data between two memory locations. This means that if we pass a parameter by reference it will copy from the variable, and if we pass it by value it will use the variable as a pointer from/to which it will copy the data.

```
Function GetIPAddress(HostAddress As Long, HostName As String) As
Boolean

  Dim nheHostRecord As NameHostEntry
  Dim lngHostRecordPointer As Long
  Dim lngHostAddressPointer As Long
  Dim lngHostAddressPointerPointer As Long

  lngHostAddressPointerPointer = 0
  lngHostAddressPointer = 0
  lngHostRecordPointer = 0
  lngHostRecordPointer = gethostbyname(HostName)
  If lngHostRecordPointer <> 0 Then
    hmemcpy nheHostRecord, ByVal lngHostRecordPointer,
        Len(nheHostRecord)
  End If
  lngHostAddressPointerPointer = nheHostRecord.AddressPointerPointer

  If lngHostAddressPointerPointer <> 0 Then
    hmemcpy lngHostAddressPointer,
        ByVal lngHostAddressPointerPointer, 4
  End If
  If lngHostAddressPointerPointer <> 0 Then
    hmemcpy HostAddress, ByVal lngHostAddressPointer, 4
  End If

  GetIPAddress = True
End Function
```

Listing 7.4 *Look up IP address*

With this technique it is not too difficult to use the function *gethostbyname* (Listing 7.4). It returns to us the *HostRecord* pointer. We copy its reference (the host record) to a local variable. We then fetch the *AddressPointer* and subsequently the address itself.

Resource Record Lookup

Other than host addresses DNS can also store additional information. It is essentially a distributed database to which all computers connected to the Internet have access, so there are good reasons to use it for other purposes. What we will be looking at next is how mail systems use DNS to route mail through the network in an efficient manner.

The reason for mail routing is simple. First imagine we only used host record to send mail to its destination. If I sent a message to A, the mail application would find the IP address for A and try to send the message there. If A was shut down the message could not be delivered. But there might be another machine B that was sitting next to A and was running fine. The optimal solution would be to transfer the message to B and for B to pass it on to A when it came back online.

The drawback to letting Winsock perform the lookups is that you are limited to only looking up host addresses. If you are interested in other resource records you are out of luck. We need to be able to obtain Mail Exchange (MX) records, so we have to find another alternative.

We could look for other software that will evaluate MX records but that would be missing half the fun. Instead we will try to do the same thing that Winsock does when it translates host names to IP addresses. We will connect directly to the DNS server and ask for the records.

The data passed between the client and server in a DNS session is purely in binary form (Figure 7.3). If you don't know the structure of the questions and answers you could spend some time trying to analyze it. Fortunately, the specifications are published in RFC 1035. We will focus on the parts that deal with MX record lookup since these are the only structures we need for mail-related DNS questions.

DNS uses the same data structure, both for queries and responses. In Figure 7.4 you can see its high level layout. After the header it contains

```
⇒    1  32    1    0    0    1    0    0      0    0    0    0    5 116 101 114
⇒  114  97    5 102 105 114 109 101      0    0   15    0    1

     1  32    1    0    0    1    0    2      0    1    0    3    5 116 101 114  ⇐
   114  97    5 102 105 114 109 101      0    0   15    0    1 192   12    0  ⇐
    15   0    1    0    1   81 128    0     15    0   10    5 109   97 105 108  ⇐
    49 192   12 192   12    0   15    0      1    0    1   81 128    0   15    0  ⇐
    10   5 109   97 105 108   50 192     12 192   12    0    2    0    1    0  ⇐
     1  81 128    0   15    6 111 114     97   99 108 101    6 100 101 108  ⇐
   112 104 105    0 192  43    0    1      0    1    0    1   81 128    0    4  ⇐
    10   1    1    3 192  65    0    1      0    1    0    1   81 128    0    4  ⇐
    10   1    1    3 192  85    0    1      0    1    0    1   81 128    0    4  ⇐
                                                                 10    1    1    3  ⇐
```

Figure 7.3 *Sample DNS session*

Header
Question Records
Answer Records
Name Server Records
Additional Information Records

Figure 7.4 *DNS Message*

ID							
QR	OPCODE	AA	TC	RD	RA	Z	RCODE
QDCOUNT							
ANCOUNT							
NSCOUNT							
ARCOUNT							

Figure 7.5 *Header Section*

a list of questions (resources being looked up). A query would typically stop here. In the case of responses the matching resources follow. First come the resource records being looked at (e.g., MX records). Then come the list of authoritative name servers for the resources. Finally, any additional resource records related to the query appear.

Now we can look at the interesting parts of the message in more detail. We start with the Header Section (Figure 7.5).

ID—unique value for this request that can be used to correlate requests and responses.

QR—bit flag that indicates whether this is a query (0) or a response (1).

OPCODE—4-bit field that specifies kind of query in this message. Possible values are:

> *0*—a standard query (QUERY)
>
> *1*—an inverse query (IQUERY)
>
> *2*—a server status request (STATUS)

AA—Authoritative Answer—one bit specifies that the responding name server is an authority for the domain name in the question section.

TC—TrunCation—specifies that this message was truncated due to length greater than that permitted on the transmission channel.

RD—Recursion Desired—directs the name server to pursue the query recursively.

RA—Recursion Available—denotes whether recursive query support is available in the name server.

Z—Zero—Must be zero in all queries and responses. (Reserved for future use.)

RCODE—Response code

> *0*—No error condition
>
> *1*—Format error
>
> *2*—Server failure
>
> *3*—Name Error
>
> *4*—Not Implemented
>
> *5*—Refused

Next we need to list the count of questions and various resource record types. Without these counts neither the client nor the server would be able to tell where the questions end and the answers begin.

QDCOUNT—number of entries in the question section.

ANCOUNT—number of resource records in the answer section.

NSCOUNT—number of name server resource records in the authority records section.

ARCOUNT—number of resource records in the additional records section.

Questions have three fields (Figure 7.6). They begin with *QNAME*, the domain name being looked up. We then have the *QTYPE*, which is the type of resource we are looking for. In our case these are Mail Exchange (MX: 15) but you will also often see Host Addresses (A: 1) and Name Servers (NS: 2).

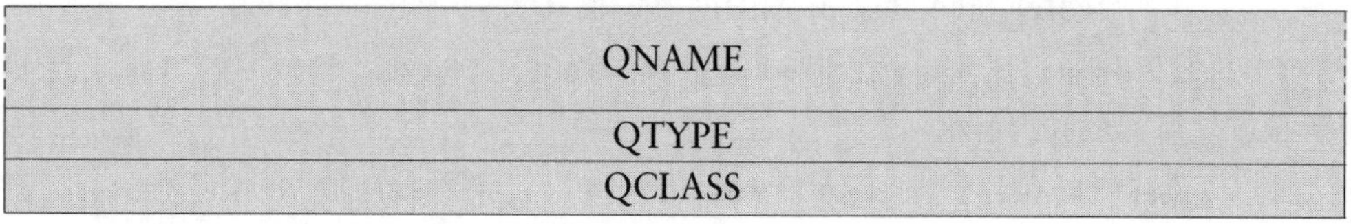

QNAME
QTYPE
QCLASS

Figure 7.6 *Question Section*

QCLASS is typically Internet (IN: 1). If you encounter any other classes there may be two reasons:

1. You have a bug in your program.
2. You are not connected to an Internet-compliant network. If you are not aware of using a very unusual network see option 1.

Resource Records begin with the name of the resource. After the type and class we find a field called TTL (Time-To-Live). This field indicates the number of seconds the resource can be held in cache before it should be revalidated from an authoritative name server. This is not of interest to us since we use the data immediately, but it

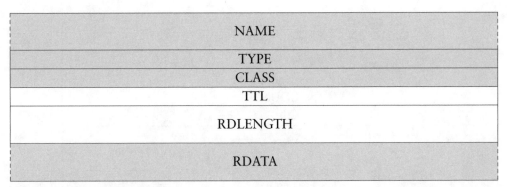

Figure 7.7 *Resource Record*

would be very important for any server that caches data for a longer period of time.

The resource data has length (RDLENTGH) and value (RDATA) fields whereby the data value will be in a particular format depending on the type and class of the resource.

In the case of MX records, the resource data consists of *Preference* and *Exchange* (Figure 7.8). The Exchange is the fully qualified domain name of an SMTP relay serving this mail domain. The Preference gives us a way of deciding the order in which we can attempt to connect to several possible relays.

Preference
Exchange

Figure 7.8 *MX Resource Data*

If we try to merge all the structures so far we should end up with something like Figure 7.9. This is the format of the data being passed between client and server with each request or response.

In order to interpret the query we scan through the data interpreting each byte as we go along. As you can see in Table 7.1, this was a request for all the MX records in the domain terra.firma.

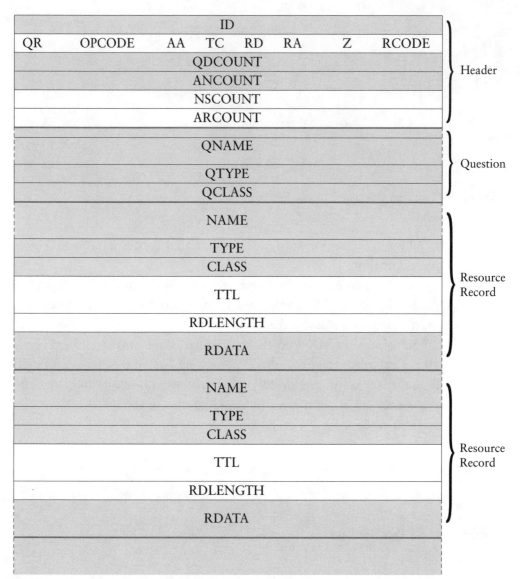

ID							
QR	OPCODE	AA	TC	RD	RA	Z	RCODE
QDCOUNT							
ANCOUNT							
NSCOUNT							
ARCOUNT							
QNAME							
QTYPE							
QCLASS							
NAME							
TYPE							
CLASS							
TTL							
RDLENGTH							
RDATA							
NAME							
TYPE							
CLASS							
TTL							
RDLENGTH							
RDATA							

Figure 7.9 *DNS Message in detail*

For example, a simple DNS query might look something like Figure 7.10.

| 1 | 32 | 1 | 0 | 0 | 1 | 0 | 0 | 0 | 0 | 0 | 0 | 5 | 116 | 101 | 114 |
| 114 | 97 | 5 | 102 | 105 | 114 | 109 | 101 | 0 | 0 | 15 | 0 | 1 |

Figure 7.10 *DNS Query in binary form*

Table 7.1 *DNS Query*

Offset	Value	Meaning	Field	Section
0	1 32		ID	
2	1		QR=OPCODE= AA=TD=0; RD=1	
3	0		RA=Z=RCODE=0	
4	0 1	1	QDCOUNT	Header
6	0 0	0	ANCOUNT	
8	0 0	0	NSCOUNT	
10	0 0	0	ARCOUNT	
12	5 116 101 114 114 97	Terra	QNAME	
18	5 102 105 114 109 97	Firma		
24	0			Question
25	0 15	MX	QTYPE	
27	0 1	IN	QCLASS	

In response we might receive Figure 7.11. We note that the ID (first 2 bytes) and the Question (starting with the 13th byte) are the same as in the request.

1	32	1	0	0	1	0	2	0	1	0	3	5	116	101	114
114	97	5	102	105	114	109	101	0	0	15	0	1	192	12	0
15	0	1	0	1	81	128	0	15	0	10	5	109	97	105	108
49	192	12	192	12	0	15	0	1	0	1	81	128	0	15	0
10	5	109	97	105	108	50	192	12	192	12	0	2	0	1	0
1	81	128	0	15	6	111	114	97	99	108	101	6	100	101	108
112	104	105	0	192	43	0	1	0	1	0	1	81	128	0	4
10	1	1	3	192	65	0	1	0	1	0	1	81	128	0	4
10	1	1	3	192	85	0	1	0	1	0	1	81	128	0	4
10	1	1	3

Figure 7.11 *DNS Response in binary form*

Table 7.2 *DNS Response*

Offset	Value	Meaning	Field	Section
0	1 32		ID	
2	1		QR=OPCODE=	
			AA=TD=0; RD=1	
3	0		RA=Z=RCODE=0	Header
4	0 1	1	QDCOUNT	
6	0 2	2	ANCOUNT	
8	0 1	1	NSCOUNT	
10	0 3	3	ARCOUNT	
12	5 116 101 114 114 97	terra	QNAME	
18	5 102 105 114 109 97	firma		
24	0			Question 1
25	0 15	MX	QTYPE	
27	0 1	IN	QCLASS	
29	192 12	→ 12 terra firma	NAME	
31	0 15	MX	CLASS	
33	0 1	IN	TYPE	
35	0 1 81 128		TTL	Answer 1
39	0 15		RDLENTH	
41	0 10		Preference	
43	5 109 97 105 108 49	mail1	Exchange	
49	192 12	→ 12 terra firma		
51	192 12	→ 12 terra firma	NAME	
53	0 15	MX	TYPE	
55	0 1	IN	CLASS	
57	0 1 81 128		TTL	Answer 2
61	0 15		RDLENTH	
63	0 10		Preference	
65	5 109 97 105 108 50	mail2	Exchange	
71	192 12	→ 12 terra firma		
73	192 12	→ 12 terra firma	NAME	
75	0 2	NS	TYPE	
77	0 1	IN	CLASS	
79	0 1 81 128		TTL	Authority 1
83	0 15		RDLENTH	
85	6 111 114 97 99 108 101	oracle		
92	6 100 101 108 112 104 105	delphi		
99	0			
100	192 43	→ 43 mail1 terra firma	NAME	
102	0 1	A	TYPE	
104	0 1	IN	CLASS	Additional 1
106	0 1 81 128		TTL	
110	0 4		RDLENTH	
112	10 1 1 3	10.1.1.3	RDATA	
116	192 65	→ 65 mail2 terra firma	NAME	
118	0 1	A	TYPE	
120	0 1	IN	CLASS	Additional 2
122	0 1 81 128		TTL	
126	0 4		RDLENTH	
128	10 1 1 3	10.1.1.3	RDATA	
132	192 85	→ 85 oracle delphi	NAME	
134	0 1	A	TYPE	
136	0 1	IN	CLASS	Additional 3
138	0 1 81 128		TTL	
142	0 4		RDLENTH	
144	10 1 1 3	10.1.1.3	RDATA	

DNS Class Modules

DNSMESSAGE

```
Public ID As Integer      ' QueryIdentifyer
Public QR As Integer      ' QueryOrResponse
Public OPCODE As Integer   ' QueryType
Public AA As Integer      ' AuthoritativeAnswer
Public TC As Integer      ' Truncation
Public RD As Integer      ' RecursionDesired
Public RA As Integer      ' RecursionAvailable
Public Z As Integer       ' UnusedZero
Public RCODE As Integer    ' ResponseCode
Public QDCOUNT As Integer ' QuestionCount
Public ANCOUNT As Integer ' AnswerCount
Public NSCOUNT As Integer ' NameServerCount
Public ARCOUNT As Integer ' AdditionalRecordCount
Private dqstQuestion() As DNSQuestion
Public Property Get Question(Index As Integer) As DNSQuestion
 Set Question = dqstQuestion(Index)
End Property
Private drrAnswer() As DNSResourceRecord
Public Property Get Answer(Index As Integer) As DNSResourceRecord
 Set Answer = drrAnswer(Index)
End Property
```

DNSQUESTION

```
Public QName As String
Public QType As Integer
Public QClass As Integer
```

DNSRESOURCERECORD

```
Public RNAME As String
Public RTYPE As Integer
Public RCLASS As Integer
Public RTTL As Long
Public RDATA As Object
```

MXRECORD

```
Public Preference As Integer
Public Exchange As String
```

Listing 7.5 *DNS Declarations*

We implement a DNS message as a set of class modules (Listing 7.5) with properties that correspond to the fields in Figure 7.5. Note that the variables are not necessarily the same size (e.g., they are specified as Integers rather than as 3-bit fields) as there is no requirement to do so. In particular, bit fields are not easy to define in Visual Basic.

As this is really a high-level class with several components (Questions, Answers, etc.) it contains these objects as properties.

DNS Client

A simple DNS client involves the following:

- Compose a DNS question.

  Set the domain name.

  Set the resource type (MX).
- Send the question to the DNS server.
- Receive the response from the server.
- Parse the response.

  Extract all the answers.

Code Example

The client in this example (Figure 7.12) allows the user to enter the DNS server and the MX domain that is to be retrieved. When the lookup is pressed it will query the server and return all matching resource records on the form.

```
Const DNS_TYPE_MX = 15
Private Sub btnLookup_Click()

Dim lngServerAddress As Long
Dim strServerName As String

Dim strSocketResponse As String
```

```
Dim strSendLine As String
Dim bytLineLength As Byte
Dim dmsgSendMessage As New DNSMessage

Dim dmsgResponseMessage As DNSMessage

lngTransmitSocket = 0

strServerName = txtServer.Text
lngStatus = GetIPAddress(lngServerAddress, strServerName)
lngStatus = CreateSocket(lngTransmitSocket, 0)
lngStatus = ConnectSocket(lngTransmitSocket, lngServerAddress, _
    DNSPort)
dmsgSendMessage.ComposeQuestion DNS_TYPE_MX, txtDomain.Text
strSendLine = dmsgSendMessage.TransferString

bytLineLength = Len(strSendLine)

strSendLine = Chr$(0) + Chr$(bytLineLength) + strSendLine + _
    Chr$(0) + Chr$(0)

lngStatus = SendSocketBinary(lngTransmitSocket, strSendLine)
lngStatus = ReceiveSocketBinary(lngTransmitSocket, strSocketResponse)
lngStatus = ReleaseSocket(lngTransmitSocket)

Set dmsgResponseMessage = New DNSMessage
dmsgResponseMessage.Parse (Mid(strSocketResponse, 3))

lstResourceRecords.Clear
For x = 1 To dmsgResponseMessage.ANCOUNT
  lstResourceRecords.AddItem Right$(Space(5) +
Str(dmsgResponseMessage.Answer(x).RDATA.Preference), 5) + _
                " " + dmsgResponseMessage.Answer(x).RDATA.Exchange
Next

End Sub
```

Listing 7.6 *Lookup MX Record*

To do this it must first compose a DNS question (Listing 7.7) reflecting the target domain. It places the associated TransferString in a buffer. When using DNS across TCP (rather than UDP) we are

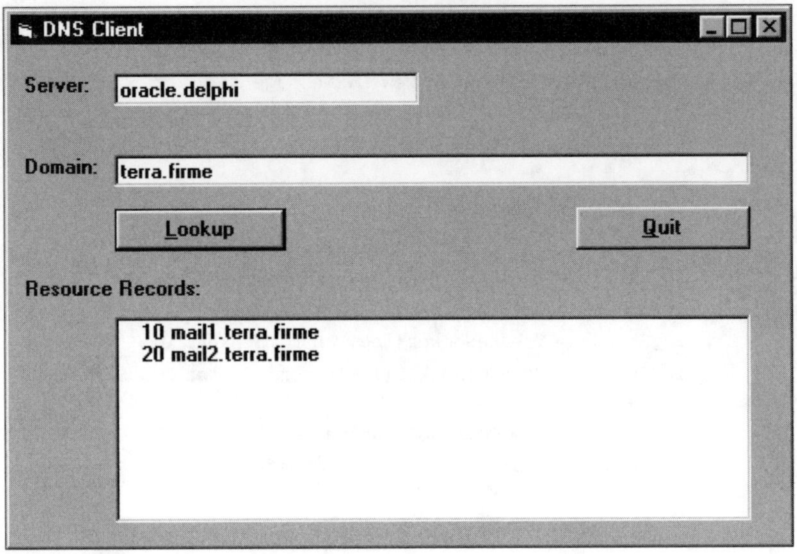

Figure 7.12 *Lookup of MX record*

required to prefix the question with a word containing its size. We add the size to the beginning and terminate with a zero-filled word.

To compose a question we need to allocate the object and fill in its properties. *QType* and *QName* (Domain) are parsed as parameters. The *QClass* is always coded as Internet.

```
Const DNS_CLASS_IN = 1
Public Sub ComposeQuestion(ResourceType As Integer, Domain As
String)
  RD = 1
  QDCOUNT = 1
  Randomize
  ID = 256 * Int(Rnd * 63) + Int(Rnd * 63)

  ReDim dqstQuestion(1)
  Set dqstQuestion(1) = New DNSQuestion

  dqstQuestion(1).QType = ResourceType
  dqstQuestion(1).QClass = DNS_CLASS_IN
  dqstQuestion(1).QName = Domain

End Sub
```

Listing 7.7 *Compose a DNS Question*

To generate the transfer string (Listing 7.8) (the actual binary string we transfer to the server) of a DNS message we fill in the Header Section (*ID, QR, OPCODE, AA, TC, RD, QDCOUNT, ANCOUNT, NSCOUNT,* and *ARCOUNT*). We then append the question (*QName, QType,* and *QClass*) and return the result.

```
Public Property Get TransferString( ) As String
 Dim HeaderSection As String
 Dim QuestionSection As String
 Dim RecordIndex As Integer

 HeaderSection = _
     PackIntegerToString(ID) + _
     Chr(QR * 128 + OPCODE * 8 + AA * 4 + TC * 2 + RD) + _
     Chr(Z * 32 + RCODE) + _
     PackIntegerToString(QDCOUNT) + _
     PackIntegerToString(ANCOUNT) + _
     PackIntegerToString(NSCOUNT) + _
     PackIntegerToString(ARCOUNT)

 QuestionSection = ""
 For RecordIndex = 1 To QDCOUNT
  QuestionSection = QuestionSection + _
     FormatDomain(dqstQuestion(RecordIndex).QName) + _
     PackIntegerToString(dqstQuestion(RecordIndex).QType) + _
     PackIntegerToString(dqstQuestion(RecordIndex).QClass)
 Next
 TransferString = HeaderSection + QuestionSection
End Property
```

Listing 7.8 *DNS Transfer String*

Note that to be complete we should also add any resource records for answers, name servers, and additional information. This example has none, so the sections have not been included.

We show the user the fully qualified domain name as a string of dot-delimited domain segments (x.y.z) as is traditional on the Internet. There is no reason DNS could not also use the syntax. However, just to make things difficult it uses counted strings.

This means, of course, that we have to change the format before we transfer it (Listing 7.9). We scan through each dot and append the size and domain segment with each iteration. When we reach the last segment (part after the final period), we also add a zero to terminate the string.

```
Private Function FormatDomain(InputDomain As String) As String
Dim strWorkBuffer As String
Dim intStartIndex As Integer
Dim intEndIndex As Integer
strWorkBuffer = ""
intStartIndex = 1
intEndIndex = InStr(intStartIndex, InputDomain, ".")
Do While intEndIndex <> 0
  strWorkBuffer = strWorkBuffer + _
         Chr(intEndIndex-intStartIndex) + _
         Mid(InputDomain, intStartIndex, _
               intEndIndex-intStartIndex)
  intStartIndex = intEndIndex + 1
  intEndIndex = InStr(intStartIndex, InputDomain, ".")
Loop

intEndIndex = Len(InputDomain) + 1
strWorkBuffer = strWorkBuffer + _
        Chr(intEndIndex-intStartIndex) + _
        Mid(InputDomain, intStartIndex, _
              intEndIndex-intStartIndex) + _
        Chr(0)

FormatDomain = strWorkBuffer
End Function
```

Listing 7.9 *Format the domain for transfer*

Visual Basic has a function to convert a byte integer to a string, namely the *Chr.* However it has none to convert a word value. Since we regularly need to convert words to string we have our own utility function (Listing 7.10) that just converts each byte and concatenates the two characters.

```
Private Function PackIntegerToString(InputInteger As Integer) As
String
  PackIntegerToString = Chr(Int(InputInteger / 256)) + _
          Chr(InputInteger And 255)

End Function
```

Listing 7.10 *Pack an Integer into a String*

To parse a DNS message (Listing 7.11) it is easiest to first convert the string to an array of bytes. Since the header has a fixed format we can extract the header fields by applying bit masks to the appropriate bytes. These include (*ID, QR, OPCODE, AA, TC, RD, QDCOUNT, ANCOUNT, NSCOUNT,* and *ARCOUNT*).

```
Public Sub Parse(InputString As String)

  Dim intQuestionIndex As Integer
  Dim intAnswerIndex As Integer
  Dim intScanIndex As Integer
  Dim HeaderByte1 As Byte
  Dim HeaderByte2 As Byte
  Dim intResourceDataLength As Integer

  intScanIndex = 1
  ID = GetWord(InputString, intScanIndex)
  HeaderByte1 = GetByte(InputString, intScanIndex)
  QR = Int(HeaderByte1 / 128) And 1
  OPCODE = Int(HeaderByte1 / 8) And 15
  AA = Int(HeaderByte1 / 2) And 1

  HeaderByte2 = GetByte(InputString, intScanIndex)
  RD = Int(HeaderByte2 / 128) And 1
  Z = Int(HeaderByte2 / 16) And 7
  RCODE = HeaderByte2 And 15
  QDCOUNT = GetWord(InputString, intScanIndex)
  ANCOUNT = GetWord(InputString, intScanIndex)
  NSCOUNT = GetWord(InputString, intScanIndex)
  ARCOUNT = GetWord(InputString, intScanIndex)
  If QDCOUNT > 0 Then ReDim dqstQuestion(QDCOUNT)
  If ANCOUNT > 0 Then ReDim drrAnswer(ANCOUNT)
  If NSCOUNT > 0 Then ReDim Nameserver(NSCOUNT)
  If ARCOUNT > 0 Then ReDim Additional(ARCOUNT)
  For intQuestionIndex = 1 To QDCOUNT
   Set dqstQuestion(intQuestionIndex) = New DNSQuestion
   dqstQuestion(intQuestionIndex).QName = GetDomain(InputString, _
      intScanIndex)
   dqstQuestion(intQuestionIndex).QType = GetWord(InputString, _
      intScanIndex)
   dqstQuestion(intQuestionIndex).QClass = GetWord(InputString, _
      intScanIndex)
  Next intQuestionIndex
```

```
For intAnswerIndex = 1 To ANCOUNT
  Set drrAnswer(intAnswerIndex) = New DNSResourceRecord
  drrAnswer(intAnswerIndex).RNAME = GetDomain(InputString, _
    intScanIndex)
  drrAnswer(intAnswerIndex).RTYPE = GetWord(InputString, _
    intScanIndex)
  drrAnswer(intAnswerIndex).RCLASS = GetWord(InputString, _
    intScanIndex)
  drrAnswer(intAnswerIndex).RTTL = GetLong(InputString, _
    intScanIndex)

  Call GetWord(InputString, intScanIndex)

  If drrAnswer(intAnswerIndex).RTYPE = 15 Then
    Set drrAnswer(intAnswerIndex).RDATA = New MXResourceData
    drrAnswer(intAnswerIndex).RDATA.Preference = GetWord(InputString, _
      intScanIndex)
    drrAnswer(intAnswerIndex).RDATA.Exchange = GetDomain(InputString, _
      intScanIndex)
  End If
Next intAnswerIndex

End Sub
```

Listing 7.11 *Parse the DNS Message*

For the remaining sections we need to scan through the data. We loop through the questions (usually only one) creating a new object for each and filling in the properties: *QName*, *QType*, and *QClass*.

The loop for the answer records creates a new resource record and also fills in the *RName*, *RType*, and *RClass*. In addition it finds the RTTL (Time-To-Live, which we ignore) and the RDATA (resource data). To simplify matters we only support MX resource records in this example (that is all we need since our question only requests them). We have finally arrived at what we are actually looking for: the *Preference* and *Exchange*.

To complete the parse we would need to extract the authority and additional-information records in the same way we parsed the answer record. That is not necessary in this example as we only use the answer.

To extract the fully qualified domain name (Listing 7.12) from a starting point in a string we need to loop through each domain part and concatenate it. We have a sequence of counted strings that will be terminated by a zero and that may be compressed (i.e., have a backwards reference to another occurrence of a subdomain). How we proceed for each domain segment depends on the first byte (n):

```
Private Function GetDomain(InputString As String, ByRef ScanIndex As
Integer) As String
 Dim strWorkBuffer As String
 Dim intScanValue As Integer
 Dim intWorkIndex As Integer

 strWorkBuffer = ""
 intScanValue = Asc(Mid(InputString, ScanIndex))
 Do While intScanValue <> 0 And intScanValue < 64
  strWorkBuffer = strWorkBuffer + _
         Mid(InputString, ScanIndex + 1, intScanValue)
  ScanIndex = ScanIndex + intScanValue + 1
  intScanValue = Asc(Mid(InputString, ScanIndex))

  If intScanValue <> 0 Then
   strWorkBuffer = strWorkBuffer + "."
  End If
 Loop

 If intScanValue > 128 Then
  intWorkIndex = Asc(Mid(InputString, ScanIndex + 1)) + 1
  strWorkBuffer = strWorkBuffer + _
         GetDomain(InputString, intWorkIndex)
  ScanIndex = ScanIndex + 2
 Else
  ScanIndex = ScanIndex + 1
 End If
 GetDomain = strWorkBuffer
End Function
```

Listing 7.12 *Extract the Domain from a String*

0—Finished. Exit the loop.

1-64—This is the size. Concatenate the next *n* bytes.

128-255—This is a compressed form of the domain. Continue parsing at byte *n*-128 and concatenate the result.

In the routine you see that the index moves along in a loop as long as there are domain segments to concatenate. When it hits a zero it terminates. And when it sees a value over 128 it calls itself to recursively retrieve the compressed segments.

We also have simple utility functions to extract the next byte, word, or longword from a string (Listing 7.13).

```
Private Function GetByte(InputString As String, ByRef ScanIndex As _
    Integer) As Byte
 GetByte = Asc(Mid(InputString, ScanIndex))
 ScanIndex = ScanIndex + 1
End Function
Private Function GetWord(InputString As String, ByRef ScanIndex As _
    Integer) As Integer
 GetWord = Asc(Mid(InputString, ScanIndex + 1)) + _
      Asc(Mid(InputString, ScanIndex)) * 256
 ScanIndex = ScanIndex + 2
End Function
Private Function GetLong(InputString As String, ByRef ScanIndex As _
    Integer) As Long
 GetLong = Asc(Mid(InputString, ScanIndex + 3)) + _
      Asc(Mid(InputString, ScanIndex + 2)) * 256 + _
      Asc(Mid(InputString, ScanIndex + 1)) * 256 ^ 2 + _
      Asc(Mid(InputString, ScanIndex)) * 256 ^ 3
 ScanIndex = ScanIndex + 4
End Function
```

Listing 7.13 *Functions to extract bytes, words, and long words from a string*

SMTP Relay

In the previous chapter we saw SMTP as a protocol to be used across a direct connection between client and server (Figure 7.13).

But in reality, mail traffic rarely takes the most direct route. For security and performance reasons, it is typically channeled along a path of several intermediate hops (Figure 7.14).

How to optimize mail flow in and outside an organization is outside the scope of this book. I assume that this has already been done in the computing environment where these mail applications are running. If we want to build a relay we just need to understand how we know where to deliver any incoming mail. All routing information for Internet Mail is stored in DNS in the form of MX records. For any

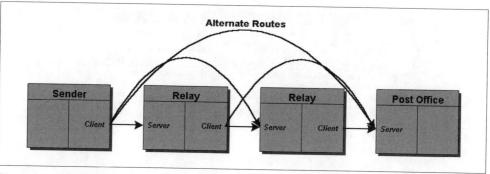

Figure 7.13 *Message Routing for SMTP*

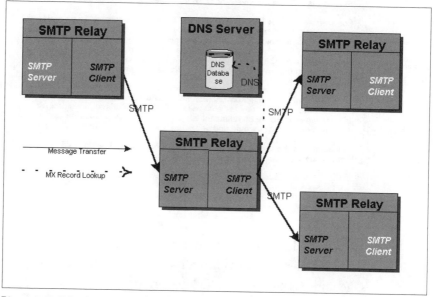

Figure 7.14 *Message flow between relays*

valid domain there will be one or more MX records. Each one of these has an associated preference.

Code Example

The SMTP relay form combines the fields (and much of the code) of the SMTP server with those of the DNS client. When an SMTP message comes in it extracts the domain from the recipient. It then issues a DNS

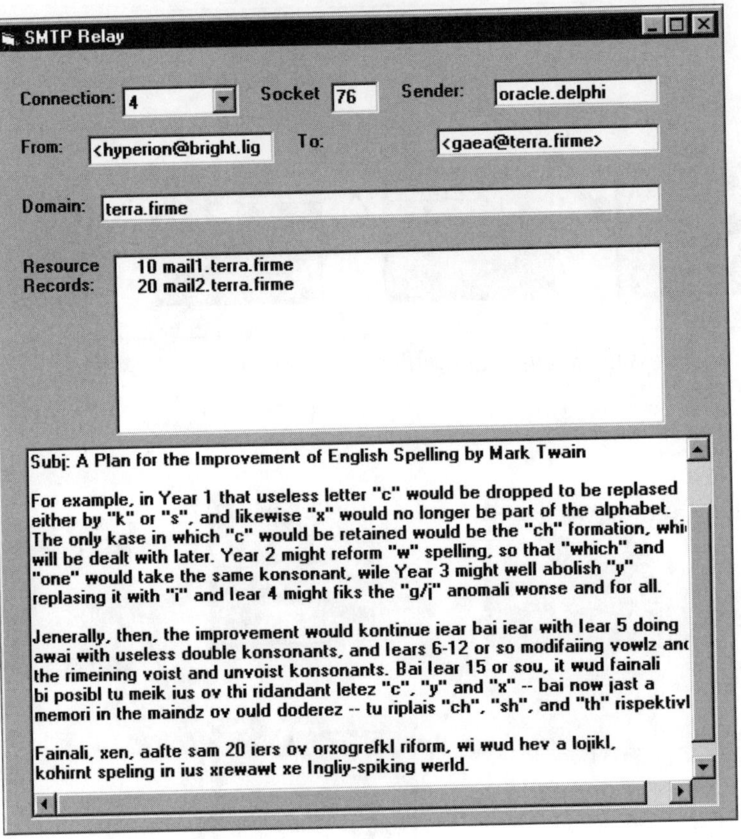

Figure 7.15 *SMTP Relay*

query for MX records for that domain. One by one it attempts to connect to the listed relays until it is successful. Then it receives the full message and passes it on as the lines arrive.

The biggest difference between a relay and a mail host is that we need to pass the message onward (Listing 7.14). After the recipient has been specified we can look up the corresponding domain name and connect to the next preferred relay. As the data is sent to us we then relay the entire message on.

```
Private Sub ProcessRequest(Index As Integer)
Dim strClientRequest As String

intStatus = ReceiveSocket(lngTransmitSocket, strClientRequest, 1)
DisplayConnection Index
txtRequest(Index).Text = strClientRequest
```

```
         strClientRequest = Trim(strClientRequest)
         Select Case Trim(UCase(Left$(strClientRequest, 4)))
          Case "HELO"
           txtSender(Index).Text = Trim(Mid(strClientRequest, 5))
           intStatus = SendSocket(lngTransmitSocket, "250 olive.tree")
          Case "MAIL"
           txtFrom(Index).Text = FormatUser(Mid(strClientRequest, 11))
           intStatus = SendSocket(lngTransmitSocket, "250 OK")
          Case "RCPT"
           txtTo(Index).Text = FormatUser(Mid$(strClientRequest, 9))
           txtDomain(Index).Text = Mid(txtTo(Index).Text, _
                       InStr(1, txtTo(Index).Text, "@") + 1)

           LookupDomain Index
           ConnectNextRelay Index

           intStatus = SendSocket(lngTransmitSocket, "250 OK")
          Case "DATA"
           RelayMessage Index
          Case "QUIT"
           intStatus = SendSocket(lngTransmitSocket, "250 OK")
           intStatus = ReleaseSocket(lngTransmitSocket)
           intStatus = SendSocket(lngRelaySocket, strClientRequest)
           intStatus = ReceiveSocket(lngRelaySocket, strClientRequest, 2)
           intStatus = ReleaseSocket(lngRelaySocket)
          Case Else
           intStatus = SendSocket(lngTransmitSocket, "250 OK")
         End Select
        End Sub
```

Listing 7.14 *Process SMTP Request*

Both the originator and recipient addresses are surrounded by
angle brackets (<>). To facilitate processing we have a routine to strip
these off (Listing 7.15).

```
Private Function FormatUser(InputUser As String) As String
 FormatUser = Trim(InputUser)

 If Left(FormatUser, 1) = "<" Then FormatUser = Mid(FormatUser, 2)
 If Right(FormatUser, 1) = ">" Then FormatUser = Left(FormatUser,
Len(FormatUser)—1)
End Function
```

Listing 7.15 *Format Username*

We look up the target domain using the same sequence of commands as the DNS client (Listing 7.16).

```
Private Sub LookupDomain(Index As Integer)

Dim lngServerAddress As Long
Dim strSocketResponse As String
Dim strSendLine As String
Dim bytLineLength As Byte
Dim dmsgSendMessage As New DNSMessage

Dim x As Integer
Dim dmsgResponseMessage As New DNSMessage

intStatus = GetIPAddress(lngServerAddress, DNSServer)
intStatus = CreateSocket(lngLookupSocket, 0)
intStatus = ConnectSocket(lngLookupSocket, lngServerAddress, DNSPort)
dmsgSendMessage.ComposeQuestion DNS_TYPE_MX, txtDomain(Index).Text
strSendLine = dmsgSendMessage.TransferString

bytLineLength = Len(strSendLine)

strSendLine = Chr$(0) + Chr$(bytLineLength) + strSendLine + _
    Chr$(0) + Chr$(0)

intStatus = SendSocketBinary(lngLookupSocket, strSendLine)
intStatus = ReceiveSocketBinary(lngLookupSocket, strSocketResponse)
intStatus = ReleaseSocket(lngLookupSocket)

dmsgResponseMessage.Parse Mid(strSocketResponse, 3)
lstResourceRecords(Index).Clear
For x = 1 To dmsgResponseMessage.ANCOUNT
  lstResourceRecords(Index).AddItem Right$(Space(5) + _
    Str(dmsgResponseMessage.Answer(x).RDATA.Preference), 5) + _
            " " + dmsgResponseMessage.Answer(x).RDATA.Exchange
Next

End Sub
```

Listing 7.16 *Look up target domain in DNS*

To connect to the next relay (Listing 7.17) we take advantage of the fact that the MX records are sorted in order of preference in our list. (It is a sorted list and each entry begins with the preference.)

```
Private Sub ConnectNextRelay(Index As Integer)
 Dim lngServerAddress As Long
 Dim strNextRelay As String
 Dim strServerResponse As String
 Dim intRelayIndex As Integer

 intRelayIndex = 0

 Do
  strNextRelay = Mid(lstResourceRecords(Index).List(intRelayIndex), 7)

  intStatus = GetIPAddress(lngServerAddress, strNextRelay)
  intStatus = CreateSocket(lngRelaySocket, 0)
  intStatus = ConnectSocket(lngRelaySocket, lngServerAddress, _
     SMTPPort)
  intRelayIndex = intRelayIndex + 1
 Loop Until intStatus
 intStatus = ReceiveSocket(lngRelaySocket, strServerResponse, 2)
 intStatus = SendSocket(lngRelaySocket, "mail from:<" + _
     txtFrom(Index).Text + ">")
 intStatus = ReceiveSocket(lngRelaySocket, strServerResponse, 2)
 intStatus = SendSocket(lngRelaySocket, "rcpt to:<" + _
     txtTo(Index).Text + ">")
 intStatus = ReceiveSocket(lngRelaySocket, strServerResponse, 2)
 intStatus = SendSocket(lngRelaySocket, "data")
 intStatus = ReceiveSocket(lngRelaySocket, strServerResponse, 2)
End Sub
```

Listing 7.17 *Connect to next relay*

We loop through the list attempting to connect to each until we
are successful. Once we have the connection we can send the *mail
from*, *rcpt to*, and *data* commands. This puts us in the same state with
respect to our server as we are with our incoming client.

To relay the message (Listing 7.18) we tell the client to start sending the data. Until we reach the final period we loop for each line
receiving it from the client and sending it on to the server.

```
Private Sub RelayMessage(Index As Integer)
 Dim strClientRequest As String
 Dim strFileName As String
 Dim intFileNumber As Integer

 intStatus = SendSocket(lngTransmitSocket, "354 Start sending...")
```

```
txtMessage(Index).Text = ""
Do
 intStatus = ReceiveSocket(lngTransmitSocket, strClientRequest, 1)
 If intStatus Then
  intStatus = SendSocket(lngRelaySocket, strClientRequest)
  If strClientRequest = "." Then Exit Do
  txtMessage(Index).Text = txtMessage(Index).Text + _
      strClientRequest + CRLF
 End If
Loop While strClientRequest <> "."

 intStatus = SendSocket(lngRelaySocket, strClientRequest)

 intStatus = SendSocket(lngTransmitSocket, "250 OK")
 intStatus = ReceiveSocket(lngRelaySocket, strClientRequest, 2)
End Sub
```

Listing 7.18 *Transfer incoming message to next relay*

Wrapping Up

SMTP relays can become quite complex. This example only illustrates
the basics. Some of the areas where production relays are further
developed are:

- *Store and Forward*—We have assumed that the next hop is always available when we receive the message from the client. This is not always
  the case. Even when it is, most relays would not make a connection
  immediately but would place all incoming messages into a queue.
  Another thread of the relay could then work on forwarding the messages
  to the next hop. A complete store-and-forward mail server needs:

  Storage for the queue and all its messages

  Standard queue processing routines (insert, remove, extract messages)

  User notification upon sustained failures (e.g., send informational
     message after 4 hours, return message after 48 hours)

  Configuration parameters (maximum size of messages, maximum num-
     ber of messages in the queue, sort order for the queue)

- *Rewrite rules*—Often relays do not simply resend messages with the same headers as they received them. They will add their own headers to record the path of transmission. Furthermore, many relays can also be configured to rewrite existing headers. This can be interesting, for example, if we would like all mail destined for one domain to be transferred to another domain.

- *Relays and Servers*—Some servers are both relays and servers at the same time. In this case the server needs to be able to detect local users and store their mail locally as well as forwarding mail for all remote users. In other words, a production server would combine the functionality of the SMTP server in the previous chapter with that of the SMTP relay in this chapter.

Chapter 8

POP3—Post Office Protocol

You probably receive most of your mail hand-delivered to your door and placed in your mailbox for you to browse through when you come home from work. But occasionally there may have been a parcel or some registered letters that need to be collected from the post office. When you go there you tell them your name and then show them some proof of identity. They verify that you are not trying to pick up someone else's mail and then give you anything they have waiting for you.

POP is a message retrieval protocol, the electronic version of the above scenario. Its purpose is to allow a user to receive messages in a central message store (Post Office) and to retrieve these on demand (Figure 8.1). The server will typically receive the messages from SMTP, although it could just as easily be X.400 or any proprietary

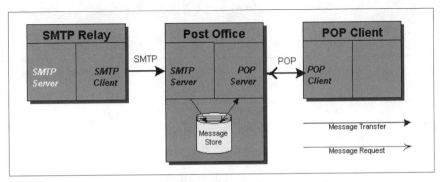

Figure 8.1 *Message request and transfer*

```
                                      +OK POP3 server version 2.0 ready⇐
⇒USER Atlas
                                                                  +OK⇐
⇒PASS forgetmenot
                                      +OK User successfully logged on⇐
⇒STAT
                                                            +OK 3 2496⇐
⇒LIST
                                                                  +OK⇐

                                                               1 892⇐
                                                               2 970⇐
                                                               3 634⇐
                                                                   .⇐
⇒RETR  3
                                                                  +OK⇐
                                      Date: Fri, 31 Dec 99 23:44 -0000⇐
                                 From: "Hestia" <hestia@eternal.flame>⇐
                                          To: "Atlas" <atlas@shrugged>⇐
                                             Subject: Courtroom quotes⇐
                                                                     ⇐
          Q. Did you ever stay all night with this man in New York?⇐
                              A. I refuse to answer that question.⇐
          Q. Did you ever stay all night with this man in Chicago?⇐
                              A. I refuse to answer that question.⇐
            Q. Did you ever stay all night with this man in Miami?⇐
                                                             A. No.⇐
                                                                     ⇐
      Q. Now, Mrs. Johnson, how was your first marriage terminated?⇐
                                                      A. By death.⇐
                      Q. And by whose death was it terminated?⇐
                                                                     ⇐
   Q. Doctor, how many autopsies have you performed on dead people?⇐
         A. All my autopsies have been performed on dead people.⇐
                                                                     ⇐
                                                                   .⇐
⇒QUIT
```

Figure 8.2 *POP session*

message transfer protocol. It then stores the messages in a temporary database and waits for client requests. When it is called it looks in the repository and retrieves any messages in the user's queue.

Figure 8.2 shows an example of a POP session. The client has authenticated to the server with a *USER*name of *Atlas* and a *PASS*word of *forgetmenot*. Then it has requested a *STATUS* of the mailbox, which showed that there were *3* messages holding *7144* bytes in this user's mailbox. It *LIST*ed them to see the sizes of each message individually. Rather than downloading all of them it only *RETR*ieved the last message and then quit the session.

Commands

Table 8.1 gives a short description of the commands that POP supports. In addition to those in the example session we will also use the *DELE* to mark a message for deletion (usually after it has been retrieved). Note that the command does not actually delete the message in the mailbox. It will only be deleted when *QUIT* is used to terminate the session and commit all deletions. If an *RSET* is sent prior to the commitment it will roll back all the deletions. *RSET* is not a commonly used command. I would wager that many POP clients (including mine) give it amiss. Nevertheless, without it the *DELE/QUIT* relationship would be incomplete.

Table 8.1 *POP Commands*

Command	Parameters	Description
APOP	Name digest	Authenticate using MD5 digest
DELE	Message	Delete this message
LIST	[Message]	List the index and byte count of message(s)
NOOP		Don't do anything—but return status
PASS	Password	Authenticate with this password
QUIT		Commit all deletions and terminate
RETR	Message	Retrieve this message
RSET		Rollback all pending deletions
STAT		Display number of messages and total size
TOP	Message Linecount	Display initial lines of this message
UIDL	Message	Display unique identifier of this message
USER	Username	Authenticate with this user

Command Flow

Figure 8.3 shows the typical sequence of commands in a POP session. Most begin by authenticating with USER and PASS (APOP is a more secure authentication mechanism but also more difficult and less commonly used). It is then useful to issue STAT since it gives a count of messages. Some clients may want the detail of LIST but it is not strictly necessary. (It would allow you to delete large messages without downloading them, for instance.)

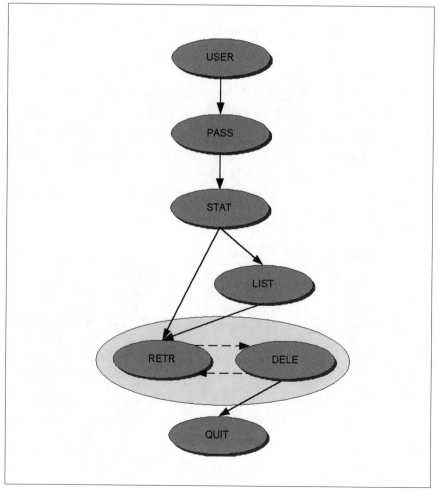

Figure 8.3 *Typical Command Flow*

Since there are typically several messages in the user's mailbox, the flow continues with a loop. After retrieving each message it is usual to also mark it for deletion. If this seems destructive keep in mind that there is no way to mark which messages have been downloaded on the server. If we don't delete the messages they will remain there and an increasing number of messages will be retrieved every session.

After downloading all the messages a QUIT will commit the deletions and then terminate.

The RFC uses a finite-state automaton to specify the sequencing of the POP commands (Figure 8.4). You could argue that POP is

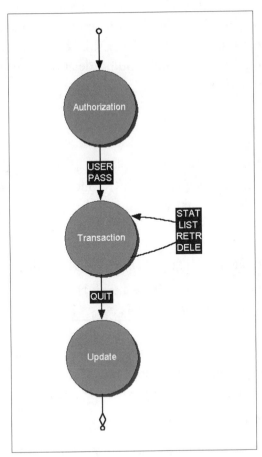

Figure 8.4 *POP State Transition Diagram*

simple enough not to require the model, yet it does unambiguously represent the protocol and it is necessary to be aware of it to follow the standard.

When the session begins it is in the *Authorization* state. This means the user has not been authenticated and cannot view or modify any mailbox. After supplying a valid username and password pair the server knows

- which mailbox to use (USER)
- that this user is authorized to use the mailbox (PASS)

We proceed to the *Transaction* state where the mailbox and its messages can be viewed. No changes can be made to the mailbox but deletions may be requested for later. The QUIT command marks the transition to the *Update* state. All pending deletions are performed and the session terminates.

Response Codes

POP response codes are relatively simple. Upon success they begin with +OK, and on failure they return –ERR. Successful responses will additionally return the data that was requested. The replies have varying formats that can be broadly classified as:

- Those that return no data (e.g., USER, PASS, DELE, QUIT)
- Those that return one line of data (e.g., STAT)
- Those that return multiple lines of data (e.g., LIST, RETR)

The first category can add any helpful text they choose to the command. It is not predefined and need not be interpreted programmatically. For instance the PASS command might return:

+OK User logged on

The second set of commands has a predefined syntax for the return line. For instance the STAT command requests the number of messages and their total size. If we have three messages of exactly 1,000 bytes each, then we should expect a response of:

+OK 3 3000

Other commands (e.g., LIST, RETR) will return multiple lines. In order to signal to the client that they have completed they use a final period. For instance the LIST command would respond with

+OK
1 1000
2 1000
3 1000
.

in the example above.

POP Client

The sequence of a POP client is:

- Identify and authenticate the user with the server.
- Determine how many messages are waiting.
- Loop through each message.
    Retrieve the message.
    Mark it for deletion.
- Commit all deletions and exit.

Download Example

The most common usage of POP is not interactive. In other words, the various commands and responses are not individually prompted by or returned to the user. Instead, the user will typically just initiate a download of the messages to a local repository. The POP client issues all the commands necessary to accomplish this and then lets the user work on the local messages.

Our first example duplicates this behavior of POP (Figure 8.5). The user specifies the POP server and authentication data. This POP downloader is not incorporated into a full mail client with its own repository, so we will just use a Windows folder and download all the messages there. The user can specify whether to delete the messages on the server or just download them. To allow the user to identify the messages in the folder we display all downloaded files on the form.

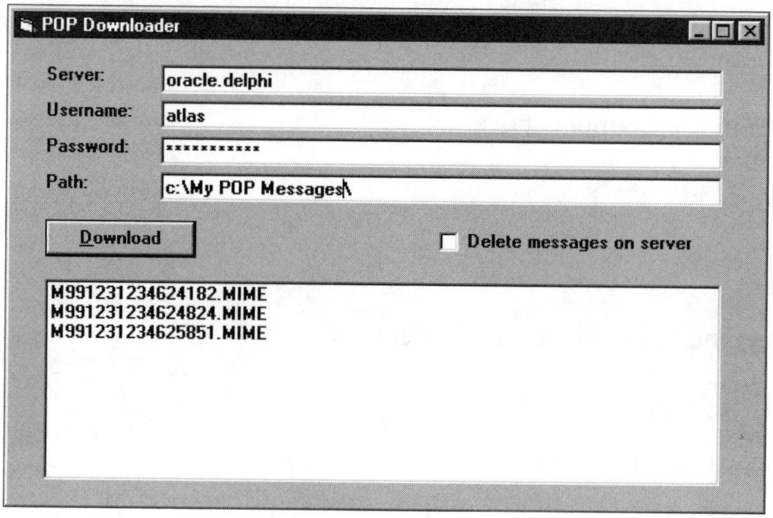

Figure 8.5 *POP Downloader*

To make this form work, we need the basic POP commands (Listing 8.1). The *USER* and *PASS* authenticate the user. We issue a *STAT* so we know how many messages to download. That means we have to parse the result. We know the first four characters are "+OK" so we start at the 5th and take everything until the next space.

We can then loop to extract each file. We have to ensure uniqueness so we concatenate a timestamp with a random number to generate each filename. If the user has asked to delete the messages from the server we also include a *DELE* command in the loop. After cycling through all the messages we *QUIT* to ensure the deletions are performed.

```
Private Sub btnDownload_Click()
Dim lngServerAddress As Long
Dim strServerName As String
Dim strSocketResponse As String
Dim intMailCountEndposition As Integer
Dim intMailCount As Integer
Dim intMessageIndex As Integer
Dim strFilename As String
lngPOPSocket= 0
strServerName = txtServer.Text
intStatus = GetIPAddress(lngServerAddress, strServerName)
intStatus = CreateSocket(lngPOPSocket, 0)

intStatus = ConnectSocket(lngPOPSocket, lngServerAddress, POP3Port)
intStatus = ReceiveSocket(lngPOPSocket, strSocketResponse)
intStatus = SendSocket(lngPOPSocket, "USER " + txtUsername.Text)
intStatus = ReceiveSocket(lngPOPSocket, strSocketResponse)
intStatus = SendSocket(lngPOPSocket, "PASS " + txtPassword.Text)
intStatus = ReceiveSocket(lngPOPSocket, strSocketResponse)
intStatus = SendSocket(lngPOPSocket, "STAT ")
intStatus = ReceiveSocket(lngPOPSocket, strSocketResponse)
intMailCountEndposition = InStr(5, strSocketResponse, " ")
intMailCount = val(Mid(strSocketResponse, 5, _
            intMailCountEndposition - 5))
For intMessageIndex = 1 To intMailCount
 strFilename = "M" + Format(Now, "yymmddhhnnss") + _
        Trim(Str(Int(Rnd * 1000))) + ".MIME"
 ExtractMessage intMessageIndex, strFilename
 If chkDelete.Value = 1 Then
  intStatus = SendSocket(lngPOPSocket, "DELE " + _
                    Str(intMessageIndex))
  intStatus = ReceiveSocket(lngPOPSocket, strSocketResponse)
 End If
 lstMessageList.AddItem strFilename
Next
 intStatus = SendSocket(lngPOPSocket, "QUIT ")
 intStatus = ReceiveSocket(lngPOPSocket, strSocketResponse)
End Sub
```

Listing 8.1 *Download a POP mailbox*

To extract a message (Listing 8.2) we ignore the first response (should be "+OK") and then loop until we encounter a final period. All the lines in between form the message, so we print them to the output file. When we hit the period we know we have finished this particular message and can close the file. Note that there is no need to print the period as it is not part of the message.

```
Private Sub ExtractMessage(MessageIndex As Integer, _
            OutputFilename As String)
Dim strSocketResponse As String
Dim strFileSpecification As String
Open txtPath + OutputFilename For Output As #1
intStatus = SendSocket(lngPOPSocket, "RETR " + Str(MessageIndex))
intStatus = ReceiveSocket(lngPOPSocket, strSocketResponse)
intStatus = ReceiveSocket(lngPOPSocket, strSocketResponse)
Do While strSocketResponse <> "."
 Print #1, strSocketResponse
 intStatus = ReceiveSocket(lngPOPSocket, strSocketResponse)
Loop
Close #1
End Sub
```

Listing 8.2 *Extract message*

Interactive POP Client

The previous example is the most typical use of POP. However, it doesn't really show the functions in operation. Figure 8.6 is an interactive version of the same thing. When the user connects, the total messages count and their total size are displayed and the messages are listed. The user has the option of Extracting one or more messages to files or viewing them interactively. He can then mark those no longer needed as deleted and commit these deletions by quitting the session.

Listing 8.3 is very similar to the Download. The only differences are:

1. It places the result of the *STAT* into the fields on the form.

2. Rather than extracting the messages we only *LIST* them. Each response represents a message and is added to the list. We ignore the first line (should be "+OK") and then continue until we reach the final period.

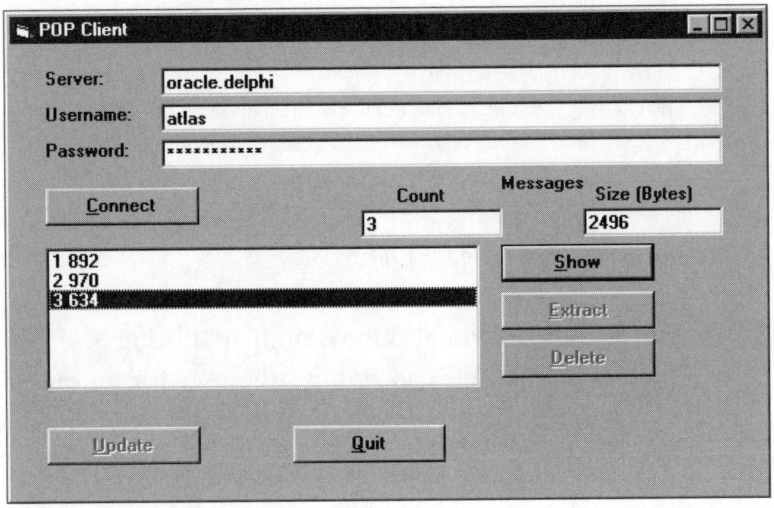

Figure 8.6 *POP Client*

```
Dim lngPOPSocket As Long
Const POP3Port = 110
Private Sub btnConnect_Click()
 Dim lngServerAddress As Long
 Dim strServerName As String
 Dim strSocketResponse As String
 Dim intMailCountEndposition As Integer
 lngPOPSocket = 0
 strServerName = txtServer.Text
 intStatus = GetIPAddress(lngServerAddress, strServerName)
 intStatus = CreateSocket(lngPOPSocket, 0)
 intStatus = ConnectSocket(lngPOPSocket, lngServerAddress, POP3Port)
 intStatus = ReceiveSocket(lngPOPSocket, strSocketResponse)
 intStatus = SendSocket(lngPOPSocket, "USER " + txtUsername.Text)
 intStatus = ReceiveSocket(lngPOPSocket, strSocketResponse)
 intStatus = SendSocket(lngPOPSocket, "PASS " + txtPassword.Text)
 intStatus = ReceiveSocket(lngPOPSocket, strSocketResponse)
 intStatus = SendSocket(lngPOPSocket, "STAT ")
 intStatus = ReceiveSocket(lngPOPSocket, strSocketResponse)
 intMailCountEndposition = InStr(5, strSocketResponse, " ")
 txtMailCount.Text = Mid(strSocketResponse, 5, _
             intMailCountEndposition - 5)
 txtMailSize.Text = Mid(strSocketResponse, intMailCountEndposition + 1)
 intStatus = SendSocket(lngPOPSocket, "LIST ")
```

```
intStatus = ReceiveSocket(lngPOPSocket, strSocketResponse)
intStatus = ReceiveSocket(lngPOPSocket, strSocketResponse)
Do While strSocketResponse <> "."
 lstMessageList.AddItem strSocketResponse
 intStatus = ReceiveSocket(lngPOPSocket, strSocketResponse)
Loop
End Sub
```

Listing 8.3 *Connect and list Inbox*

The *Extract* should also look familiar (Listing 8.4). Since this is a one-time extraction we can prompt the user for an output file. This would have been tedious for the user in the bulk download but it makes sense here.

```
Private Sub btnExtract_Click()
Dim strSocketResponse As String
Dim strFileSpecification As String
strFileSpecification = InputBox("Please enter file: ")
Open strFileSpecification For Output As #1
intStatus = SendSocket(lngPOPSocket, "RETR " + _
            Str(lstMessageList.ListIndex + 1))
intStatus = ReceiveSocket(lngPOPSocket, strSocketResponse)
intStatus = ReceiveSocket(lngPOPSocket, strSocketResponse)
Do While strSocketResponse <> "."
 Print #1, strSocketResponse
 intStatus = ReceiveSocket(lngPOPSocket, strSocketResponse)
Loop
Close #1
End Sub
```

Listing 8.4 *Extract selected message to a file*

In addition to letting the users save the messages to files we also give them the opportunity to view the messages (Listing 8.5). To make this easier we use the MIME reader. Similar to the Extraction, we ask the POP server to *RETR* the message and then loop to receive all the lines in the message (until, but not including, the final period). But rather than sending them to a file, we add each of the lines to the MIME message and then *Show* the form.

```
Private Sub btnShow_Click()
 Dim strSocketResponse As String
 Load frmReadMIMEMessages
 intStatus = SendSocket(lngPOPSocket, "RETR " + _
          Str(lstMessageList.ListIndex + 1))
 intStatus = ReceiveSocket(lngPOPSocket, strSocketResponse)
 intStatus = ReceiveSocket(lngPOPSocket, strSocketResponse)
 Do While strSocketResponse <> "."
  frmReadMIMEMessages.DisplayMessage.Lines.Add strSocketResponse
  intStatus = ReceiveSocket(lngPOPSocket, strSocketResponse)
 Loop
 frmReadMIMEMessages.Show

End Sub
```

Listing 8.5 _Display selected message_

Marking a message as deleted is quite straightforward (Listing 8.6). We issue a _DELE_ and should receive a response of "+OK."

```
Private Sub btnDelete_Click()
 Dim strSocketResponse As String
 Dim intRetrieveIndex As Integer
 intRetrieveIndex = lstMessageList.ListIndex + 1
 intStatus = SendSocket(lngPOPSocket, "DELE " + Str(intRetrieveIndex))
 intStatus = ReceiveSocket(lngPOPSocket, strSocketResponse)
End Sub
```

Listing 8.6 _Mark selected message as deleted_

The _QUIT_ is just as simple (Listing 8.7). When we have finished we send it, receive back the status, and then can release the socket.

```
Private Sub btnQuit_Click()

 Dim strSocketResponse As String
 intStatus = SendSocket(lngPOPSocket, "QUIT ")
 intStatus = ReceiveSocket(lngPOPSocket, strSocketResponse)
 intStatus = ReleaseSocket(lngPOPSocket)
 End
End Sub
```

Listing 8.7 _Commit deletions and terminate_

POP Server

In order to be able to service POP requests a server needs to have:

- Command dispatching routine
- Mailbox storage system supporting
    - Multiple users
    - Multiple messages per user
- Means to maintain Client State

Note that it is not part of the POP server's responsibilities to populate the mailbox store. Incoming messages are delivered to the mailbox by another application (typically an SMTP server). The only issue is ensuring that both servers can share the store and that there are no locking problems.

Code Example

Figure 8.7 shows the information this POP server maintains to help process user requests. The most fundamental is the State, as this shows whether the user has been authenticated. The username is extracted from the USER command but not used until authenticated with a (PASS) password. The server can then locate the mailbox and load all the messages in preparation for the LIST. By totaling the list it also has what it needs for the STAT.

There are three columns holding the information we need for each message. The first column holds a deletion flag, which may be blank (not marked for deletion) or D (marked for deletion). The second holds the byte size of the message. It would be returned in response to any LIST commands. Finally, we have the file name. If any messages need to be retrieved the server will lookup the filename, open it, and return the contents.

In addition to some generic server functions, the POP server has some POP-specific tasks to be performed upon accepting a user connection (Listing 8.8):

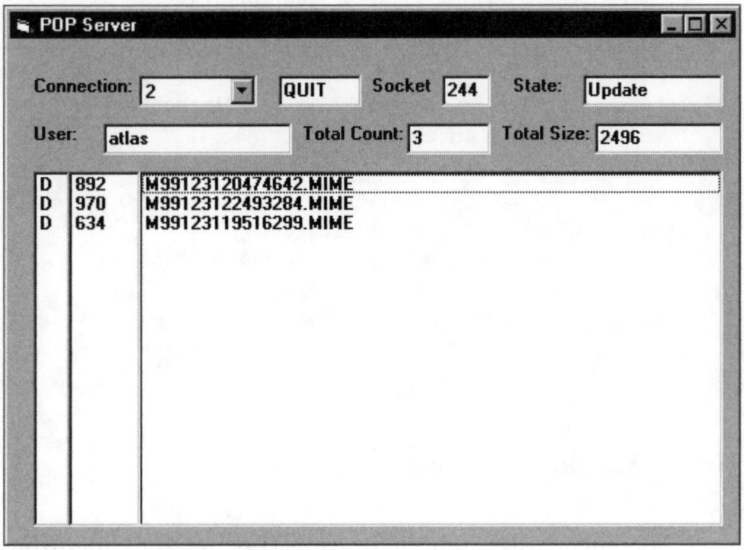

Figure 8.7 *POP Server*

- It initializes the internal state to *Authorization*.
- It issues the first reply to the client. Only the "*+OK*" is necessary, but it is customary to add some helpful text to identify the POP server.

```
Private Sub AcceptConnection()
Dim sotTransmitSocketAddress As OutputSocketDescriptor
Dim intTransmitSocketAddressSize As Integer
Dim intCurrentConnection As Integer
intTransmitSocketAddressSize = LenB(sotTransmitSocketAddress)
intTransmitSocketAddressSize = 20
lngTransmitSocket = accept(lngListenSocket, _
    sotTransmitSocketAddress, intTransmitSocketAddressSize)
intCurrentConnection = cboConnection.ListCount

cboConnection.AddItem Trim(Str(intCurrentConnection))
Load txtSocket(intCurrentConnection)
Load txtRequest(intCurrentConnection)
Load txtState(intCurrentConnection)
Load txtUser(intCurrentConnection)
Load txtTotalCount(intCurrentConnection)
Load txtTotalSize(intCurrentConnection)
Load lstDeletionList(intCurrentConnection)
```

```
Load lstSizeList(intCurrentConnection)
Load lstFileList(intCurrentConnection)
txtSocket(intCurrentConnection) = Trim(Str(lngTransmitSocket))
txtState(intCurrentConnection).Text = "Authorisation"
DisplayConnection intCurrentConnection
intStatus = SendSocket(lngTransmitSocket, "+OK POP server here")

If WSAAsyncSelect(lngTransmitSocket, _
         txtRequest(intCurrentConnection).hwnd, _
         WM_MBUTTONDBLCLK, FD_READ) Then
   MsgBox "Unable to set Asynch mode"
End If


End Sub
```

Listing 8.8 *Accept user connection*

The central dispatching routine (Listing 8.9) identifies the POP command and performs processing specific to it:

USER—Set the user field on the form for correlation with *PASS*.

PASS—Verify password. In this ultrasecure server the password must be the same as the username. The state is updated to Transaction and the user files are loaded.

STAT—The total count and size are retrieved from the form and sent to the user.

RETR—The requested message is sent to the user.

DELE—The requested message is marked for deletion by placing a *"D"* in the corresponding entry of the deletion list.

QUIT—The state is changed to *Update* and all marked messages are deleted.

```
Private Sub ProcessRequest(Index As Integer)
 Dim strSendLine As String
 Dim strClientRequest As String
 Dim strCommand As String
 Dim strParameters As String
 DisplayConnection Index
 intStatus = ReceiveSocket(lngTransmitSocket, strClientRequest)
 strClientRequest = Trim(strClientRequest)
```

```
txtRequest(Index).Text = strClientRequest
strCommand = Trim(UCase(Left$(strClientRequest, 4)))
strParameters = Trim(Mid(strClientRequest, 6))
Select Case strCommand
 Case "USER"
  txtUser(Index).Text = strParameters
  intStatus = SendSocket(lngTransmitSocket, "+OK")
 Case "PASS"
  If strParameters = txtUser(Index).Text Then
   intStatus = SendSocket(lngTransmitSocket, "+OK")
   txtState(Index).Text = "Transaction"
   LoadUserFiles Index
  Else
   intStatus = SendSocket(lngTransmitSocket, "-ERR")
  End If
 Case "STAT"
  strSendLine = "+OK " + txtTotalCount(Index).Text + _
          " " + txtTotalSize(Index).Text
  intStatus = SendSocket(lngTransmitSocket, strSendLine)
 Case "LIST"
  ListMessages Index
 Case "RETR"
  RetrieveMessage Index, val(strParameters)
 Case "DELE"
  lstDeletionList(Index).List(val(strParameters) - 1) = "D"
  intStatus = SendSocket(lngTransmitSocket, "+OK")
 Case "QUIT"
  txtState(Index).Text = "Update"
  DeleteMessages Index
 Case Else
  intStatus = SendSocket(lngTransmitSocket, "-ERR " + _
             strCommand + " not supported")
 End Select
End Sub
```

Listing 8.9 *Dispatch user request*

Once the user has been authenticated we cache the list of messages in
the mailbox for quick and easy retrieval (Listing 8.10). After constructing
the user's path we loop through the files. With each iteration we increment the cumulative totals for the number and size of the files and add
the file name, file size, and a blank deletion flag to the respective lists. We
finish by displaying the totals on the form for future reference.

```
Const PostOfficeDirectory = "C:\Post Office\"

Private Sub LoadUserFiles(intCurrentConnection As Integer)
 Dim strCurrentUser As String
 Dim strCurrentDirectory As String
 Dim strCurrentFile As String
 Dim intCurrentFileSize As Integer
 Dim intTotalCount As Integer
 Dim intTotalSize As Integer
 strCurrentUser = txtUser(intCurrentConnection).Text
 strCurrentDirectory = PostOfficeDirectory + strCurrentUser + "\"
 strCurrentFile = Dir(strCurrentDirectory + "*")
 intTotalCount = 0
 intTotalSize = 0
 Do Until strCurrentFile = ""
  intTotalCount = intTotalCount + 1
  intCurrentFileSize = FileLen(strCurrentDirectory + strCurrentFile)
  intTotalSize = intTotalSize + intCurrentFileSize

  lstDeletionList(intCurrentConnection).AddItem Space(1)
  lstSizeList(intCurrentConnection).AddItem Str(intCurrentFileSize)
  lstFileList(intCurrentConnection).AddItem strCurrentFile
  strCurrentFile = Dir

 Loop
 txtTotalCount(intCurrentConnection).Text = Trim(Str(intTotalCount))
 txtTotalSize(intCurrentConnection).Text = Trim(Str(intTotalSize))
 End Sub
```

Listing 8.10 *Load mailbox into cache*

When we receive a request to the *List* all the messages in a user's
mailbox (Listing 8.11) our first reply line is a confirmation ("+OK")
as well as the count of messages. We then loop for each message and
display an index and the size of that particular message. To terminate
the list we send a period.

```
Private Sub ListMessages(intCurrentConnection As Integer)
 Dim strSendLine As String
 Dim intMessageIndex As Integer
 strSendLine = "+OK " + txtTotalCount(intCurrentConnection).Text + _
        " Messages"
 intStatus = SendSocket(lngTransmitSocket, strSendLine)
 For intMessageIndex = 0 To _
```

```
                  val(txtTotalCount(intCurrentConnection).Text) - 1
      strSendLine = Str(intMessageIndex + 1) + " " + _
          lstSizeList(intCurrentConnection).List(intMessageIndex)
      intStatus = SendSocket(lngTransmitSocket, strSendLine)
    Next
    intStatus = SendSocket(lngTransmitSocket, ".")
  End Sub
```

Listing 8.11 *List messages in mailbox*

To retrieve (*RETR*) a message (Listing 8.12) we optimistically begin by confirming with "+OK." Then we determine the full path (Post Office path, username for folder, and unique filename from list). We open the file and loop through each line of the file sending it to the client as is. To terminate we again send a single period.

```
    Private Sub RetrieveMessage(intCurrentConnection As Integer,
    MessageIndex As Integer)
     Dim strSendLine As String
     Dim strCurrentFile As String
     Dim intCurrentFileNumber As Integer
     Dim strCurrentUser As String
     Dim strCurrentDirectory As String
     intStatus = SendSocket(lngTransmitSocket, "+OK ")
     strCurrentUser = txtUser(intCurrentConnection).Text
     strCurrentDirectory = PostOfficeDirectory + strCurrentUser + "\"
     strCurrentFile = strCurrentDirectory + _
             lstFileList(intCurrentConnection).List(MessageIndex - 1)
     intCurrentFileNumber = FreeFile
     Open strCurrentFile For Input As #intCurrentFileNumber
     Do While Not EOF(intCurrentFileNumber)
       Line Input #intCurrentFileNumber, strSendLine
       intStatus = SendSocket(lngTransmitSocket, strSendLine)
     Loop
     Close #intCurrentFileNumber
     intStatus = SendSocket(lngTransmitSocket, ".")
    End Sub
```

Listing 8.12 *Retrieve requested message*

Deleting the marked messages (Listing 8.13) means we need to loop through the deletion list. Wherever there is a deletion flag (*D*) we delete the corresponding file using the Visual Basic *Kill* command.

```
Private Sub DeleteMessages(intCurrentConnection As Integer)
 Dim strCurrentUser As String
 Dim strCurrentDirectory As String
 Dim intMessageIndex As Integer
 intStatus = SendSocket(lngTransmitSocket, "+OK ")
 strCurrentUser = txtUser(intCurrentConnection).Text
 strCurrentDirectory = PostOfficeDirectory + strCurrentUser + "\"
 For intMessageIndex = 0 To _
     val(txtTotalCount(intCurrentConnection).Text) - 1
  If lstDeletionList(intCurrentConnection).List(intMessageIndex) _
                               = "D" Then
   Kill strCurrentDirectory + _
      lstFileList(intCurrentConnection).List(intMessageIndex)
  End If
 Next
End Sub
```

Listing 8.13 *Delete marked messages*

Wrapping Up

Some loose ends for the POP examples include:

- *Embedded periods*—Just like SMTP, POP uses a line with a single period to designate the end of a message (in multiline responses, RETR, in particular). In order to support messages with embedded periods the server must "byte-stuff" the line by inserting an additional period and the client must remove the first byte. The technique is the same as with SMTP, however the roles are reversed. With SMTP the client pads and the server removes the padding. POP requires the server to pad and the client to remove the padding.

- *Authentication*—The sample server uses a very primitive form of authentication. Production servers must have a secure means of authenticating a user.

- *Permanent Identifiers*—The UIDL command allows a permanent number to be associated with a message. This is primarily useful for clients that do not delete the messages after they have been downloaded. If the client caches the message header and the associated UIDL, then it can allow the user to download the specific message at his or her discretion at some later time.

Chapter 9

IMAP—Interactive Mail Access Protocol

POP and IMAP are both protocols that allow a remote client to access messages stored in a mailbox on a server. In both cases mail is delivered to the post office and stays there until the user has a chance to connect and retrieve messages. The most fundamental difference between the two protocols is the structure of the mailbox and the functions that support this structure.

A POP mailbox is simply a queue of messages (Figure 9.1). It only allows the client to retrieve the entries and remove them from the queue. IMAP stores the messages in a folder hierarchy. This implies the need for a number of functions to manipulate the hierarchy and move messages between folders.

Figure 9.2 shows an example of an IMAP session. The client has authenticated to the server with a *USER*name of *Poseidon* and a

POP Mail Queue	IMAP Mailbox Hierarchy		
Message 1	*Folder 1*		
Message 2		Message 1	
Message 3		Message 2	
Message 4	*Folder 2*		
Message 5		Message 1	
Message 6		*Subfolder 1*	
Message 7			Message 1
Message 8		*Subfolder 2*	

Figure 9.1 *POP and IMAP mailbox structures*

*PASS*word of *forgetmenot*. Then it has *FETCH*ed the fifth message from the mailbox. After retrieving the message it has *STORE*d the *Deleted* and *Seen* flags on the message. The client then terminated the session with the *LOGOUT* command.

At this point you should see a resemblance to the functionality that can be provided by POP. Note that there are more commands and that they allow more parameters. This means a greater challenge for

```
                                          * OK IMAP4rev1 server ready⇐
⇒0024 LOGIN "Poseidon" "forgetmenot"
                                          0024 OK LOGIN completed.⇐
⇒0025 SELECT "test"
                        * FLAGS (\Seen \Answered \Flagged \Deleted \Draft)⇐
            * OK [PERMANENTFLAGS (\Seen \Answered \Flagged \Deleted \Draft)]⇐
                        * OK [UIDVALIDITY 851] UIDVALIDITY value.⇐
                        0025 OK [READ-WRITE] SELECT completed.⇐
⇒0026 UID FETCH 5 (RFC822.HEADER RFC822.SIZE UID FLAGS INTERNALDATE)
                              * 5 FETCH (RFC822.HEADER {559}⇐
                              Date: Fri, 31 Dec 99 23:55 -0000⇐
                              From: "Hera" <hera@sweet.vengeance>⇐
                              To: "Poseidon" <poseidon@three.teeth>⇐
                              Subject: Ways to Confuse Your Roommate⇐
                                                                    ⇐
              Whenever your roommate walks in, wait one minute and then⇐
              stand up. Announce that you are going to take a shower.⇐
                   Whenever your roomate comes in lower your eyes and⇐
                                             giggle to yourself.⇐
                   Whenever the phone rings, get up and answer the door.⇐
                        Whenever someone knocks, answer the phone.⇐
                   Tell your roommate that someone called and said⇐
                                   that it was really important⇐
                              but you can't remember who it was.⇐
                                                                 ⇐
        RFC822.SIZE 559 UID 10 FLAGS (\Seen) INTERNALDATE "31-Dec-1999 23:55:09⇐
                                                          +0000")⇐
                                         0026 OK FETCH completed.⇐
⇒002A UID STORE 5 +FLAGS (\Deleted \Seen)
                                         002A OK STORE completed.⇐
⇒9999 LOGOUT
                              * BYE IMAP4rev1 server signing off⇐
                              9999 OK LOGOUT completed.⇐
```

Figure 9.2 *Sample IMAP session*

parsing, but it also implies that more functionality can be made available to the end-user.

Command Flow

IMAP uses a state diagram not too different from POP (Figure 9.3). There are more functions, but the first two states (Nonauthenticated/ Authenticated) roughly correspond to the POP3 Authorization and

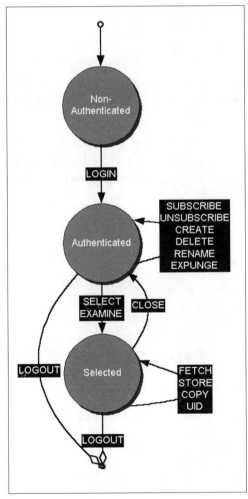

Figure 9.3 *IMAP State Diagram*

Transaction states. In addition, we have a selected state, which indicates that a specific folder in the mailbox has been selected.

Folders (Mailboxes)

An IMAP mailbox is structured in terms of a container hierarchy that I call *Folders*. Note that in the RFC, as well as the bulk of the literature, these are called mailboxes. I prefer to limit the use of the word *Mailbox* to the set of folders associated with a particular user (the top-level IMAP mailbox).

Commands

We have a number of functions that allow us to manipulate folders. Although their mnemonic names make most of them self-explanatory, I would like to draw attention to a few of them.

The EXPUNGE and CLOSE commands roughly correspond to the (POP) QUIT command. When we issue either of these the server will delete all messages *in that folder* that were previously *marked for deletion*.

Table 9.1 *Folder Operations*

Command	Description
CHECK	Request a checkpoint
CLOSE	Remove deleted messages and deselect folder
CREATE	Create a new folder
DELETE	Delete a folder
EXAMINE	Select the folder in read-only mode so that messages can be read
EXPUNGE	Remove deleted messages
RENAME	Rename a folder
SEARCH	Search folder for messages satisfying given criteria
SELECT	Select the folder so that messages can be accessed
STATUS	Request the status of the mailbox
SUBSCRIBE	Add to server's list of active folders
UID SEARCH	Similar to SEARCH but using permanently unique message identifiers
UNSUBSCRIBE	Remove from server's list of active folders

You should also be aware of the idea of a subscribed folder. The rationale behind it is that a user may have a large number of folders and subfolders in his mailbox. It would be inefficient to retrieve the entire folder list each time the user logs in. We therefore let the user specify a list of folders that are marked as subscribed. Subsequently, the user can choose to only download the list of subscribed folders.

Attributes

Folders, beyond the data (messages and subfolders) they contain, also have a set of server-defined attributes (Table 9.2). In this book we will ignore the flags, but you will still see them and could take advantage of them to refine the programs.

Table 9.2 *Folder Attributes*

Attribute	Description
Marked	Marked as interesting by the server (e.g., new messages have arrived)
Noinferiors	No subfolders exist (nor may any be created)
Noselect	Not possible to *SELECT* folder
Unmarked	Does not contain new messages since last selection

Messages

Commands

There are fewer functions on messages than folders (Table 9.3). Unfortunately, what it lacks in number the *FETCH* command more than makes up for in complexity. Some points to be aware of:

- *APPEND* will create a new message in a folder. This is not a typical command. Usually messages are stored automatically on the server as they arrive from the mail system (SMTP). Client only needs to read, refile, and delete them. Client-initiated creation is therefore the exception (e.g., moving a message from another mail store into an IMAP mailbox).

- *FETCH* can be used both to fetch the message content (RFC 822/MIME) as well as to view a subset of message properties.
- *UID* uses a permanent (session-independent) message identifier. In other words, a *UID FETCH 1* will always fetch the same message in every session. In contrast, a *FETCH 1* would always fetch the same message in the same session but might fetch another message in the next session.

Table 9.3 *Message Operations*

Command		Description
APPEND		Append a new message to a folder
COPY		Copy message to another folder
FETCH		Retrieve contents and attributes of messages in a folder
STORE		Alter attributes associated with messages in a folder
UID	COPY	Same as COPY, FETCH, and STORE except that permanently unique message identifiers
	FETCH	(rather than message sequence numbers) are used
	STORE	

Attributes

The only flag we will use in these examples is "/Deleted." A functional client would also need support of "/Seen." The other flags are not always implemented but do enhance the user interface when available.

Table 9.4 *Message Attributes*

Attribute	Description
Answered	Message has been answered
Deleted	Message has been marked for deletion
Draft	Message has not completed composition
Flagged	Message has been flagged for special attention
Recent	Message arrived since last session
Seen	Message has been read

Components

As alluded to above, the *FETCH* command can be used to retrieve a subset of the message. A number of different message components are defined (Table 9.5), so that the client can easily fetch only the data it needs. This helps a client with limited bandwidth to optimize response time by retrieving only the required data from many messages (e.g., to build a list of messages in the folder).

Table 9.5 *Summary of Message Components*

Component	Description
ALL	Equivalent to (FLAGS INTERNALDATE RFC822.SIZE ENVELOPE)
BODY	Nonextensible form of BODYSTRUCTURE
BODY.PEEK	Alternate form of BODY that does not mark the message *Seen*
BODYSTRUCTURE	Parsed MIME Structure of the message
ENVELOPE	Envelope structure of the message
FAST	Equivalent to (FLAGS INTERNALDATE RFC822.SIZE)
FLAGS	The flags (attributes) of the message
INTERNALDATE	Internal date of the message
RFC822	Complete RFC 822 message
RFC822.HEADER	RFC 822 Headers of the message
RFC822.SIZE	Size of the RFC 822 message
RFC822.TEXT	Text body of the message
UID	Permanently unique identifier for the message

Syntax

Commands

IMAP commands take the form

Command-Identifier Command-Verb Parameter-List

The Command-Identifier is a (frequently numeric) identifier that is guaranteed to be unique with each command. It is usually incremental (an easy way to guarantee its uniqueness) but need not be.

The command-verb is one of the commands that we have seen in the previous section, or one of the general-purpose commands (Table 9.6).

Table 9.6 *Miscellaneous Commands*

Command	Description
AUTHENTICATE	Indicates an authentication mechanism to the server
CAPABILITY	Requests a listing of capabilities supported by the server
LOGIN	Identifies and authenticates the client to the server
LOGOUT	Informs server that the client is done with the connection
NOOP	Does nothing

Each command-verb has its own syntax for parameters. However, they have a lot in common:

- Parameters are separated by a single space.
- Flag lists are enclosed in parentheses (/Deleted /Seen).
- Parameters with special characters (e.g., spaces, punctuation) are surrounded by quotes.
- Sizes are surrounded by braces {233}.

Responses

Responses are also verb-specific. Nonetheless the two share some common syntax.

- Interim responses are preceded by an asterisk.
- Final responses are preceded by the command-identifier and command-verb of the command to which they respond.
- There must be a final response for every command. There need not be any interim responses.
- There is no guarantee that multiple outstanding commands will be answered in the order requested. This means that a client that issues multiple requests in parallel (to optimize response time) will need to be able to correlate the responses.

IMAP Client

A possible sequence of an IMAP client is:

- Identify and authenticate the user with the server.
- Request a listing of all the folders in the mailbox.
  Display the folder listing to the user.
  Allow the user to select a folder.

Select the folder on the server.

Request a listing of the messages in the folder.

Display the listing to the user.

Allow the user to select a message.

Fetch the message from the server.

Display the message to the user.

However, in contrast to POP, we must remember that IMAP is highly interactive. In other words, rather than following a prescribed sequence we must provide the user with options to perform any of several functions at any time. In addition to the above, some of the functions we should support include:

- Folder creation
- Folder deletion
- Folder subscription
- Folder unsubscription
- Message deletion
- Message copy from one folder to another

Code Example

The User Interface of an IMAP client (Figure 9.4) needs to provide:

- Mechanism for authentication (*Username, Password*)
- Listing of folders with possibility for user to select one (*Folders*)
- Display of messages in the folder (*Messages*)
- Option to view or extract a message (*Show, Extract*)

When we connect to the server (Listing 9.1) we immediately issue a *LOGIN* and *List* the *Folders* in the mailbox.

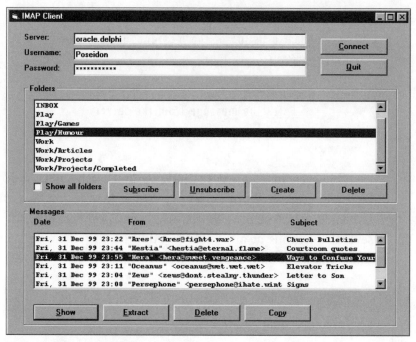

Figure 9.4 *IMAP Client*

```
Private Sub btnConnect_Click()
 Dim lngServerAddress As Long
 Dim strServerName As String
 Dim strSocketResponse As String
 lngIMAPSocket = 0
 strServerName = txtServer.Text
 intStatus = GetIPAddress(lngServerAddress, strServerName)
 intStatus = CreateSocket(lngIMAPSocket, 0)
 intStatus = ConnectSocket(lngIMAPSocket, lngServerAddress, IMAPPort)
 intStatus = ReceiveSocket(lngIMAPSocket, strSocketResponse)
 intStatus = SendSocket(lngIMAPSocket, _
            NextIndex + _
            "LOGIN " + _
            Quote + txtUsername.Text + Quote + Blank + _
            Quote + txtPassword.Text + Quote)
 intStatus = ReceiveSocket(lngIMAPSocket, strSocketResponse)
 ListFolders
 End Sub
```

Listing 9.1 *Connect to IMAP Mailbox*

In order to generate unique command identifiers (Listing 9.2) we use a module-level variable: *intCommandIndex*. To obtain the current index we create a string with the value of the variable and one trailing space. The function *NextIndex* increments this index and returns the new *CurrentIndex*. Each time we call *NextIndex* we are therefore sure to have an identifier that is unique within that session.

```
Dim intCommandIndex As Integer
Private Function CurrentIndex() As String
 CurrentIndex = Trim(Str(intCommandIndex)) + Blank
End Function

Private Function NextIndex() As String
 intCommandIndex = intCommandIndex + 1
 NextIndex = CurrentIndex
End Function
```

Listing 9.2 *Generate Unique Command Identifiers*

When listing folders in a mailbox we have the choice of two commands:

1. LIST—lists all folders in the mailbox
2. LSUB—lists only the subscribed folders

Both commands have the same syntax:

LIST *(flags) folder-reference folder-name*

Depending on whether the option to show all folders is checked, we issue the appropriate command (Listing 9.3). We then loop through all the interim responses and place them in the folder list. Each *untagged* response will be of the format:

*LIST *(flags) folder-reference folder-name*

We therefore extract the text after the folder-reference (the first "/").

```
Private Sub ListFolders()
 Dim strSocketResponse As String
 lstFolderList.Clear
 If chkShowAllFolders.Value = 0 Then
  intStatus = SendSocket(lngIMAPSocket, _
        NextIndex + _
        "LSUB " + QuoteQuote + Blank + QuoteStarQuote)
  lstFolderList.AddItem "INBOX"
```

```
 Else
  intStatus = SendSocket(lngIMAPSocket, _
        NextIndex + _
         "LIST " + QuoteQuote + Blank + QuoteStarQuote)
 End If
 intStatus = ReceiveSocket(lngIMAPSocket, strSocketResponse)
 Do While Left(strSocketResponse, Len(CurrentIndex)) <> CurrentIndex
  lstFolderList.AddItem _
       Mid(strSocketResponse, _
         InStr(5, strSocketResponse, QuoteSlashQuote) + 4)
  intStatus = ReceiveSocket(lngIMAPSocket, strSocketResponse)
 Loop
End Sub
```

Listing 9.3 *List Folders*

To create a folder (Listing 9.4) we only need to issue the *CREATE* command with the folder name as a parameter. We issue an InputBox to allow the user to specify the required folder.

```
LIST "" "*"
LSUB "" "*"
Private Sub btnCreateFolder_Click()
 Dim strSocketResponse As String
 intStatus = SendSocket(lngIMAPSocket, _
        NextIndex + _
         "CREATE " + Quote + InputBox("Folder Name:") + Quote)
 intStatus = ReceiveSocket(lngIMAPSocket, strSocketResponse)
 ListFolders
End Sub
```

Listing 9.4 *Create a folder*

Folder deletion (Listing 9.5) is accomplished with the *DELETE* command. We supply the currently selected folder name as a parameter.

```
Private Sub btnDeleteFolder_Click()
 Dim strSocketResponse As String
 intStatus = SendSocket(lngIMAPSocket, _
        NextIndex + _
         "DELETE " + Quote + lstFolderList.Text + Quote)
 intStatus = ReceiveSocket(lngIMAPSocket, strSocketResponse)

 ListFolders
End Sub
```

Listing 9.5 *Delete selected folder*

Listing 9.6 shows folder subscription with the *SUBSCRIBE* command. We supply the currently selected folder name as a parameter.

```
Private Sub btnSubscribeFolder_Click()
 Dim strSocketResponse As String
 intStatus = SendSocket(lngIMAPSocket, _
      NextIndex + _
      "SUBSCRIBE " + Quote + lstFolderList.Text + Quote)
 intStatus = ReceiveSocket(lngIMAPSocket, strSocketResponse)

 ListFolders
 End Sub
```

Listing 9.6 *Subscribe to selected folder*

To remove a folder (Listing 9.7) from the subscription list we use the *UNSUBSCRIBE* command. We supply the currently selected folder name as a parameter.

```
Private Sub btnUnsubscribeFolder_Click()
 Dim strSocketResponse As String
 intStatus = SendSocket(lngIMAPSocket, _
      NextIndex + _
      "UNSUBSCRIBE " + Quote + lstFolderList.Text + Quote)
 intStatus = ReceiveSocket(lngIMAPSocket, strSocketResponse)

 ListFolders
 End Sub
```

Listing 9.7 *Unsubscribe selected folder*

When the user double-clicks a folder (Listing 9.8) we go ahead and *SELECT* the folder. We then issue a *FETCH* command on all the messages in the folder (range 1:*) to obtain the headers of the messages. These are then placed in the Message List for viewing by the user.

```
Private Sub lstFolderList_DblClick()
 Dim strSocketResponse As String
 Dim strMessageDate As String
 Dim strMessageSubject As String
 Dim strMessageFrom As String
 lstMessageList.Clear
 intStatus = SendSocket(lngIMAPSocket, _
      NextIndex + _
      "SELECT " + lstFolderList.Text)
```

```
intStatus = ReceiveSocket(lngIMAPSocket, strSocketResponse)
Do While Left(strSocketResponse, Len(CurrentIndex)) <> CurrentIndex
 intStatus = ReceiveSocket(lngIMAPSocket, strSocketResponse)
Loop
intStatus = SendSocket(lngIMAPSocket, _
        NextIndex + _
        "FETCH 1:* (BODY[HEADER.FIELDS (DATE SUBJECT FROM)])")
intStatus = ReceiveSocket(lngIMAPSocket, strSocketResponse)
Do While Left(strSocketResponse, Len(CurrentIndex)) <> CurrentIndex
 intStatus = ReceiveSocket(lngIMAPSocket, strSocketResponse)
 strMessageDate = Mid(strSocketResponse, _
            InStr(5, strSocketResponse, ":") + 2)

 intStatus = ReceiveSocket(lngIMAPSocket, strSocketResponse)
 strMessageSubject = Mid(strSocketResponse, _
            InStr(5, strSocketResponse, ":") + 2)

 intStatus = ReceiveSocket(lngIMAPSocket, strSocketResponse)
 strMessageFrom = Mid(strSocketResponse, _
            InStr(5, strSocketResponse, ":") + 2)

 lstMessageList.AddItem Left(strMessageDate + Space(20), 20) + " " + _
            Left(strMessageFrom + Space(35), 35) + " " + _
            Left(strMessageSubject, 20)
 Do While Left(strSocketResponse, 1) <> "*" And _
        Left(strSocketResponse, Len(CurrentIndex)) <> CurrentIndex
     intStatus = ReceiveSocket(lngIMAPSocket, strSocketResponse)
 Loop
Loop
End Sub
```

Listing 9.8 *Select folder on double click*

To show a message (Listing 9.9) we first need to *FETCH* the RFC
822 component. This will return the RFC 822 formatted message. We
add all the lines to the DisplayMessage object and then display the
MIME Reader.

```
Private Sub btnShow_Click()
Dim strSocketResponse As String
Dim intWorkIndex As Integer
Dim intRetrieveIndex As Integer
Dim strRetrieveMessage As String
intRetrieveIndex = lstMessageList.ListIndex + 1
strRetrieveMessage = ""
Load frmReadMIMEMessages
```

```
intStatus = SendSocket(lngIMAPSocket, _
        NextIndex + _
        "FETCH " + Trim(Str(intRetrieveIndex)) + " " + "(RFC822)")
intStatus = ReceiveSocket(lngIMAPSocket, strSocketResponse)
intStatus = ReceiveSocket(lngIMAPSocket, strSocketResponse)
Do
 frmReadMIMEMessages.DisplayMessage.Lines.Add strSocketResponse
 intStatus = ReceiveSocket(lngIMAPSocket, strSocketResponse)
Loop While Left(Trim(strSocketResponse), 5) <> CurrentIndex
frmReadMIMEMessages.Show

End Sub
```

Listing 9.9 *Show selected message*

To copy a message (Listing 9.10) we use the *COPY* command. We supply the ID of the current message and the requested target folders as a parameters.

```
Private Sub btnCopy_Click()
 Dim strSocketResponse As String
 Dim intRetrieveIndex As Integer
 intRetrieveIndex = lstMessageList.ListIndex + 1
 intStatus = SendSocket(lngIMAPSocket, _
        NextIndex + _
        "COPY " + Trim(Str(intRetrieveIndex)) + " " + Quote + _
        InputBox("Folder Name:") + Quote)
 intStatus = ReceiveSocket(lngIMAPSocket, strSocketResponse)
 End Sub
```

Listing 9.10 *Copy selected message to a new folder*

To extract a message (Listing 9.11) we first need to *FETCH* the RFC 822 component. This will return the RFC 822 formatted message. We print all the output lines to the requested output file.

```
Private Sub btnExtract_Click()
 Dim strSocketResponse As String
 Dim intWorkIndex As Integer
 Dim intRetrieveIndex As Integer
 intRetrieveIndex = lstMessageList.ListIndex + 1
 strFileSpecification = InputBox("Please enter file: ")
 Open strFileSpecification For Output As #1
 intStatus = SendSocket(lngIMAPSocket, _
        NextIndex + _
        "FETCH " + Trim(Str(intRetrieveIndex)) + " " + "(RFC822)")
```

```
intStatus = ReceiveSocket(lngIMAPSocket, strSocketResponse)
intStatus = ReceiveSocket(lngIMAPSocket, strSocketResponse)
Do
 Print #1, strSocketResponse
 intStatus = ReceiveSocket(lngIMAPSocket, strSocketResponse)
Loop While Left(Trim(strSocketResponse), 5) <> CurrentIndex
Close #1
End Sub
```

Listing 9.11 *Extract selected message to a file*

Listing 9.12 deletes a message by requesting a *STORE* of the
"\Deleted" flag with the message. It is now marked for deletion. If we
were to *CLOSE* the folder it would permanently delete the message.
But rather than waiting we go ahead and issue an *EXPUNGE*, which
deletes the message while keeping the folder selected.

```
Private Sub btnDelete_Click()
Dim strSocketResponse As String
Dim intRetrieveIndex As Integer
intRetrieveIndex = lstMessageList.ListIndex + 1
intStatus = SendSocket(lngIMAPSocket, _
      NextIndex + _
      "STORE " + Trim(Str(intRetrieveIndex)) + " " + _
      "+FLAGS (\Deleted)")
intStatus = ReceiveSocket(lngIMAPSocket, strSocketResponse)
intStatus = SendSocket(lngIMAPSocket, NextIndex + "EXPUNGE")
intStatus = ReceiveSocket(lngIMAPSocket, strSocketResponse)

End Sub
```

Listing 9.12 *Permanently delete selected message*

IMAP Server

In order to be able to service IMAP requests a server needs to have:

- Command dispatching routine
    - IMAP command parser
- Mailbox storage system supporting
    - Multiple users
    - Multiple folders per user

Multiple messages per folder
- Means to maintain Client State

As in the case of the POP server, IMAP is not responsible for populating the mailbox store.

Code Example

This implementation of an IMAP server uses the Windows file system to represent a user's mailbox. Each subfolder of the mailbox is also a subdirectory of the root directory. The messages are stored as RFC822/MIME files in the folders.

For simplicity we will not distinguish between subscribed and not subscribed folders. We will also not store any of the folders/File attributes other than the "\Deleted" flag. Others could easily be added later, but we'll have our hands full with this much to start with.

For every connection an IMAP server must potentially store at least the state, the username, and the selected folder. In addition, we cache the list of folders for the user, and the list of message files for the selected folder.

The dispatching function (Listing 9.13) recognizes five basic commands:

CAPABILITY—This command typically initiates the session. It doesn't provide any useful information but many clients will require us to support it. In reality (since we don't fully implement IMAP) we have no capability at all. We will bend the truth, however, and pretend to support IMAP4 and IMAP4rev1.

LOGIN—When the client authenticates we extract out the Username. We won't validate the password. We then load the user (fill with Username and cache the folders in the user's mailbox).

LIST, LSUB—We list all the folders, which are cached on the form.

SELECT—We load the requested folder (fill in Selected Folder and cache the list of files found in that directory).

UID FETCH, FETCH—We determine the message range and requested components, then we retrieve them and return them to the client.

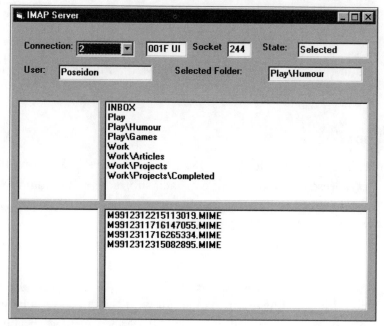

Figure 9.5 *IMAP Server*

```
Private Sub ProcessRequest(Index As Integer)
 Dim SendLine As String
 Dim ClientRequest As String
 Dim CommandIdentifier As String
 Dim CommandKeyword As String
 Dim StatusResponse As String
 Status = ReceiveSocket(TransmitSocket, ClientRequest)
 DisplayConnection Index
 txtRequest(Index).Text = ClientRequest
 CommandIdentifier = GetToken(ClientRequest, 1)
 CommandKeyword = UCase(GetToken(ClientRequest, 2))
 If CommandKeyword = "UID" Then
  CommandKeyword = "UID " + UCase(GetToken(ClientRequest, 3))
 End If
 Select Case CommandKeyword
  Case "CAPABILITY"
   Status = SendSocket(TransmitSocket, "* CAPABILITY IMAP4 IMAP4rev1")
  Case "LOGIN"
   LoadUser Index, GetToken(ClientRequest, 3)
  Case "LIST", "LSUB"
```

```
      ListFolders Index, ClientRequest
   Case "SELECT"
      LoadFolder Index, GetToken(ClientRequest, 3)
   Case "UID FETCH"
      FetchMessageRange Index, GetToken(ClientRequest, 4), _
                   GetToken(ClientRequest, 5)
   Case "CREATE"
      MkDir PostOfficeDirectory + "\" + txtUser(Index).Text _
         + "\" + GetToken(ClientRequest, 3)
   Case "DELETE"
      RmDir PostOfficeDirectory + "\" + txtUser(Index).Text _
         + "\" + GetToken(ClientRequest, 3)
   Case "STORE"
      lstFileFlags(Index).List(GetToken(ClientRequest, 3)) = _
            GetToken(ClientRequest, 3)
   Case "COPY"
       FileCopy GetToken(ClientRequest, 3), GetToken(ClientRequest, 3)
   Case "SUBSCRIBE"
   Case "UNSUBSCRIBE"
   Case Else
      ' Status = SendSocket(TransmitSocket, "+OK")
   End Select
   StatusResponse = CommandIdentifier + " OK " + CommandKeyword + _
      " completed"
   Status = SendSocket(TransmitSocket, StatusResponse)
End Sub
```

Listing 9.13 *IMAP Command Dispatcher*

In order to extract a given token from a command we have no choice but to attempt to parse the string. In Listing 9.14 I have included a simple parsing function using a finite-state machine. While the topic of parsing is not trivial, it is fortunately an area where much work has been done and many books have been written. Rather than attempt to treat the topic here I will therefore only give a rough overview. In this example, we scan the string from left to right. As we encounter any characters that could begin a token (*Left* Parentheses, Braces, Quotes, or any text) we set a state variable indicating which kind of token we have. We then continue to scan until we find the corresponding end of the token (e.g., the *Right* counterpart of the beginning character). Each time we complete a token we increment the token count. When we arrive at the token index requested, then we return the value of the token.

```
Private Enum ParseStateType
 WhiteSpace = 0
 SimpleString = 1
 QuotedString = 2
 Parentheses = 3
 Braces = 4
End Enum
Private Function GetToken(SearchString As String, _
            TokenIndex As Integer) As String
 Dim ScanState As ParseStateType
 Dim CurrentCharacter As String
 Dim ScanIndex As Integer
 Dim TokenFound As Boolean
 Dim ScanToken As Integer
 Dim TokenBegin As Integer
 Dim NestDepth As Integer
 Dim WorkToken As String
 WorkToken = ""
 ScanIndex = 1
 ScanToken = 0
 TokenFound = False
 ScanState = WhiteSpace
 Do While ScanIndex <= Len(SearchString)
  CurrentCharacter = Mid(SearchString, ScanIndex, 1)
  Select Case ScanState
   Case WhiteSpace
    If Not CurrentCharacter = " " Then
     ScanToken = ScanToken + 1
     WorkToken = CurrentCharacter
     Select Case CurrentCharacter
      Case "("
       ScanState = Parentheses
       NestDepth = 1
      Case """"
       ScanState = QuotedString
       WorkToken = ""
      Case "{"
       ScanState = Braces
       NestDepth = 1
      Case Else
       ScanState = SimpleString
```

```
    End Select
   End If
   ScanIndex = ScanIndex + 1
 Case SimpleString
  Select Case CurrentCharacter
   Case " "
     ScanState = WhiteSpace
     If ScanToken = TokenIndex Then
      GetToken = WorkToken
      Exit Function
     End If
   Case Else
     WorkToken = WorkToken + CurrentCharacter
     ScanIndex = ScanIndex + 1
  End Select
 Case QuotedString
  If CurrentCharacter = """" Then
   ScanState = WhiteSpace
   If ScanIndex < Len(SearchString) Then
    If Mid(SearchString, ScanIndex + 1, 1) = """" Then
     ScanIndex = ScanIndex + 1
     ScanState = QuotedString
    End If
   End If
   If ScanState = WhiteSpace And ScanToken = TokenIndex Then
    GetToken = WorkToken
    Exit Function
   End If
  End If
  WorkToken = WorkToken + CurrentCharacter
  ScanIndex = ScanIndex + 1
 Case Parentheses
  Select Case CurrentCharacter
   Case "("
    NestDepth = NestDepth + 1
   Case ")"
    NestDepth = NestDepth - 1
  End Select
  WorkToken = WorkToken + CurrentCharacter
  If NestDepth = 0 Then
   ScanState = WhiteSpace
   If ScanToken = TokenIndex Then
    GetToken = WorkToken
    Exit Function
```

```
      End If
    End If
  Case Braces
   Select Case CurrentCharacter
    Case "{"
     NestDepth = NestDepth + 1
    Case "}"
     NestDepth = NestDepth - 1
   End Select
   WorkToken = WorkToken + CurrentCharacter
   If NestDepth = 0 Then
    ScanState = WhiteSpace
    If ScanToken = TokenIndex Then
     GetToken = WorkToken
     Exit Function
    End If
   End If
  End Select
 Loop
 If ScanToken = TokenIndex Then
  GetToken = WorkToken
 Else
  GetToken = ""
 End If
End Function
```

Listing 9.14 *Get requested token from string*

Once a user has been authenticated we load the username into the
textbox (Listing 9.15). We then loop through all the files (and subdi-
rectories) in the user's root directory. Each file is checked to see if it is
a subdirectory and, if so, it is added to the folder list.

```
Private Sub LoadUser(Index As Integer, UserName As String)
 Dim CurrentDirectory As String
 Dim CurrentFile As String
 txtUser(Index).Text = UserName
 CurrentDirectory = PostOfficeDirectory + UserName + "\"
 CurrentFile = Dir$(CurrentDirectory, vbDirectory)
 Do Until CurrentFile = ""
  If CurrentFile <> "." And CurrentFile <> ".." And _
    (GetAttr(CurrentDirectory & CurrentFile) And vbDirectory) = _
    vbDirectory Then
   lstFolders(CurrentConnection).AddItem CurrentFile
```

```
      CurrentFile = Dir$
    End If
  Loop
End Sub
```

Listing 9.15 *Load Authenticated User*

When the client requests a set of folders (Listing 9.16) we loop through all the entries in the folder list. Those that match the request are then returned to the client.

```
Private Sub ListFolders(Index As Integer, ClientRequest As String)
  Dim strResponseLine As String
  Dim strRequestedFolder As String
  Dim strCurrentFolder As String
  Dim intFolderIndex As Integer
  strRequestedFolder = GetToken(ClientRequest, 4)
  For intFolderIndex = 1 To lstFolders.Count
    strCurrentFolder = lstFolders(intFolderIndex)
    strResponseLine = "* " + GetToken(ClientRequest, 2) + _
            "()""/" """" + strCurrentFolder + """"
    Status = SendSocket(TransmitSocket, strResponseLine)
  Next
End Sub
```

Listing 9.16 *List requested folders*

When the client selects a folder we load that folder into the corresponding textbox (Listing 9.17). We then loop through all the files in the folder and cache them in the file list.

```
Private Sub LoadFolder(CurrentConnection As Integer, FolderName As
String)
  Dim CurrentUser As String
  Dim CurrentDirectory As String
  Dim CurrentFile As String
  Dim CurrentFileSize As Integer
  Dim ListEntry As String
  txtSelectedFolder(CurrentConnection).Text = FolderName
  CurrentUser = txtUser(CurrentConnection).Text
  CurrentDirectory = PostOfficeDirectory + CurrentUser + "\" + _
        FolderName + "\"
  CurrentDirectory = PostOfficeDirectory + CurrentUser + "\"
  CurrentFile = Dir$(CurrentDirectory + "*")
```

```
  Do Until CurrentFile = ""
   ListEntry = Right$(Space$(6) + Str(CurrentFileSize), 6) + Chr$(9) + _
      CurrentFile
   lstFiles(CurrentConnection).AddItem ListEntry
   lstFileFlags(CurrentConnection).AddItem ListEntry
   CurrentFile = Dir$


 Loop
End Sub
```

Listing 9.17 *Load selected folder*

The *FETCH* and *UID FETCH* commands request us to fetch
components from a message range (Listing 9.18). This range can
either be a single message (e.g., 3) or a colon-delimited range (e.g.,
3:7). We search for a colon in the string. If it is there, then we loop
through all the messages from the beginning of the range to the end
of the range. Otherwise we simply fetch the message requested.

```
Private Sub FetchMessageRange(CurrentConnection As Integer,
MessageRange As String, MessageComponents As String)
 Dim intBeginIndex As Integer
 Dim intEndIndex As Integer
 Dim intCurrentIndex As Integer
 If InStr(1, MessageRange, ":") = 0 Then
  FetchMessage CurrentConnection, Int(val(MessageRange)), _
        MessageComponents
 Else
  intBeginIndex = _
     Int(val(Left(MessageRange, InStr(1, MessageRange, ":"))))
  intEndIndex = _
     Int(val(Mid(MessageRange, InStr(1, MessageRange, ":") + 1)))
  For intCurrentIndex = intBeginIndex To intEndIndex
   FetchMessage CurrentConnection, intCurrentIndex, _
        MessageComponents
  Next
 End If
End Sub
```

Listing 9.18 *Fetch requested message range*

To fetch a particular message we need to loop through all the
requested components and retrieve them one by one (Listing 9.19). In

each case we determine the component and return the appropriate data. In this example, we do not support all possible components that might be requested. We have reduced the code to some of the most common:

- *RFC822, BODY, BODY.PEEK*—Return the entire message
- *RFC822.HEADER*—Returns only the header lines from the message (to the first blank line)
- *RFC822.SIZE*—Returns the number of bytes in the message (the size of the file)
- *INTERNALDATE*—Returns the modification date of the file
- *UID*—Returns the index of the message (should return a permanent ID but it doesn't)
- FLAGS—Returns all the flags that are set for the message

```
Private Sub FetchMessage(CurrentConnection As Integer, MessageIndex As
Integer, MessageComponents As String)
 Dim strSendLine As String
 Dim strMessageFile As String
 Dim intMessageFileNumber As Integer
 Dim strCurrentUser As String
 Dim strCurrentDirectory As String
 Dim strComponents As String
 Dim strCurrentComponent As String
 Dim intComponentIndex As Integer
 Dim strCurrentHeader As String
 Dim strHeaders As String
 intComponentIndex = 1
 strComponents = Trim(UCase(MessageComponents))
 If Left(strComponents, 1) = "(" Then
  strComponents = Trim(Mid(strComponents, 2, Len(strComponents) - 2))
 End If
 strCurrentComponent = GetToken(strComponents, intComponentIndex)
 strCurrentUser = txtUser(CurrentConnection).Text
 strCurrentDirectory = PostOfficeDirectory + strCurrentUser + "\"
 strMessageFile = strCurrentDirectory + _
    lstFiles(CurrentConnection).List(MessageIndex - 1)
 strSendLine = "* " + Trim(Str(MessageIndex)) + " FETCH ("
 Do While strCurrentComponent <> ""
  Select Case strCurrentComponent
   Case "RFC822", "BODY[]", "BODY.PEEK[]"
```

```
  strSendLine = strSendLine + strCurrentComponent + _
        " {" + Trim(Str(FileLen(strMessageFile)) + "}")
Status = SendSocket(TransmitSocket, strSendLine)
intMessageFileNumber = FreeFile
Open strMessageFile For Input As #intMessageFileNumber
Do While Not EOF(intMessageFileNumber)
 Line Input #intMessageFileNumber, strSendLine
 Status = SendSocket(TransmitSocket, strSendLine)
Loop
Close #intMessageFileNumber
strSendLine = " "

Case "RFC822.HEADER"
 strHeaders = ""
 intMessageFileNumber = FreeFile
 Open strMessageFile For Input As #intMessageFileNumber
 Do
 Line Input #intMessageFileNumber, strCurrentHeader
 strHeaders = strHeaders + CRLF + strCurrentHeader
 Loop While Not EOF(intMessageFileNumber) And strCurrentHeader <> ""
 Close #intMessageFileNumber
 strHeaders = strHeaders + CRLF
 strSendLine = strSendLine + strCurrentComponent + _
        " {" + Trim(Str(Len(strHeaders)) + "}")
 Status = SendSocket(TransmitSocket, strSendLine)
 Status = SendSocket(TransmitSocket, Mid(strHeaders, 3))
 strSendLine = " "

Case "RFC822.SIZE"
 strSendLine = strSendLine + strCurrentComponent + " " + _
        Trim(Str(FileLen(strMessageFile))) + " "

Case "INTERNALDATE"
 strSendLine = strSendLine + strCurrentComponent + " """ + _
        Format(FileDateTime(strMessageFile), _
            "dd-mmm-yy hh:mm:ss") + " +0000"" "

Case "UID"
 strSendLine = strSendLine + strCurrentComponent + " " + _
        Trim(Str(MessageIndex)) + " "

Case "FLAGS"
 strSendLine = strSendLine + strCurrentComponent + " (\Seen) "
```

```
   End Select

   intComponentIndex = intComponentIndex + 1
   strCurrentComponent = GetToken(strComponents, intComponentIndex)
  Loop
  strSendLine = RTrim(strSendLine) + ")"
  Status = SendSocket(TransmitSocket, strSendLine)
End Sub
```

Listing 9.19 *Fetch individual message*

Wrapping Up

IMAP is a very comprehensive protocol. To fully support it you must expect to write a lot of code—probably more than for any of the other protocols covered in this book. Some areas for further development include:

- *Parsing*—IMAP is a text-based protocol. It is fairly easy to read and understand but not quite as easy to parse. In particular, you must consider a proper analysis of:

    IMAP commands and responses—These consist of a number of lexical tokens with a precise formal syntax. We have taken a shortcut by extracting the information we needed without performing a full parse. Not only is this risky, since it is easy to miss some commands with a nontypical syntax, but we are also much more restricted from extending our code by adding new functionality.

    MIME components—IMAP assumes we are able to fully parse our MIME messages into a very low-level set of components. In order to fully support some of the MIME commands we would need to first parse the message in detail and then map each component to the structure provided by IMAP.

- *Authentication*—As with POP, IMAP is intended to be a protocol for private (not anonymous) use. In other words, each user should only be able to access a predefined mailbox or set of mailboxes. In order to ensure this we need to provide a secure form of authentication.

- *Supplementary Mailbox information*—IMAP specifies for the server to store more information than just the mailbox hierarchy and the messages in it. The server should also store and, when requested, be able to provide:

    UID—We have cheated in our support of UIDs since our Ids are not really permanent. Many clients would use the UID to be able to create a link between a local cached copy of (at least parts of) the message and the actual message on the server.

    Subscription—Likewise, clients assume that the server is storing the list of subscribed folders for each user.

    Attributes/Flags—Ideally the server should support all the flags, including items such as Seen.

Chapter 10

ASN.1—Abstract Syntax Notation One

ASN.1 is specified in X.208 but it relies on an unspecified set of encoding rules. Generally, the (BER) Basic Encoding Rules (X.209) are used. Since LDAP also uses X.209 I will use the term ASN.1 to refer to both X.208 and X.209 collectively.

If you need to devise a way to store data you will always be confronted with the same trade-offs.

1. *How rigid should the definition be?* If we make assumptions about our information (e.g., we only need the last two digits of the calendar year) we can make the encoding and entry easier. On the other hand, if those assumptions turn out to be misguided, it means we may have to redesign the application.

2. *How compact should the data be?* In order to ensure maximum flexibility we can attempt to remove as many assumptions as possible. A four-digit year may be enough for now but in a mere 8,000 years we will have another problem. What if we change to a different calendar counting up from the big bang? What if an undiscovered alien civilization uses a different date and time format? Clearly we need to draw the line somewhere, or we could have thousand-byte date fields and still be worried.

ASN.1 (Abstract Syntax Notation One) tries to allow maximum freedom of implementation in encoding. The BER (Basic Encoding Rules) provide us with a succinct encoding of any data item, while at the same time maximizing extensibility.

Figure 10.1 shows some sample ASN.1 data. As you can see, it is not particularly intuitive. We will look at what it means later, but first we need to understand how ASN.1 is structured.

99	43	4	0	10	1	2	10	1	3	2	1	10	2	1	30
1	1	0	164	12	4	2	99	110	48	6	128	4	100	105	111
110	48	10	4	2	99	110	4	4	109	97	105	108			

Figure 10.1 *Sample ASN.1 data*

Structure

At the highest level every structure is encoded in three parts (Figure 10.2). Starting from the end we have the actual data (could be numeric, string, or many other types of data). Prefixed to the data we have its length. This facilitates parsing since it lets us know where this structure ends and the next begins. Before the length is the identifier. It may give us a clue about the meaning of the data, but in every case it will tell us its format.

Identifier	Length	Contents

Figure 10.2 *Encoding structure*[1]

Identifier

Each Identifier is a single byte (Figure 10.3), which is composed of three parts.

The first two bits identify the class of the tag (Table 10.1). These indicate the scope of the validity of a tag. A context-specific tag is mean-

---

[1] The encoding structure is defined in X.209 §6.

8	7	6	5	4	3	2	1
Class		P/C		Number of Tag			

Figure 10.3 *Bits of Identifier octet[2]*

ingful only in the context of one specific ASN.1 definition. Application level tags apply to the entire application (e.g., LDAP). Finally, there are also universal tags that are defined for all ASN.1 definitions.

Table 10.1 *Classes of ASN.1 Tags[3]*

Class	Bit 8	Bit 7
Universal	0	0
Application	0	1
Context-specific	1	0
Private	1	1

To illustrate, let us use a tag number of 1 (Table 10.2).

- The identifier 1 is a universal tag (bits 7 and 8 both set to 0) meaning Boolean Type (see Table 10.3 for the list of universal tags).

- 65 is an application tag (bit 7 set to 1, bit 8 set to 0). This means that every application will have a different interpretation of this tag. LDAP, for example, uses tag 1 to mean a *BindResponse*.

- 129 is context-specific (bit 8 set to 1, bit 7 set to 0). In an LDAP message it can mean *"krbv42LDAP," "or,"* or *"any,"* depending on where it occurs in an LDAP message.

Table 10.2 *Tag of Value 1 Illustrated with Different Classes*

Class		P/C	Tag					Tag	Identifier
8	7	6	5	4	3	2	1		
0	0	0	0	0	0	0	1	1	1
0	1	0	0	0	0	0	1	1	65
1	0	0	0	0	0	0	1	1	129

---

[2] The set of identifiers is specified in X.209 § 6.2.5.
[3] See X.209 §6.2.4 for the formal specification of the ASN.1 tags.

The Identifier also has a 1-bit field labeled P/C. This stands for Primitive/Constructed and indicates whether the type is atomic or whether it consists of subtypes. This is a particularly useful field for parsing, since it permits an application-independent analysis of the structure without any knowledge of the individual tags.

Most ASN.1 structures are directly or indirectly built from Universal tags (Table 10.3). The Primitive types (Boolean, Integer, OctetString, Enumerated) are fairly intuitive in meaning There are two composite types that we will encounter. They are:

- *SEQUENCE*—all subvalues occur in sequence
- *SET*—any of the subvalues may occur in any order

In ASN.1 definitions you will also come across references to

- *CHOICE*—only one of the subvalues occurs

Table 10.3 *Universal ASN Tags[4]*

Universal Tags	Description
1	Boolean type
2	Integer type
3	Bistring type
4	Octetstring type
5	Null type
6	Object identifier type
7	Object descriptor type
8	External type
9	Real type
10	Enumerated type
12-15	Reserved
16	Sequence type
17	Set type
18-22, 25-27	Character string types
23, 24	Time types
28-	Reserved

---

[4] The list of ASN.1 tags can be found in X.208 §5.7.

Note that although CHOICE seems similar to the above constructs, it is not a tag and it is not composite. Every instance of a choice will be the particular subtype that occurs. Therefore we will only see the tag of the subtype.

Length

The length field is an encoding that indicates the length of the following contents. Again we encounter the issue of knowing the bounds of the length in order to determine the length field. If we use a one-byte length field the maximum would be 256 (2^8). With two bytes it would be 65536 (2^{16}). We can allocate a dozen bytes for the length field. It would take care of the problem for the foreseeable future. But it would also mean that to send a single byte we would need a structure of 14 (1-Identifier, 12-Length, 1-Contents) bytes.

The compromise between efficiency and scalability is a dual-encoding scheme.[5]

We have a short form with a one-byte length field (Figure 10.4). The first bit must be 0, which leaves 7 bits and allows us to encode length of up to 128 (2^7).

5							
0	0	0	0	0	1	0	1

Figure 10.4 *Short encoding of length 5*

If bit 8 is set (i.e., the value of the first Length byte is greater than 128) then we are using the long form of encoding (Figure 10.5). In this case, the lower 7 bits give the length of the remaining length bytes. So, conceivably, we could have 127-length bytes that would accommodate a length of 2^{1016} content octets—probably enough to satisfy today's needs.

---

[5] Both of these forms are actually subforms of the definite form of length encoding. There is also another "indefinite" form, which uses termination octets rather than length octets. LDAP only uses the definite form, so I have limited my discussion to it.

132=128+4	0	0	0	5
1 0 0 0 0 1 0 0	0 0 0 0 0 0 0 0	0 0 0 0 0 0 0 0	0 0 0 0 0 0 0 0	0 0 0 0 0 1 0 1

Figure 10.5 *Long encoding of length 5*

In Figure 10.6 you can see what the whole encoding looks like. We are encoding an OctetString (Universal 4) of length 2 (using the short encoding) and a value of "Hi."

Identifier	Length	Contents	
4	2	72 = 'H'	105 = 'i'
0 0 0 0 0 1 0 0	0 0 0 0 0 0 1 0	0 1 0 0 1 0 0 0	0 1 1 0 1 0 0 1

Figure 10.6 *Encoding of string "Hi"*

Now that you have the basics it is time to look at an actual ASN.1 syntax definition (Listing 10.1). It looks a little like a programming language or possibly a data definition language.

```
SearchRequest ::=
      [APPLICATION 3] SEQUENCE {
        baseObject  LDAPDN,
        scope       ENUMERATED {
                baseObject       (0),
                singleLevel      (1),
                wholeSubtree     (2)
              },
        derefAliases ENUMERATED {
                    neverDerefAliases    (0),
                    derefInSearching     (1),
                    derefFindingBaseObj  (2),
                    derefAlways          (3)
                  },
        sizeLimit   INTEGER (0 .. maxInt),
        timeLimit   INTEGER (0 .. maxInt),
        attrsOnly   BOOLEAN,
        filter      Filter,
        attributes  SEQUENCE OF AttributeType
      }
Filter ::=
```

```
        CHOICE {
            and         [0] SET OF Filter,
            or          [1] SET OF Filter,
            not         [2] Filter,
            equalityMatch    [3] AttributeValueAssertion,
            substrings       [4] SubstringFilter,
            greaterOrEqual   [5] AttributeValueAssertion,
            lessOrEqual      [6] AttributeValueAssertion,
            present       [7] AttributeType,
            approxMatch      [8] AttributeValueAssertion
        }
SubstringFilter ::=
        SEQUENCE {
            type         AttributeType,
            SEQUENCE OF CHOICE {
                initial     [0] LDAPString,
                any         [1] LDAPString,
                final       [2] LDAPString
            }
        }
AttributeValueAssertion ::=
        SEQUENCE {
            attributeType     AttributeType,
            attributeValue    AttributeValue
        }
AttributeType ::= LDAPString
AttributeValue ::= OCTET STRING
```

Listing 10.1 *Sample ASN.1 definitions*

You see definitions for six ASN.1 structures: *SearchRequest, Filter, SubstringFilter, AttributeValueAssertion, AttributeType,* and *AttributeValue.* The best way to understand these definitions it to see how they are encoded. In Figure 10.1 you saw one possible encoding using these rules. If you are ambitious, you might want to decipher it yourself before you continue. Just in case you don't know where to start, I have correlated the binary data with the syntax specification in Figure 10.7.

Each of the tags is calculated based on the parameter shown in Table 10.4.

```
 99   43            Application 3 (SearchRequest), Length: 47
  4    0            OctetString (baseObject), Length: 0
 10    1   2        Enumerated (scope), Length: 1, Value: 2(wholeSubtree)
 10    1   3        Enumerated (derefAliases), Length: 1, Value: 3 (derefAlways)
  2    1  10        Integer (sizeLimit), Length: 1, Value: 10
  2    1  30        Integer (timeLimit), Length: 1, Value: 30
  1    1   0        Boolean (attrsOnly), Length: 1, Value: 0 (False)
164   12            ContextSpecific 4 (substrings), Length: 12
  4    2  99 110    OctetString (type), Length: 2, Value: "cn"
 48    6              Sequence (SubstringFilter), Length: 6
128    4 100 105 111 110  ContextSpecific 0 (initial), Length: 4, Value:"dion"
 48   10              Sequence (attributes), Length: 10,
  4    2  99 110        OctetString (AttributeType), Length: 2, Value: "cn"
  4    4 109  97 105 108  OctetString (AttributeType), Length: 4, Value: "mail"
```

Figure 10.7 *Analysis of ASN.1 data*

Table 10.4 *Identifier Calculations*

Structure	Identifier		Clan	Constructed	Tag
SearchRequest	99	64+32+3	APPLICATION(64)	Yes (32)	3
baseObject	4	0+0+4	UNIVERSAL (0)	No (0)	4
scope	10	0+0+10	UNIVERSAL (0)	No (0)	10
derefAliases	10	0+0+10	UNIVERSAL (0)	No (0)	10
sizeLimit	2	0+0+2	UNIVERSAL (0)	No (0)	2
timeLimit	2	0+0+2	UNIVERSAL (0)	No (0)	2
attrsOnly	1	0+0+1	UNIVERSAL (0)	No (0)	1
substrings	164	128+32+4	Context-Specific (128)	Yes (32)	4
type	4	0+0+4	UNIVERSAL (0)	No (0)	4
SubstringFilter	48	0+32 + 16	UNIVERSAL (0)	Yes (32)	0
initial	128	128+0+0	Context-Specific (128)	No (0)	0
attributes	48	0+32 + 16	UNIVERSAL (0)	Yes (32)	0
AttributeType	4	0+0+4	UNIVERSAL (0)	No (0)	4
AttributeType	4	0+0+4	UNIVERSAL (0)	No (0)	4

Let's walk through each line.

- We can tell that this structure is a *SearchRequest* since it begins with an Application 3. It is constructed and the length of its value is 43. Since that is the length of the remaining byte stream we know all the other types are subordinates.

- The first subtype is the *baseObject*. As we should expect from the definition it is an OctetStream (Universal 4). It has a zero length so we need not look for a value.

- Next comes the *scope*. The enumerated type (Universal 10) has a length of 1 and a value of 2. Looking at the syntax definition we see that a 2 means *wholeSubtree*.

- The *derefAliases* is also an enumerated type with a length of 1 and a value of 3 (meaning *derefAlways*).

- The *sizeLimit* and *timeLimit* entries are integer (Universal 2) of length 1 with values of 10 and 30 respectively.

- The Boolean (Universal 1) type *attrsOnly* always has a length of 1. A value of 0 means False, while any other value would mean True.

- The syntax definition has Filter next, but we don't see any reference to one in the data. This is because Filter is a Choice. We only see the particular Filter used, which in this case is *Substrings* (Context-specific 4). It is implemented as a *SubstringFilter* so we continue our parsing from there.

- We have an Octetstring "type" with length of 2 and a value of "cn" followed by a *sequence* of choice of (*initial*, *any*, or *final*). In this case our sequence only has one entry having one initial with length 4 and value "dion."

- Having completed parsing the *substrings* we finish the *SearchRequest* where there was still an entry of attributes. It is also a *sequence*. Its two entries have a total length of 10.

- First we have an *AttributeType* of "cn," followed by an *AttributeType* of "mail."

Encoding ASN.1

There are two challenges to encoding ASN.1 that we need to consider. First of all, we need to know how to encode any particular item into its TLV set. This would be sufficient if we only had a linear sequence of atomic data items to encode. In order to accommodate the structural types we need to be able to accept structured input and encode the subitems into the appropriate hierarchies.

Code Example

Figure 10.7 shows a simple form that will allow you to add multiple data items to a structure. By indicating the depth it knows at which hierarchical level to insert the item. You can see the values added (S=String, N=Numeric, C=Composite) in the lower left-hand textbox. The middle pane (ASN) shows the ASN.1 interpretation of the structure, while the right textbox (Binary) shows the binary output of the ASN.1 encoding.

The sample ASN.1 composer (Figure 10.8) lets a user add, delete, and update substructures to the ASN.1 structure shown on the form. When all the components are complete the binary structure can be saved to a file.

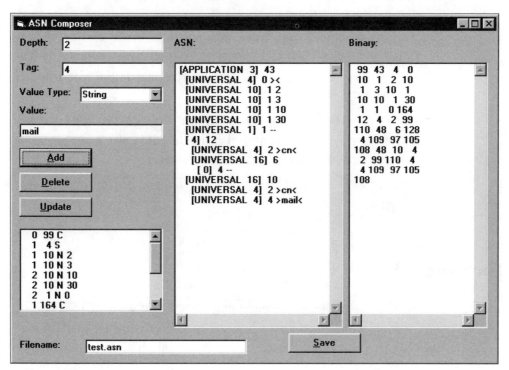

Figure 10.8 *ASN Composer*

To facilitate user entry of structured information we have introduced the notion of depth (an entry of depth n+1 is a component of the previous entry of depth n). All the components are shown in the record list (lower-left panel) with their depth, tag, value type (whether the data the user is entering is string, numeric, or composed).

```
Public Const ASN_SCOPE_MASK = 192
Public Const ASN_UNIVERSAL_MASK = 0
Public Const ASN_APPLICATION = 64
Public Const ASN_CONTEXT_SPECIFIC = 128
Public Const ASN_PRIVATE = 192
Public Const ASN_COMPOSITE = 32
Public Const ASN_BOOLEAN_TAG = 1
Public Const ASN_INTEGER_TAG = 2
Public Const ASN_OCTETSTRING_TAG = 4
Public Const ASN_ENUMERATED_TAG = 10
Public Const ASN_SEQUENCE_TAG = 16 + ASN_COMPOSITE
Public Const ASN_SET_TAG = 17 + ASN_COMPOSITE
```

Listing 10.2 *ASN.1 Constants*

To add an entry (Listing 10.3) to the structure we first create the line (depth, tag, value type, value) and add it to the list (lstRecords). We then refresh the form, which updates the other controls as well as the underlying ASN.1 structure.

```
Private Sub btnAdd_Click()
Dim strAddLine As String
strAddLine = Right(Space(4) + txtDepth.Text, 4) + _
    Right(Space(4) + txtTag.Text, 4) + _
    Right(Space(2) + Left(cboValueType.Text, 1), 2) + _
    " " + txtValue.Text

If lstRecords.ListIndex = -1 Then
 lstRecords.AddItem strAddLine
Else
 lstRecords.AddItem strAddLine, lstRecords.ListIndex
End If

RefreshForm

End Sub
```

Listing 10.3 *Add ASN.1 structure*

To delete a component we simply remove the currently selected item from the list and refresh the form (Listing 10.4).

```
Private Sub btnDelete_Click()
If lstRecords.ListIndex <> -1 Then
 lstRecords.RemoveItem lstRecords.ListIndex
End If


RefreshForm


End Sub
```

Listing 10.4 *Delete ASN.1 structure*

The update replaces the currently selected item in the list with the values entered by the user (Listing 10.5). Again the RefreshForm does all the real work.

```
Private Sub btnUpdate_Click()
If lstRecords.ListIndex <> -1 Then
 lstRecords.List(lstRecords.ListIndex) = _
     Right(Space(4) + txtDepth.Text, 4) + _
     Right(Space(4) + txtTag.Text, 4) + _
     Right(Space(2) + Left(cboValueType.Text, 1), 2) + _
     " " + txtValue.Text
End If
RefreshForm
End Sub
```

Listing 10.5 *Update ASN.1 Structure*

When we need to refresh the form we first update the underlying structure (Listing 10.6). This means we fill an array with all records of the structure and use it to *Compose* our underlying ASN structure. We can load the ASN description directly from the *Dump* property. The binary version is derived from the *TransferString*. Since the property is binary we need to convert the values to decimal and add formatting (spaces and line-feeds) for visual clarity.

```
Private Sub RefreshForm()
Dim strTransferString As String
Dim intScanIndex As Integer
```

```
FillArray MainArray, 0

asnMain.Compose MainArray
txtASN.Text = asnMain.Dump

strTransferString = asnMain.TransferString
txtBinary.Text = ""
For intScanIndex = 1 To Len(strTransferString)
 txtBinary.Text = txtBinary.Text + Right(Space(3) + _
      Str(Asc(Mid(strTransferString, intScanIndex, 1))), 4)
 If Int(intScanIndex / 4) = intScanIndex / 4 Then
  txtBinary.Text = txtBinary.Text + Chr(13) + Chr(10)
 End If
Next

txtASN.Refresh
txtBinary.Refresh

End Sub
```

Listing 10.6 *Refresh the form*

Our work arrays contain a minimum of two entries for the structure they describe (Listing 10.7). The first is simply the tag of the structure. In the case of an atomic tag (e.g., numeric or string) the second entry is the value of the structure.

```
Private Sub FillArray(ByRef WorkArray, ByRef LineIndex As Integer)
Dim intArrayIndex As Integer
Dim intLineDepth As Integer
Dim varSubordinateArray() As Variant
ReDim Preserve WorkArray(2)
WorkArray(1) = val(Mid(lstRecords.List(LineIndex), 5, 4))

intArrayIndex = 1
intLineDepth = GetDepth(LineIndex)

Select Case Mid(lstRecords.List(LineIndex), 10, 1)
 Case "N"
  WorkArray(2) = Chr(Mid(lstRecords.List(LineIndex), 12))
 Case "S"
  WorkArray(2) = Mid(lstRecords.List(LineIndex), 12)
 Case "C"
  Do While GetDepth(LineIndex + 1) > intLineDepth
```

```
            intArrayIndex = intArrayIndex + 1
            LineIndex = LineIndex + 1
            ReDim Preserve WorkArray(intArrayIndex)
            FillArray varSubordinateArray, LineIndex
            WorkArray(intArrayIndex) = varSubordinateArray
        Loop
   End Select

End Sub
Private Function GetDepth(LineIndex As Integer) As Integer
 If LineIndex <= lstRecords.ListCount Then
  GetDepth = val(Left(lstRecords.List(LineIndex), 4))
 Else
  GetDepth = -1
 End If
End Function
```

Listing 10.7 *Fill array from record list*

When the structure is constructed, then all the subordinate constituents are loaded into the remaining slots of the array. In order to determine which entries are subordinate, we examine the depth of all subsequent entries until we find one of equal or less depth.

The Compose method of an ASN class takes the InputList and extracts the first value into the tag (Listing 10.8).

If the second entry is an array, this is a sign that we are dealing with a composite type. We loop through all the subentries and recursively *Compose* them. In the case that the second entry was not an array (an atomic type) we put its value into the value of the object.

```
   Public Sub Compose(InputList As Variant)
    Dim intIndexCounter As Integer
    Dim bolEndInputList As Boolean

    intIndexCounter = 0
    intTag = InputList(1)

    If VarType(InputList(2)) And vbArray Then
     Do
       intIndexCounter = intIndexCounter + 1
       ReDim Preserve asnSubItem(intIndexCounter)
       Set asnSubItem(intIndexCounter) = New ASN1
       asnSubItem(intIndexCounter).Compose (InputList(intIndexCounter + 1))
```

```
    bolEndInputList = True
       If intIndexCounter + 2 <= UBound(InputList) Then
        If Not IsEmpty(InputList(intIndexCounter + 2)) Then
         bolEndInputList = False
        End If
       End If
     Loop Until bolEndInputList
    Else
     strValue = InputList(2)
    End If
    bolComplete = True
    intTotalSubItems = intIndexCounter
   End Sub
```

Listing 10.8 *Compose ASN.1 structure*

The *TransferString* is a concatenation of tag, length, and value
(Listing 10.9). The *Tag* and *Value* are both stored in variables and
easy enough to obtain.

Only the length is derived and must be calculated. We look at the
actual length of the value. If it is less than 128 we can use it without
any transformation. Otherwise, we create a 4-byte length and use the
long form of the length. This means an initial length field indicator (4
is the length of the length field; 128 indicates this is the long form)
plus the 4 bytes.

Note that we could possibly use length fields of other sizes than 4
bytes. However, in most cases the economy in the transfer load does
not offset the added processing.

```
   Public Property Get TransferString() As String
    Dim intShortLength As Integer
    Dim strValueLength As String

    Dim bytLength(1 To 4) As Byte

    intShortLength = Me.Length

    If intShortLength < 128 Then
     strValueLength = Chr(intShortLength)
    Else
     bytLength(4) = intShortLength And 255
```

```
bytLength(3) = Int(intShortLength / (2 ^ 8)) And 255
bytLength(2) = Int(intShortLength / (2 ^ 16)) And 255
bytLength(1) = Int(intShortLength / (2 ^ 24)) And 255

strValueLength = Chr(4 + 128) _
      + Chr(bytLength(1)) _
      + Chr(bytLength(2)) _
      + Chr(bytLength(3)) _
      + Chr(bytLength(4))
End If


TransferString = Chr(Me.Tag) + strValueLength + Me.Value
End Property
```

Listing 10.9 *ASN.1 Transfer String*

Given the terseness of ASN.1 data it is worthwhile having a way to examine the contents in human-readable form. The *Dump* property (Listing 10.10) is purely for display and debugging purposes. There is no required or even preferred way in which we must present the data.

- In this implementation we start with the tag. In the case of an Application or Universal tag we add the clan to the tag to avoid making the reader having to calculate it.

- We continue with the value. We know that integers and enumerated tags have numeric values. Octetstrings have string values. Since we are unsure of the rest, we don't display the values.

- We compose a temporary string with an appropriate amount of indentation, tag, and length.

- If we are dealing with a constructed type we need to append all the subtypes. We obtain these by recursively requesting the *Dump* property of each.

```
Public Property Get Dump(Optional level) As String
  Dim intIndexCounter As Integer

  Dim strWorkText As String

  Dim strDisplayTag As String
```

```
    Dim strDisplayValue As String

    If IsMissing(level) Then
     level = 0
    End If

    If Not Me.Complete Then
     Exit Property
    End If

    Select Case intTag And ASN_SCOPE_MASK
     Case ASN_APPLICATION
      strDisplayTag = "[APPLICATION " + Str(intTag And 31) + "] "
     Case ASN_UNIVERSAL
      strDisplayTag = "[UNIVERSAL " + Str(intTag And 31) + "] "
     Case Else
      strDisplayTag = "[" + Str(intTag And 31) + "] "
    End Select

    Select Case intTag
     Case ASN_INTEGER_TAG, ASN_ENUMERATED_TAG
      strDisplayValue = Str(Asc(strValue))
     Case ASN_OCTETSTRING_TAG
      strDisplayValue = " >" + strValue + "<"
     Case Else
      strDisplayValue = " —"
    End Select

    strWorkText = Space$(1 + level * 2) + strDisplayTag +
    Str(Me.Length)

    If Me.Composite Then
     strDisplayValue = Chr$(13) + Chr$(10)
     For intIndexCounter = 1 To intTotalSubItems
      strDisplayValue = strDisplayValue + _
              asnSubItem(intIndexCounter).Dump(level + 1)
     Next
     Dump = strWorkText + strDisplayValue
    Else
     Dump = strWorkText + strDisplayValue + Chr$(13) + Chr$(10)
    End If

    If level = 0 Then Dump = Dump + Chr$(13) + Chr(10)
    End Property
```

Listing 10.10 *Dump ASN.1 Structure*

If the user wants to save the binary data, we open a file and *Put* the *TransferString* to the file (Listing 10.11).

```
Private Sub btnSave_Click()
Dim intOutputFileNumber As Integer
intOutputFileNumber = FreeFile
Open txtFilename.Text For Binary As #intOutputFileNumber
Put #intOutputFileNumber, , asnMain.TransferString
Close #intOutputFileNumber

End Sub
```

Listing 10.11 *Save ASN.1 Structure to File*

Decoding ASN.1

Code Example

To illustrate decoding an ASN.1 structure we have a form (Figure 10.9) that lets the user read the binary data from a file and displays both the ASN.1 parsed fields as well as the source.

When the user reads the file we open it in binary mode and *Get* the contents (Listing 10.12). These are *parsed* by our main ASN.1 object.

```
Dim asnMain As New ASN1
Private Sub btnRead_Click()
Dim intInputFileNumber As Integer
Dim strInputString As String * 10000
intInputFileNumber = FreeFile
Open txtFilename.Text For Binary As #intInputFileNumber
Get #intInputFileNumber, , strInputString
Close #intInputFileNumber
asnMain.Parse strInputString
RefreshForm

End Sub
```

Listing 10.12 *Read ASN.1 from file*

The *RefreshForm* (Listing 10.13) works similarly to the one in the composer (Listing 10.6) except that there is no need to compose the ASN.

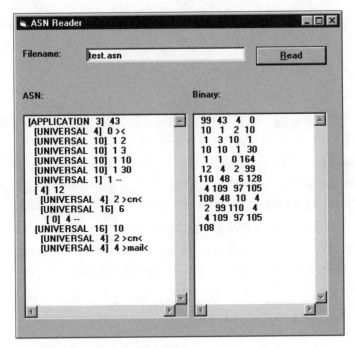

Figure 10.9 *ASN Reader*

```
Private Sub RefreshForm()
 Dim strTransferString As String
 Dim intScanIndex As Integer
 txtASN.Text = asnMain.Dump
 strTransferString = asnMain.TransferString

 txtBinary.Text = ""
 For intScanIndex = 1 To Len(strTransferString)
  txtBinary.Text = txtBinary.Text + Right(Space(3) + _
      Str(Asc(Mid(strTransferString, intScanIndex, 1))), 4)
  If Int(intScanIndex / 4) = intScanIndex / 4 Then
   txtBinary.Text = txtBinary.Text + Chr(13) + Chr(10)
  End If
 Next

 txtASN.Refresh
 txtBinary.Refresh

 End Sub
```

Listing 10.13 *Refresh Form*

The biggest task in reading an ASN.1 encoded structure is parsing it (Listing 10.14). We know that it consists of a tag, length, and value, in that order.

- The first byte is always the *tag*.

- The real work starts with the *length*. If it is less than 128, it is a short length field and requires no extra work. Otherwise, we need to subtract 128 to determine the size of the length field. We calculate the length by starting at the final length byte and adding any additional bytes multiplied by their coefficient (factor of 256).[6]

- The *value* is extracted using the size we have just obtained.

- If our type is composite then we need to continue the parse for all subitems. This means recursively calling the parse routine.

```
Public Sub Parse(ByRef InputText As String)
Dim bytLength1 As Byte
Dim intLength2 As Integer
Dim intIndexCounter As Integer
Dim strParseText As String

strParseText = InputText
intLength2 = 0

If Len(strParseText) < 2 Then
 bolComplete = False
 Exit Sub
End If

intTag = Asc(Left$(strParseText, 1))
bytLength1 = Asc(Mid$(strParseText, 2, 1))
strParseText = Mid$(strParseText, 3)

If bytLength1 < 128 Then
 intLength2 = bytLength1
Else
 bytLength1 = bytLength1 - 128
 If Len(strParseText) < bytLength1 Then
```

---

[6] Note that in this example we only support a maximum of two *significant* bytes. This accommodates lengths of up to 65,536.

```
   bolComplete = False
   Exit Sub
  End If
  intLength2 = Asc(Mid$(strParseText, bytLength1, 1))
  If bytLength1 > 1 Then intLength2 = intLength2 + _
       256 * Asc(Mid$(strParseText, bytLength1 - 1, 1))
  strParseText = Mid$(strParseText, bytLength1 + 1)
 End If

 If Len(strParseText) < intLength2 Then
  bolComplete = False
  Exit Sub
 Else
  strValue = Left$(strParseText, intLength2)
  strParseText = Mid$(strParseText, intLength2 + 1)
 End If
 If intTag And ASN_COMPOSITE Then
  Dim RemainingSubItems As String
  intIndexCounter = 0
  RemainingSubItems = strValue
  Do
   intIndexCounter = intIndexCounter + 1
   ReDim Preserve asnSubItem(intIndexCounter)
   Set asnSubItem(intIndexCounter) = New ASN1
   asnSubItem(intIndexCounter).Parse RemainingSubItems
  Loop While RemainingSubItems <> "" And _
       asnSubItem(intIndexCounter).Complete
  intTotalSubItems = intIndexCounter
 Else
  intTotalSubItems = 0
 End If

 InputText = strParseText
 bolComplete = True
End Sub
```

Listing 10.14 *Parse ASN.1 Structure*

Wrapping Up

ASN.1 is actually not that difficult to work with at the syntactic level.
It isn't easy to debug, since you have to try to correlate a binary

stream of values to your data structure. But once the basics are there, I find it much easier to parse than a text protocol (e.g., IMAP).

If you are looking for ways to improve the applications you could consider:

- *Length encodings*—While LDAP only uses the definite form of length encoding, ASN.1 also allows an indefinite length. If you wanted to use ASN.1 for other protocols you might consider adding support for the indefinite length.

- *ASN.1 compiler*—Ideally we would be able to provide an ASN.1 definition to the program with some data and it could generate the structure complete with all the tags. This is not a trivial task and requires an ASN.1 compiler that is able to parse an ASN.1 definition. You then need to parse the ASN.1 data and correlate the two.

Chapter 11

LDAP—Lightweight Directory Access Protocol

The main purpose of any directory is to provide users the facility to look up correspondents in order to be able to send mail to them correctly. A primitive directory would contain nothing more than a search key (e.g., full name) and an E-mail address as in Dionysus (dionysus@fruitofthe.vine). This would allow anyone to address messages knowing only each subscriber's full name.

There are a couple of limitations to this approach. Firstly, the full name may not be unique. There may be more than one John Smith in the organization. How would the user know which to select? Secondly, we may not know the full name but only other information about the user (surname, phone-extension, etc.).

To address these issues we expand the database of the directory by adding more columns, or properties of the user. By including personal details such as location, department, and job title, it is easy to select the correct match when a search returns multiple users. We can also include the properties in the search to refine a search (e.g., find all users with surname Smith and location Sydney) or broaden a search (e.g., find all users with surname Smith or surname Schmidt).

As we alluded to in the previous chapter, an LDAP session uses ASN.1 to encode the data transferred between client and server (Figure 11.1). Each command or response is in the form of an LDAP message.

```
⇒
LDAPMessage
  messageID=1
  BindRequest
    version=3
    name=''
    authentication=simple
                                                                        ⇐
                                        LDAPMessage
                                          messageID=1
                                          BindResponse
                                            resultCode=success
                                            matchedDN=''
                                              errorMessage=''

⇒
LDAPMessage
  messageID=2
  SearchRequest
    baseObject=''
    scope=wholeSubtree
    derefAliases=derefAlways
    sizeLimit=10
    timeLimit=30
    attrsOnly=False
    Filter
      substrings
        type='cn'
        Sequence
          initial='dion'
    Sequence
      AttributeType='cn'
      AttributeType='mail'
                                                                        ⇐
                              LDAPMessage
                                messageID=2
                                SearchResponse entry
                                  objectName='cn=Dionysus'
                                  Sequence
                                    Sequence
                                      AttributeType='cn'
                                      Set
                                        AttributeValue='Dionysus'
                                    Sequence
                                      AttributeType='mail'
                                      Set
                                        AttributeValue=
                                        'dionysus@fruitofthe.vine'
                                                                        ⇐
                                  LDAPMessage
                                    messageID=2
                                    SearchResponse resultCode
                                      resultCode=success
                                      matchedDN=''
                                      errorMessage=''
```

Figure 11.1 *Sample LDAP session*

LDAP Messages

The ASN.1 definition of an LDAP message is shown in Figure 11.2. It is a very high-level definition with only two components.

The *messageID* is an arbitrary number assigned by the client when making a request and is retained by the server when creating the response. It allows clients to correlate responses to multiple outstanding requests.

The *protocolOp* is the substance of the message. It reflects a different ASN.1 structure, depending on the request or response it indicates, so we shall look at the primary functions individually.

First you should be aware of the typical sequence of LDAP requests (Figure 11.3). The client begins by binding to the directory of an LDAP server. The purpose of binding is to establish a context for the session. The user can authenticate and specify parameters that should apply to any of

```
LDAPMessage ::=
      SEQUENCE {
          messageID    MessageID,
          protocolOp   CHOICE {
                              bindRequest         BindRequest,
                              bindResponse        BindResponse,
                              unbindRequest       UnbindRequest,
                              searchRequest       SearchRequest,
                              searchResponse      SearchResponse,
                              modifyRequest       ModifyRequest,
                              modifyResponse      ModifyResponse,
                              addRequest          AddRequest,
                              addResponse         AddResponse,
                              delRequest          DelRequest,
                              delResponse         DelResponse,
                              modifyRDNRequest    ModifyRDNRequest,
                              modifyRDNResponse   ModifyRDNResponse,
                              compareDNRequest    CompareRequest,
                              compareDNResponse   CompareResponse,
                              abandonRequest      AbandonRequest
                         }
          }

      MessageID ::= INTEGER (0 .. maxInt)
```

Figure 11.2 *LDAP Message definition*

the following queries. It can issue one or more directory requests. We will only look at the most frequent: search. However, it would be possible to add, modify, or delete entries, too. To terminate the session the client issues an unbind request and releases the port. With this sequence in mind, we can look at some of the requests and responses in more detail.

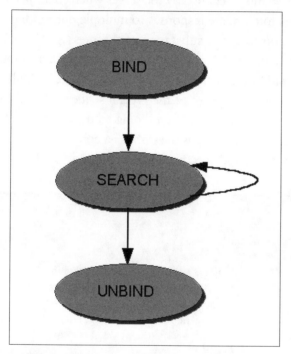

Figure 11.3 *Typical LDAP Request Flow*

LDAP Requests

The purpose of the bind twofold:

- Establish the *version* of LDAP. This implies the set of supported proto-col operations.

- Authenticate the user. This can be done with or without encryption. Rather than spending much time on security, we will access LDAP anonymously as is most frequently the case. To do this we leave the *name* empty and specify *simple* authentication.

```
BindRequest ::=
        [APPLICATION 0] SEQUENCE {
                        version   INTEGER (1 .. 127),
                        name      LDAPDN,
                        authentication CHOICE {
                            simple        [0] OCTET STRING,
                            krbv42LDAP    [1] OCTET STRING,
                            krbv42DSA     [2] OCTET STRING
                        }
        }
```

Figure 11.4 *Bind Request definition*

The search request is the most complex of the definitions we need. It is composed of several items:

- *baseObject*—a base object entry relative to which the search may be performed.

- *scope*—indicates whether the search should be performed on only the baseObject, a single level beneath the baseObject, or the whole subtree beneath the baseObject.

- *derefAliases*—indicates how alias objects should be handled in searching.

- *sizelimit*—restricts the maximum number of entries returned.

- *timelimit*—restricts the maximum time (in seconds) allowed for a search.

- *attrsOnly*—indicates whether to return both attribute types and values, or just attribute types.

- *filter*—defines search criteria.

- *attributes*—indicates a list of attributes that may be returned in the result.

The unbind request is only used to clean up the connection before terminating. It does not pass any data.

```
UnbindRequest ::= [APPLICATION 2] NULL227
```

Figure 11.5 *Unbind Request definition*

```
SearchRequest ::=
        [APPLICATION 3] SEQUENCE {
            baseObject    LDAPDN,
            scope         ENUMERATED {
                                baseObject            (0),
                                singleLevel           (1),
                                wholeSubtree          (2)
                          },
            derefAliases  ENUMERATED {
                                    neverDerefAliases     (0),
                                    derefInSearching      (1),
                                    derefFindingBaseObj   (2),
                                    derefAlways           (3)
                          },
            sizeLimit     INTEGER (0 .. maxInt),
            timeLimit     INTEGER (0 .. maxInt),
            attrsOnly     BOOLEAN,
            filter        Filter,
            attributes    SEQUENCE OF AttributeType
        }

    Filter ::=
        CHOICE {
            and               [0] SET OF Filter,
            or                [1] SET OF Filter,
            not               [2] Filter,
            equalityMatch     [3] AttributeValueAssertion,
            substrings        [4] SubstringFilter,
            greaterOrEqual    [5] AttributeValueAssertion,
            lessOrEqual       [6] AttributeValueAssertion,
            present           [7] AttributeType,
            approxMatch       [8] AttributeValueAssertion
        }

    SubstringFilter
        SEQUENCE {
            type              AttributeType,
            SEQUENCE OF CHOICE {
                initial       [0] LDAPString,
                any           [1] LDAPString,
                final         [2] LDAPString
            }
        }

AttributeValueAssertion ::=
        SEQUENCE {
            attributeType     AttributeType,
            attributeValue    AttributeValue
        }

    AttributeType ::= LDAPString

        AttributeValue ::= OCTET STRING
```

Figure 11.6 *Search Request definition*

LDAP Responses

LDAP responses depend on the request that initiated them. But in all cases they must return the status of the action. This is presented in the form of an LDAP Result. As you can see in Figure 11.7, there are a number of possible failure codes with which the server may respond to the client. To keep the example simple, we will limit

```
LDAPResult ::=
      SEQUENCE {
         resultCode      ENUMERATED {
                          success                       (0),
                          operationsError               (1),
                          protocolError                 (2),
                          timeLimitExceeded             (3),
                          sizeLimitExceeded             (4),
                          compareFalse                  (5),
                          compareTrue                   (6),
                          authMethodNotSupported        (7),
                          strongAuthRequired            (8),
                          noSuchAttribute               (16),
                          undefinedAttributeType        (17),
                          inappropriateMatching         (18),
                          constraintViolation           (19),
                          attributeOrValueExists        (20),
                          invalidAttributeSyntax        (21),
                          noSuchObject                  (32),
                          aliasProblem                  (33),
                          invalidDNSyntax               (34),
                          isLeaf                        (35),
                          aliasDereferencingProblem     (36),
                          inappropriateAuthentication   (48),
                          invalidCredentials            (49),
                          insufficientAccessRights      (50),
                          busy                          (51),
                          unavailable                   (52),
                          unwillingToPerform            (53),
                          loopDetect                    (54),
                          namingViolation               (64),
                          objectClassViolation          (65),
                          notAllowedOnNonLeaf           (66),
                          notAllowedOnRDN               (67),
                          entryAlreadyExists            (68),
                          objectClassModsProhibited     (69),
                          other                         (80)
                          },
         matchedDN       LDAPDN,
         errorMessage    LDAPString
      }
```

Figure 11.7 *LDAP Result definition*

ourselves to the success code, which is obviously indispensable in any working session.

The bind response (Figure 11.8) is really nothing more than an LDAPResult with its tag attached to the beginning.

```
BindResponse ::= [APPLICATION 1] LDAPResult
```

Figure 11.8 *Bind Response definition*

The search response also contains the result code at the end, but the bulk of the response is the entry, which is a sequence of matching directory entries. Each match is presented as an object name followed by a sequence of attributes. Note that there is no response to the *UnbindRequest* as it only signals the end of the session.

```
SearchResponse ::=
    CHOICE {
        entry          [APPLICATION 4] SEQUENCE {
                           objectName    LDAPDN,
                           attributes    SEQUENCE OF SEQUENCE {
                                             AttributeType,
                                             SET OF AttributeValue
                                         }
                       },
        resultCode    [APPLICATION 5] LDAPResult
    }
```

Figure 11.9 *Search Response definition*

In order to make our code more readable, it is useful to define constants for all the tags. This makes reading and writing the programs much easier and less error-prone. Listing 11.1 shows some of the ones we will encounter in our examples.

```
Public Const LDAP_BINDREQUEST_TAG = 0 + ASN_APPLICATION
Public Const LDAP_BINDRESPONSE_TAG = 1 + ASN_APPLICATION
Public Const LDAP_UNBINDREQUEST_TAG = 2 + ASN_APPLICATION
Public Const LDAP_SEARCHREQUEST_TAG = 3 + ASN_APPLICATION
Public Const LDAP_SEARCHRESPONSEENTRY_TAG = 4 + ASN_APPLICATION
```

```
Public Const LDAP_SEARCHRESPONSERESULT_TAG = 5 + ASN_APPLICATION
Public Const LDAP_ABANDONREQUEST_TAG = 16 + ASN_APPLICATION
Public Const LDAP_SEARCH_AND = 0 + ASN_CONTEXT_SPECIFIC + _
    ASN_COMPOSITE
Public Const LDAP_SEARCH_OR = 1 + ASN_CONTEXT_SPECIFIC + _
    ASN_COMPOSITE
Public Const LDAP_SEARCH_NOT = 2 + ASN_CONTEXT_SPECIFIC
Public Const LDAP_SEARCH_EQUALITYMATCH = 3 + ASN_CONTEXT_SPECIFIC
Public Const LDAP_SEARCH_SUBSTRINGS = 4 + ASN_CONTEXT_SPECIFIC + _
    ASN_COMPOSITE
Public Const LDAP_SUBSTRING_INITIAL = 0 + ASN_CONTEXT_SPECIFIC
Public Const LDAP_SUBSTRING_ANY = 1 + ASN_CONTEXT_SPECIFIC
Public Const LDAP_SUBSTRING_FINAL = 2 + ASN_CONTEXT_SPECIFIC
```

Listing 11.1 *Subset of LDAP Constants*

LDAP Client

The steps of an LDAP client are:

- Allow the user to specify a search string.
- Connect to the LDAP server.
- Compose and Issue an LDAP Bind.
- Accept the Bind response.
- Compose and Issue an LDAP Search.
- Accept the Search responses.
- Display each response to the user.

Client Example

The form (Figure 11.10) for the LDAP client allows the user to enter a search string. This is then passed to the server and the distinguished name of all matches is displayed. If the user selects one of the matches, then the attributes of that match are also presented. To assist in debugging and understanding LDAP we have a panel on the right that shows the ASN.1 encoded data being passed with each request and response.

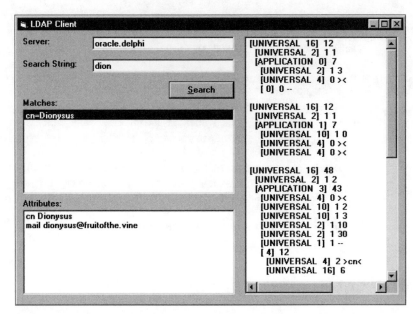

Figure 11.10 *Example LDAP client*

When the search button is pressed (Listing 11.2) the LDAP session is executed. This means that the client has to send a *BindRequest*, *SearchRequest*, and *UnbindRequest*.

```
Private Sub btnSearch_Click()
Dim lngServerAddress As Long
Dim strServerName As String

lngLDAPSocket = 0

strServerName = txtServer.Text
intStatus = GetIPAddress(lngServerAddress, strServerName)
intStatus = CreateSocket(lngLDAPSocket, 0)
intStatus = ConnectSocket(lngLDAPSocket, lngServerAddress, _
    LDAPPort)

intStatus = SendBindRequest()
intStatus = SendSearchRequest(txtSearchString.Text)
intStatus = SendUnBindRequest()

intStatus = ReleaseSocket(lngLDAPSocket)

End Sub
```

Listing 11.2 *Search for user*

The bind request is first (Listing 11.3). It is composed according to the definition we saw earlier (Figure 11.4) and then sent to the server. Note that we leave the name and authentication blank, since we are binding anonymously. We wait for the response but don't attempt to process it other than displaying it on the form.

```
Const LDAP_VERSION = 3
Dim RequestMessageID As Integer
Private Function SendBindRequest() As Integer

 Dim asnBindRequest As New ASN1
 Dim asnBindResponse As New ASN1
 Dim strServerResponse As String
 intRequestMessageID = intRequestMessageID + 1

 asnBindRequest.Compose ( _
  Array(ASN_SEQUENCE_TAG, _
   Array(ASN_INTEGER_TAG, Chr(intRequestMessageID)), _
   Array(LDAP_BINDREQUEST_TAG, _
    Array(ASN_INTEGER_TAG, Chr(LDAP_VERSION)), _
    Array(ASN_OCTETSTRING_TAG, ""), _
    Array(ASN_CONTEXT_SPECIFIC, "")))))
 txtASNDialog.Text = txtASNDialog.Text + asnBindRequest.Dump
 intStatus = SendSocketBinary(lngLDAPSocket, _
               asnBindRequest.TransferString)
 intStatus = ReceiveSocketBinary(lngLDAPSocket, strServerResponse)

 asnBindResponse.Parse (strServerResponse)
 txtASNDialog.Text = txtASNDialog.Text + asnBindResponse.Dump
 txtASNDialog.Refresh

End Function
```

Listing 11.3 *Send Bind Request*

The search request must also be composed. We have a few more fields to deal with, but most of them are not overly exciting. The most important points to note are that we are looking for all entries that have a *cn* matching our SearchString and that we wish to see only the attributes *cn* and *mail*.

When we receive the response we have to do a little processing to be able to present it to the user. We cycle through all the subentries that have a tag denoting that they are a response-entry (rather than the final result code). For each entry we add the *name* to the list of matches and then cycle through any *attributes* present. Each one of these is added to the corresponding list in the control array.[1]

```
Const LDAP_SIZELIMIT = 10
Const LDAP_TIMELIMIT = 30
Const LDAP_BASEOBJECT = ""
Private Function SendSearchRequest(SearchString As String) As
Integer

Dim asnRequest As New ASN1
Dim asnResponse As New ASN1
Dim strServerResponse As String
Dim strServerNextResponse As String
Dim intMatchIndex As Integer
Dim intAttributeIndex As Integer
Dim asnAttribute As New ASN1
intRequestMessageID = intRequestMessageID + 1

asnRequest.Compose ( _
 Array(ASN_SEQUENCE_TAG, _
  Array(ASN_INTEGER_TAG, Chr(intRequestMessageID)), _
  Array(LDAP_SEARCHREQUEST_TAG, _
   Array(ASN_OCTETSTRING_TAG, LDAP_BASEOBJECT), _
   Array(ASN_ENUMERATED_TAG, Chr(LDAP_SCOPE_WHOLESUBTREE)), _
   Array(ASN_ENUMERATED_TAG, Chr(LDAP_DEREFALIASES_ALWAYS)), _
   Array(ASN_INTEGER_TAG, Chr(LDAP_SIZELIMIT)), _
   Array(ASN_INTEGER_TAG, Chr(LDAP_TIMELIMIT)), _
   Array(ASN_BOOLEAN_TAG, Chr(LDAP_FALSE)), _
   Array(LDAP_SEARCH_SUBSTRINGS, _
    Array(ASN_OCTETSTRING_TAG, "cn"), _
    Array(ASN_SEQUENCE_TAG, _
     Array(ASN_CONTEXT_SPECIFIC, SearchString))), _
   Array(ASN_SEQUENCE_TAG, _
    Array(ASN_OCTETSTRING_TAG, "cn"), _
    Array(ASN_OCTETSTRING_TAG, "mail")))))
txtASNDialog.Text = txtASNDialog.Text + asnRequest.Dump
intStatus = SendSocketBinary(lngLDAPSocket, _
```

---

[1] To cache the attributes of all the matches on the form while displaying them simultaneously we use a control array. Each match has one entry (i.e., one list of attributes). These lists are positioned on top of each other with only one visible at any given moment.

```
                          asnRequest.TransferString)

       intStatus = ReceiveSocketBinary(lngLDAPSocket, strServerResponse)
       asnResponse.Parse strServerResponse
       txtASNDialog.Text = txtASNDialog.Text + asnResponse.Dump


       For intMatchIndex = 1 To lstAttributes.UBound
        Unload lstAttributes(intMatchIndex)
       Next
       lstMatches.Clear

       intMatchIndex = 0
       Do While asnResponse.SubItem(2).Tag = LDAP_SEARCHRESPONSEENTRY_TAG

         DoEvents
         lstMatches.AddItem asnResponse.SubItem(2).SubItem(1).Value

         intMatchIndex = intMatchIndex + 1
         Load lstAttributes(intMatchIndex)
         Set asnAttribute = asnResponse.SubItem(2).SubItem(2)
         For intAttributeIndex = 1 To asnAttribute.SubItemCount
          lstAttributes(intMatchIndex).AddItem _
            asnAttribute.SubItem(intAttributeIndex).SubItem(1).Value + _
            " " + _
       asnAttribute.SubItem(intAttributeIndex).SubItem(2).SubItem(1).Value
         Next

         asnResponse.Parse strServerResponse

         txtASNDialog.Text = txtASNDialog.Text + asnResponse.Dump

       Loop

       ShowMatch (intMatchIndex)
       lstMatches.ListIndex = intMatchIndex - 1
       txtASNDialog.Refresh
     End Function
```

Listing 11.4 *Send Search Request*

Whenever a user clicks on one of the matches, we need to ensure that the attributes list corresponding to that match is visible and the previous match is no longer visible.

```
Private Sub ShowMatch(MatchIndex As Integer)
 Static intOldMatchIndex As Integer
 If intOldMatchIndex > lstAttributes.UBound Then intOldMatchIndex =
lstAttributes.UBound
 lstAttributes(intOldMatchIndex).Visible = False
 lstAttributes(MatchIndex).Visible = True

 intOldMatchIndex = MatchIndex

 lstMatches.ToolTipText = lstMatches.Text

End Sub
```

Listing 11.5 *Show Matches*

LDAP Server

In order to support LDAP a server must:

- Accept LDAP requests
- Dispatch according to the operation (Bind, Search, etc.)
- Have a store containing all the directory information
    - One record for each directory entry
    - Each record should have an X.500 distinguished name
    - Must be able to search the store with partial information

Server Example

Figure 11.11 shows the form for the LDAP server. It displays the ASN.1 encoded dialog for each connection.

For this example, I have used an Excel spreadsheet as the store for the directory (Figure 11.12), since it will be a familiar concept for most readers and is relatively easy to work with from Visual Basic.

Each client request must be dispatched to the appropriate routine (Listing 11.6). We only support two requests, Bind and Search, and ignore the rest. The only other one we would expect to receive is

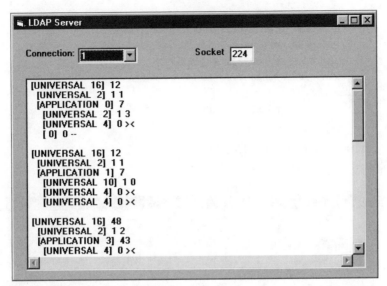

Figure 11.11 *LDAP Server*

Unbind, but since we do not need to acknowledge it and have no special need for it, there is no reason to have a separate procedure.

```
Private Sub ProcessRequest(Index As Integer)
 Dim strClientRequest As String
 Dim strRequestMessageID As String

 Dim asnRequest As New ASN1
 Dim asnResponse As New ASN1


 lngTransmitSocket = val(txtSocket(intCurrentConnection))

 intStatus = ReceiveSocketBinary(lngTransmitSocket, _
              strClientRequest)
 DisplayConnection Index

 asnRequest.Parse (strClientRequest)

 strRequestMessageID = asnRequest.SubItem(1).Value

 txtRequest(Index).Text = txtRequest(Index).Text + asnRequest.Dump
 txtRequest(Index).Refresh
```

```
Select Case asnRequest.SubItem(2).Tag
  Case LDAP_BINDREQUEST_TAG
    ProcessBindRequest Index, asnRequest
  Case LDAP_SEARCHREQUEST_TAG
    ProcessSearchRequest Index, asnRequest
End Select
txtRequest(Index).Refresh
End Sub
```

Listing 11.6 *Process Client Request*

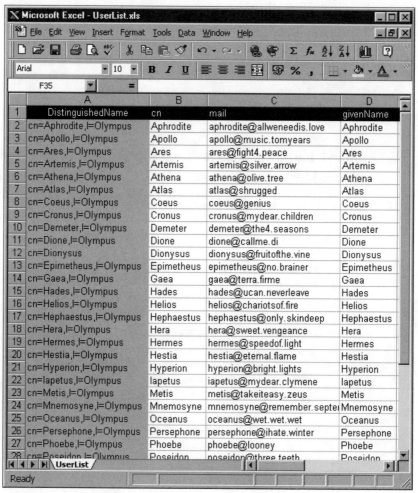

Figure 11.12 *Directory store as Excel spreadsheet*

Our processing of the bind request is strictly limited to sending a positive response (Listing 11.7). We need the parsed request but only to ensure we maintain the same *messageID* as the request (first subitem of the request). We leave both the *matchedDN* and *errorMessage* fields empty.

```
Private Sub ProcessBindRequest(Index As Integer, BindRequest As
ASN1)
 Dim asnBindResponse As New ASN1
 asnBindResponse.Compose ( _
  Array(ASN_SEQUENCE_TAG, _
   Array(ASN_INTEGER_TAG, BindRequest.SubItem(1).Value), _
   Array(LDAP_BINDRESPONSE_TAG, _
    Array(ASN_ENUMERATED_TAG, Chr(LDAP_RESULT_SUCCESS)), _
    Array(ASN_OCTETSTRING_TAG, ""), _
    Array(ASN_OCTETSTRING_TAG, ""))))
 txtRequest(Index).Text = txtRequest(Index).Text + _
                asnBindResponse.Dump
 intStatus = SendSocketBinary(lngTransmitSocket, _
                asnBindResponse.TransferString)
End Sub
```

Listing 11.7 *Process Bind Request*

To process the search request (Listing 11.8) we loop through every entry in our directory. If it matches the filter specified in the request, then we compose a response entry for the match.

In addition to the matches, we also have to compose a response result with a status of success. We can then concatenate all the entries into one transfer string and send the response to the client.

```
Private Sub ProcessSearchRequest(Index As Integer, SearchRequest As
ASN1)
 Dim intUserIndex As Integer
 Dim intMatchCount As Integer

 Dim asnSearchResponseEntry() As ASN1
 Dim asnSearchResponseResult As New ASN1
 Dim strTransferString As String
 intMatchCount = 0
 For intUserIndex = 2 To xwsUserListSheet.Cells(1, 1).End(xlDown).Row
  If MatchFilter(intUserIndex, SearchRequest.SubItem(2).SubItem(7))
```

```
Then
    intMatchCount = intMatchCount + 1
    ReDim Preserve asnSearchResponseEntry(intMatchCount)

    Set asnSearchResponseEntry(intMatchCount) = New ASN1
    ComposeResponseEntry SearchRequest, intUserIndex, _
            asnSearchResponseEntry(intMatchCount)
    txtRequest(Index).Text = txtRequest(Index).Text + _
                asnSearchResponseEntry(intMatchCount).Dump
  End If
Next


asnSearchResponseResult.Compose _
 Array(ASN_SEQUENCE_TAG, _
  Array(ASN_INTEGER_TAG, SearchRequest.SubItem(1).Value), _
  Array(LDAP_SEARCHRESPONSERESULT_TAG, _
   Array(ASN_ENUMERATED_TAG, Chr(LDAP_RESULT_SUCCESS)), _
   Array(ASN_OCTETSTRING_TAG, ""), _
   Array(ASN_OCTETSTRING_TAG, "")))
txtRequest(Index).Text = txtRequest(Index).Text + _
            asnSearchResponseResult.Dump
strTransferString = ""
For intUserIndex = 1 To intMatchCount
 strTransferString = strTransferString + _
        asnSearchResponseEntry(intUserIndex).TransferString
Next
strTransferString = strTransferString + _
        asnSearchResponseResult.TransferString
 intStatus = SendSocketBinary(lngTransmitSocket, strTransferString)
End Sub
```

Listing 11.8 *Process Search Request*

To determine whether a given user matches the supplied filter
(Listing 11.9), we need to first examine the tag of the filter:

- AND—we set the default to TRUE and loop through the subitems. If
  any of them do not match, then we set the value to FALSE
- OR—we set the default to FALSE and loop through the subitems. If
  any of them matches, then we set the value to TRUE
- NOT—we invert the match of the subitems

- SUBSTRINGS—We loop through all the subitems, and if we find any containing the searched substring then we set the result to TRUE. Note that there are three possible places to look for the substring:

    INITIAL—at the beginning of the target

    FINAL—at the end of the target

    ANY—anywhere within the target

```
Private Function MatchFilter(UserIndex As Integer, SearchFilter As
ASN1) As Boolean
Dim bolPartialMatch As Boolean
Dim intIndexCounter As Integer
Dim strMatchString As String


Select Case SearchFilter.Tag
  Case LDAP_SEARCH_AND
    bolPartialMatch = True
    For intIndexCounter = 1 To SearchFilter.SubItemCount
      If Not MatchFilter(UserIndex, _
             SearchFilter.SubItem(intIndexCounter)) Then _
                 bolPartialMatch = False
    Next
  Case LDAP_SEARCH_OR
    bolPartialMatch = False
    For intIndexCounter = 1 To SearchFilter.SubItemCount
      If MatchFilter(UserIndex, _
             SearchFilter.SubItem(intIndexCounter)) Then _
                 bolPartialMatch = True
    Next
  Case LDAP_SEARCH_NOT
    bolPartialMatch = Not MatchFilter(UserIndex, _
                     SearchFilter.SubItem(1))
  Case LDAP_SEARCH_SUBSTRINGS
    Dim SubstringCandidateList As ASN1
    Dim SubstringCandidate As ASN1
    Set SubstringCandidateList = SearchFilter.SubItem(2)
    strMatchString = Trim(FindAttribute(UserIndex, _
       SearchFilter.SubItem(1).Value))
    bolPartialMatch = False
    For intIndexCounter = 1 To SubstringCandidateList.SubItemCount
      Set SubstringCandidate = _
         SubstringCandidateList.SubItem(intIndexCounter)
      Select Case SubstringCandidate.Tag
```

```
        Case LDAP_SUBSTRING_INITIAL
        If strMatchString Like Trim(SubstringCandidate.Value) + "*"
Then
          bolPartialMatch = True
        End If
        Case LDAP_SUBSTRING_ANY
        If strMatchString Like "*" + Trim(SubstringCandidate.Value) + "*"
Then
          bolPartialMatch = True
        End If
        Case LDAP_SUBSTRING_FINAL
        If strMatchString Like "*" + Trim(SubstringCandidate.Value)
Then
          bolPartialMatch = True
        End If
      End Select
    Next
  End Select
  MatchFilter = bolPartialMatch
End Function
```

Listing 11.9 *Match Filter*

The simplest (although not necessarily most efficient) way to find a given named attribute for a user in our spreadsheet is to loop through all the column headings. If we find a match then we return the cell for that column and the row of the user (Listing 11.10).

```
Private Function FindAttribute(UserIndex As Integer, AttributeName)
As String
 Dim intAttributeIndex As Integer
 FindAttribute = ""
 For intAttributeIndex = 2 To _
            xwsUserListSheet.Cells(1, 1).End(xlToRight).Column
   If Trim(UCase(xwsUserListSheet.Cells(1, intAttributeIndex).Value)) = _
     Trim(UCase((AttributeName))) Then
    FindAttribute = xwsUserListSheet.Cells(UserIndex, _
                       intAttributeIndex).Value
   End If
 Next
End Function
```

Listing 11.10 *Find Attribute*

In composing a response entry for a given match, we begin by compiling the sequence of attributes for that user (Listing 11.11). This entails looping through the list of attributes in the directory and verifying for each whether it was requested by the client. If so, we create an entry in a temporary array that defines the sequence of AttributeType (name) and AttributeValue.

```
Private Sub ComposeResponseEntry(SearchRequest As ASN1, _
                UserIndex As Integer, _
                ByRef ResponseEntry As ASN1)
Dim intAttributeIndex As Integer
Dim intMatchAttributeIndex As Integer
Dim varAttributeList() As Variant
ReDim varAttributeList(xwsUserListSheet.Cells(1, _
  1).End(xlToRight).Column)
intMatchAttributeIndex = 1
varAttributeList(1) = ASN_SEQUENCE_TAG
For intAttributeIndex = 2 To _
            xwsUserListSheet.Cells(1, 1).End(xlToRight).Column
  If MatchAttribute(xwsUserListSheet.Cells(1, _
          intAttributeIndex).Value, _
          SearchRequest.SubItem(2).SubItem(8)) Then
intMatchAttributeIndex = intMatchAttributeIndex + 1
  varAttributeList(intMatchAttributeIndex) = _
   Array(ASN_SEQUENCE_TAG, _
     Array(ASN_OCTETSTRING_TAG, _
       xwsUserListSheet.Cells(1, intAttributeIndex).Value), _
     Array(ASN_SET_TAG, _
      Array(ASN_OCTETSTRING_TAG, _
        xwsUserListSheet.Cells(UserIndex, _
                  intAttributeIndex).Value)))
  End If
Next

ResponseEntry.Compose _
 Array(ASN_SEQUENCE_TAG, _
  Array(ASN_INTEGER_TAG, SearchRequest.SubItem(1).Value), _
  Array(LDAP_SEARCHRESPONSEENTRY_TAG, _
   Array(ASN_OCTETSTRING_TAG, _
            xwsUserListSheet.Cells(UserIndex, 1).Value), _
          varAttributeList))
End Sub
```

Listing 11.11 *Compose response entry for user*

After finishing the loop we can compose the response entry with the distinguished name of the user and the attribute list we just generated.

To determine if a particular stored attribute was requested by the client, we loop through the requested attributes returning a value of TRUE if any of them match (Listing 11.12).

```
Private Function MatchAttribute(StoredAttribute As String, _
                RequestedAttributes As ASN1) As Boolean
Dim intRequestedAttributeIndex As Integer
MatchAttribute = False
For intRequestedAttributeIndex = 1 To
RequestedAttributes.SubItemCount
  If StoredAttribute = _
     RequestedAttributes.SubItem(intRequestedAttributeIndex).Value
Then
    MatchAttribute = True
  End If
Next
End Function
```

Listing 11.12 *Determine if stored attribute was requested*

Wrapping Up

Some areas to explore for further LDAP development are:

- *Writable LDAP*—We have used LDAP in the read-only mode alone, and we have only looked up entries in the directory. However, it is also possible to update the directory via LDAP. In order to add, modify, or delete entries we would need to send LDAP messages with the corresponding protocol operations.

- *Authentication*—We only support anonymous LDAP, which is quite common for read-only mode, since most directories are meant primarily for public browsing. Nonetheless, many production servers also provide a means of authentication. For writable LDAP directories, secure authentication is virtually indispensable.

- *Production store*—The Excel spreadsheet is easy to understand and use but is not efficient or suitable for a large directory. It would be possible to make use of a commercial database (like Microsoft SQL Server), or you could develop your own and store it in simple files.

If you intend to write a significant amount of code using LDAP, you might be interested in looking at the LDAP Application Program Interface, specified in RFC 1823. It defines a C-language application program interface to LDAP. To use it, you would link against a DLL (Windows Dynamic Link Library) containing LDAP API (e.g., WLDAP32.DLL).

Chapter 12

The Complete Picture

Integration

In the examples provided, I have dealt with each protocol somewhat independently. I have written an SMTP client that sends a message, POP and IMAP clients that retrieve messages, and an LDAP client that looks up users in the directory. For testing and illustration it is useful to look at each of these protocols independently. In a typical user environment, however, no user will want to call up three different programs to process mail. We will need to integrate all these functions into one application.

Integrating these functions means more than just adding all the forms into a Visual Basic project. We need to make it as easy as possible for the user to invoke the functions required (Figure 12.1). For example, we can make IMAP the initial form, as most users will want to begin by viewing their mailbox. The user could read the MIME messages in Chapter 9 so we needn't make any changes on that account.

At some point the user may decide to compose a new message. We can create a menu option (*mnuCreateMessage*). When clicked it will load the SMTP form and show it to the user (Listing 12.1). The user can then fill in the text and recipients and send the message in the same way as our previous examples.

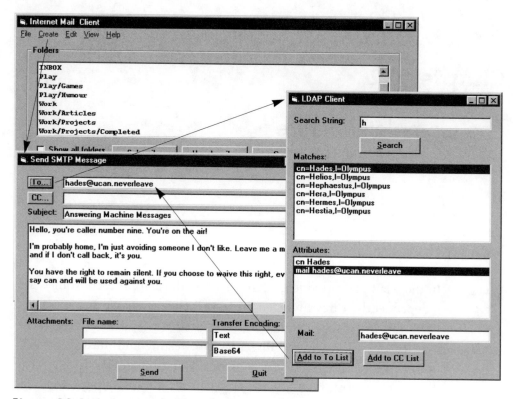

Figure 12.1 *Integrating the client forms*

```
Private Sub mnuCreateMessage_Click()
 Load frmSendSMTPMessage
 frmSendSMTPMessage.Show
End Sub
```

Listing 12.1 *Create a new message*

```
Private Sub btnCC_Click()
 Load frmLDAPClient
 frmLDAPClient.Show
End Sub
Private Sub btnTo_Click()
 Load frmLDAPClient
 frmLDAPClient.Show
End Sub
```

Listing 12.2 *Look up recipient*

In some cases, the user may not know the E-mail address of the intended recipient. We can change the *To* and *CC* labels from the original form to buttons. When they are pressed they will invoke the LDAP form to allow the user to access the directory (Listing 12.2).

At this point, the user could look up the directory entry and then return to the SMTP form to manually add the E-mail address. We can make this a little easier on the user by automatically placing the address on the SMTP form when the user presses one of the *Add* buttons (Listing 12.3).

```
Private Sub btnAddCC_Click(Index As Integer)
  frmSendSMTPMessage.txtCCRecipient = txtMailAddress.Text
End Sub
Private Sub btnAddTo_Click(Index As Integer)
  frmSendSMTPMessage.txtToRecipient = txtMailAddress.Text
End Sub
```

Listing 12.3 *Add new recipient to message header*

Production Quality

Error Processing

In these examples we have focused on simplicity and have neglected error processing. I have assumed the most favorable conditions possible to illustrate how the protocols should work. Any production code would emphasize robustness and fault tolerance. In particular, we should cover:

- *Error Recovery*—trapping errors to allow the function to continue
- *Error Reporting*—displaying meaningful messages to the user
- *Error Logging*—recording errors and other important events in a log file to facilitate tracing
- *Error Isolation*—ensuring that errors provoked or experienced by one user do not affect other users
- *Fully asynchronous (nonblocking) operation*—ensuring that network problems or other systems do not cause an application to hang

Protocol Compliance

While the examples have illustrated the main commands and responses of the protocols, a production client should implement all functions required by the specification. It must also implement each function thoroughly: that is, it must allow for all exceptions and unexpected circumstances.

- Implementation of all commands and responses
- Support for all exceptions (embedded periods, boundaries)

Sound Development Platform

We have used VB and the Windows file system for illustrative purposes. These are useful tools since they are easy to understand and familiar for most developers. However, this does not mean they are ideal for production code. Some components to consider if we are developing mission-critical applications might include:

- *C, Visual C++*—These are the most popular languages for production development at present. You might consider another language too, but you would want to ensure that it is both robust and efficient.
- *Portability*—Visual Basic only runs on Microsoft Windows operating systems. For the servers in particular, it is worth serious thought to make them available on UNIX, considered by many to be more stable and reliable for mission-critical applications. If the code is written to be portable (which already implies that you don't use Visual Basic) then moving it to another operating system is significantly easier.
- *Database storage*—Windows files are easy to use. However they do not easily provide some of the functions that we may require for a production mail store or directory:

  Transactions—In order to ensure the integrity of our databases, we may need to be able to group database operations into transactions with commit/rollback capability.

  Security—Production mail systems require strong security precautions, preferably with very fine degree of granularity in access control.

- *Data caching*—We might consider caching data from our databases into memory in order to optimize the response time for our users. However, we must ensure that all changes are also stored to the database in the case of a system failure. We would also need to guarantee that any other clients accessing the same data before it is committed to disk receive the cached data.

Emerging Directions

Extended Functionality

ESMTP

RFC 1651, and its successor RFC 1869, define a mechanism for extending SMTP services. A client supporting service extensions may start a session by issuing an *EHLO* rather than a *HELO*. If the SMTP server supports any extensions it will list them in its response.

Table 12.1 lists some of the extensions currently in use. Of particular interest is DSN (Domain Name System), since the absence of delivery notifications in SMTP has long been considered one of its weaknesses (particularly when compared to X.400).

Table 12.1 *ESMTP Extensions*

Extension	Description	RFCs
8BITMIME	8bit-MIME transport	1426, 1652
SIZE	Message Size Declaration	1653, 1870
DSN	Delivery Status Notifications	1891

IMAP Extensions

IMAP continues to be a protocol in development. In order to make new implementations compatible with the old, the changes are implemented as extensions. The server can opt to support any of these enhancements, in which case it makes this support known to the client as an entry in the CAPABILITY response.

Some of the extensions listed below have already made their way into RFCs and will, no doubt, soon become standard to all IMAP products. Others are only experimental and may either fall into disuse or be surpassed by other extensions.

- *UIDPLUS*—reduces the amount of time used by (primarily disconnected) clients
- *NAMESPACE*—allows client to request prefixes of namespaces used by the server
- *CHILDREN*—allows client to efficiently determine if a particular mailbox has children
- *LANGUAGE*—allows client and server to negotiate a language for human-readable responses
- *LOGIN-REFERRALS*—allow client to transparently failover (connect to an alternate server when the primary server becomes unavailable)
- *QUOTA*—permits client to manipulate limits on mailbox resources

Security

As networks and messaging systems grow in size and complexity, it becomes more and more difficult to ensure that they are not compromised. More and more business-critical applications are automated. Sensitive information is increasingly passed electronically. It is no surprise that the need to address problems of security has become more acute.

The main focus in standardization has been on:

- *Authentication*—Ensuring that all participants are who they purport to be
- *Privacy*—Ensuring that it is not possible to intercept information in transit between participants
- *Integrity*—Ensuring that information sent between participants cannot be altered en route

In order to guarantee these three requirements it is necessary for both participants to have a secret password, called a key, with which all data is encrypted. At a high level, there are two types of approaches to encryption, symmetric (or private, e.g., DES, IDEA, AES) and asymmetric (or public, e.g., RSA, ECC).

In a private-key encryption scheme both participants have the same key. The encryption algorithm is two-way. In other words you can use the same key to decrypt as you use to encrypt. The weakness of this approach is that it requires you to agree on a secret key with every possible correspondent.

Public-key encryption uses a pair of keys called the private and public key, respectively. The algorithm is asymmetric in that something encrypted with one key can only be decrypted with the other. You can therefore give your public key to everyone and keep your private key for yourself. Anything someone wants to send to you they encrypt with your public key and only you can decrypt it.

This scheme works well when you have a limited set of possible correspondents. You can ensure they have your public key and you have theirs. However, the goal of cryptologists is much greater than this. They would like you to be able to correspond with people you have never met before and to do so in a secure fashion. In theory, you can exchange public keys with anyone, but if you do so electronically you will want to ensure that the key really belongs to the person you assume before you send any sensitive information.

When the ITU (International Telegraphic Union) designed the X.500 directory, they saw this need coming, so they made provision for storing the user's public key in an attribute in the directory. Instead of asking the user to provide you with his or her public key, you would be able to query the directory for the key and be confident that it was authentic.

The attribute holding the key is actually called an *X.509 Certificate* and holds a substantial amount of information relating to the key, including:

- Issuer of the key
- Encryption algorithm
- Validity of the key
- Name of the holder of the key

Even though it was originally intended as part of the X.500 directory, there is no requirement for the certificate to actually be stored there or retrieved from there. It is self-contained and can be presented using any mechanism. An issuer of digital certificates is referred to as a Certification Authority (CA). As it is not realistic to expect all users worldwide to use the same authority, the CAs have begun to establish a complex network of trusts among them. All the user needs to do is confirm the public key with his or her CA to be able to securely correspond with another user.

SSL/TLS

SSL (Secure Sockets Layer) is an interface designed by Netscape to provide secure transactions across a network. It uses both public and private key encryption techniques to ensure that all communication across a network link is secure.

The SSL protocol was developed to authenticate network peers and provide both privacy and reliability across connections. It attempts to balance several goals (cryptographic security, interoperability, extensibility, and efficiency), with the highest priority being that of security.

Architecturally, it is divided into two layers:

- The SSL Handshake Protocol provides a mechanism for mutual authentication and the negotiation of an encryption algorithm.
- The SSL Record Protocol specifies how to format and interpret the encrypted data.

Based on SSL V3.0, and very similar to it (although incompatible), is TLS (Transport Layer Security) V1.0. TLS was published as an Internet standard in January 1999 as RFC 2246. Time will measure its success, but the first indicators look positive as it is already being examined in the context of IMAP, POP, and LDAP. You can find more information about SSL on Netscape's Web site (http://home.netscape.com/eng/ssl3) and about TLS in RFC 2246.

S/MIME AND PGP

Secure Multipurpose Internet Mail Extensions and Pretty Good Privacy are two means of end-to-end encryption that are currently receiving Internet attention. Both of these make use of MIME to include encrypted messages and signatures, however they use difference formats of data within these bodyparts and are therefore not compatible.

At present, neither S/MIME nor PGP are recognized as an Internet standard. There are, however, informational RFCs describing their use in the Internet.

- *RFC 2311*—S/MIME Version 2 Message Specification
- *RFC 2312*—S/MIME Version 2 Certificate Handling
- *RFC 2313*—PKCS #1: RSA Encryption Version 1.5
- *RFC 2314*—PKCS #10: Certification Request Syntax Version 1.5
- *RFC 2315*—PKCS #7: Cryptographic Message Syntax Version 1.5
- *RFC 2268*—Description of the RC2 Encryption Algorithm

There are six S/MIME RFCs (2311-2315, 2268) describing the use of S/MIME version 2. The current intent is for S/MIME version 3 to be proposed as an Internet standard. You can find more information on the status of S/MIME from RSA (http://www.rsa.com) or from the IETF (Internet Engineering Task Force) (http://www.ietf.org/html. charters/smime-charter.html).

- *RFC 1991*—PGP Message Exchange Formats
- *RFC 2015*—MIME Security with Pretty Good Privacy

PGP has two RFCs. Although RFC 1991 is only informational, RFC 2015 is a Proposed Standard. However, RFC 2015 has not been well accepted and there are questions about its adoption as a Standard. At the same time, the IETF OpenPGP Working Group is working on a standards track protocol (RFC 2440) that may have better prospects for adoption.

At present, most of the big players are endorsing S/MIME. Only time will tell, however, which of these two approaches will be the long-term winner.

LDAP

Most data in a directory is not particularly sensitive. If we are looking up people's E-mail addresses, the server doesn't care who we are or whether anyone is intercepting our request. However, LDAP directories are being increasingly used as distributed databases holding a variety of types of information. Security is therefore becoming more important.

Some possible misuses of a directory include:

- Intercepting sensitive data between client and server
- Monitoring client authentication and impersonating the client to access data
- Impersonating the server to gain authentication information from the client
- Impersonating the server to provide the client with false information

These and other security risks are currently being addressed by the IETF. There are presently draft specifications (see Web site at http://www.ietf.org/internet-drafts/) but eventually you can expect a revision to LDAP or an additional standard outlining a secure LDAP implementation.

IMAP/POP

While there are already secure means of authentication for both IMAP and POP, the current effort is to bring these in line with the Internet standard. There are currently drafts in progress specifying a means of incorporating TLS (Transport Layer Security) into both protocols.

GroupWare

We need only look at the major mail systems of today (e.g., Lotus Notes, Microsoft Exchange) to note that E-mail is inextricably entwined with other GroupWare functions. While the initial focus of the standards has been on mail, there has been a recent push to standardize the interfaces to other GroupWare functions as well.

Electronic Business Cards

Versit (a consortium including Apple Computer, IBM Corporation, Lucent Technologies, and Siemens) laid the groundwork for an electronic form of the ubiquitous business card. In 1996 they joined the Internet Mail Consortium (IMC)[1] and transferred the rights to their specifications.

These electronic cards, called vCards, can carry personal information including name, addresses, telephone numbers, E-mail addresses, and Internet URLs. The data can be text in any language, pictures as well as audio, and even multimedia clips. All this information is included in standard vCard format as a MIME bodypart. Mail clients that are vCard-aware recognize the MIME content-type and are able to add the contact information to the recipient's personal information manager.

The vCard has now been released as an IETF specification and includes two parts:

- *RFC 2425—MIME Content-Type for Directory Information*
- *RFC 2426—vCard MIME Directory Profile*

Cross-Platform Scheduling

Versit also developed a specification called vCalendar to exchange calendaring and scheduling information across platforms, thus facilitating tasks such as

---

[1] http://www.imc.org/pdi

- Meeting Schedule
- Project Management
- Event Planning
- Delegation of Tasks and Action Items

Similar to vCard, vCalendar also packages these items as MIME bodyparts. The receiver's mail client recognizes the items and offers the user the possibility of accepting the task or appointment. Once accepted, the local calendar is updated and a response may be sent.

The specifications have been extended, renamed (to iCalendar), and submitted to the IETF.

- *RFC 2445—iCalendar—Internet Calendaring and Scheduling Core Object Specification*
- *RFC 2446—iTIP—iCalendar Transport Independent Interoperability Protocol: Scheduling Events, BusyTime To-Dos, and Journal Entries*
- *RFC 2447—iMIP—iCalendar Message-based Interoperability Protocol*

Workflow

Workflow is still a technology in development. Many business applications have been automated with it. Yet there are no fixed approaches that have been proven to be optimal. This makes it difficult to standardize its encoding.

The most extensive work in the area of standardization has been on the part of the Workflow Management Coalition.[2] They have published several documents on the subject. One of the more interesting in the context of E-mail is Interface 4 (WFMC-TC-1018) "*Internet E-mail MIME Binding,*" which specifies how to store Workflow objects inside a MIME message.

---

[2] http://www.aiim.org/wfmc

Appendix A

Library Functions

The Winsock routines are quite complete as they are. In order to use them with Visual Basic you need to have the following:

- The Winsock DLL (Wsock32.DLL is provided with Windows 95, Windows 98, Windows NT, and Windows 2000).
- All the Winsock routine declarations. The usual place to start is wsksock.bas (use your favorite Internet search engine to locate one of the many versions available for downloading).

Additionally, I have added a thin layer on top of the Winsock routines that, in my opinion, makes them easier to use—particularly for illustration, testing, and debugging.

Monitoring Dialog

One feature I have added is to display all the inbound and outbound data on all the sockets I have open. I have found this quite valuable in debugging my code, so I have included it with my source files. In Figure A.1 you can see an example: [52—>] signifies outbound data from socket 52; [—>52] means data inbound to socket 52.

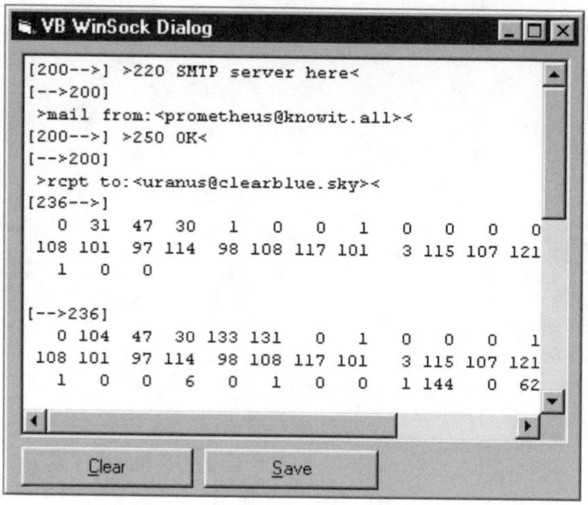

Figure A.1 *Monitoring the connection*

```
Sub DialogPrint(ByVal PrintPrefix As String, _
        ByVal PrintText As String)

    Dim strDialogText As String
    Dim strPrintLine As String

    strDialogText = frmVBWinSockDialog!txtDialog.Text

    strPrintLine = PrintPrefix + " " + Trim$(PrintText)

    If Right(strPrintLine, 2) <> CRLF Then
        strPrintLine = strPrintLine + CRLF
    End If

    strDialogText = strDialogText + strPrintLine
    frmVBWinSockDialog!txtDialog.Text = strDialogText
    frmVBWinSockDialog!txtDialog.Refresh
End Sub
```

Listing A.1 *Logging the dialog*

Error Checking

While I have not included much error-checking in the examples, it is clearly something that needs to go into production code, and sometimes even prototyping is easier with a few checks. I have a few functions in Listing A.2. *SocketError* simply maps a numeric routine code to a human readable string. *LastSocketError* calls Winsock to retrieve the last error condition.

```
Function SocketError(ErrorCode) As String

 Select Case ErrorCode
  Case 0:    SocketError = "OK"
  Case 10004: SocketError = "WSAEINTR"
  Case 10009: SocketError = "WSAEBADF"
  Case 10013: SocketError = "WSAEACCES"
  ...
  Case Else
    SocketError = "UNKNOWN ERROR CODE" + Str$(ErrorCode)
 End Select
End Function
Function LastSocketError() As String
 Status = WSAGetLastError()
 LastSocketError = SocketError(Status)
End Function
Sub DebugLastError(Action As String)
 Debug.Print "Error during " + Action + ": " + LastSocketError
End Sub
```

Listing A.2 *Error-Trapping Routines*

DebugLastError is the procedure I usually call. It prints the last error message to the immediate Window. You could easily modify it to print to a log file or display the message to a console.

Wrapping Socket Calls

The rest of my functions are primarily wrapper functions. They call the associated Winsock routines and do some additional work like displaying to the dialog window and performing some simple error-trapping.

Listing A.3 shows an initialization routine. Other than initializing Winsock (*WSAStartup*) it ensures that the Dialog form is displayed.

```
Type WSADataType
 wVersion As Integer
 wHighVersion As Integer
 szDescription As String * 257
 szSystemStatus As String * 129
 iMaxSockets As Integer
 iMaxUdpDg As Integer
 lpVendorInfo As String * 200
End Type
Global WSAData As WSADataType

Function StartWinSock()

 Dim intRequestedVersion As Integer

 frmVBWinSockDialog.Show

 intRequestedVersion = &H101
 Status = WSAStartup(intRequestedVersion, WSAData)

 If Status Then
  DebugLastError "WinSock startup "
  StartWinSock = False
  Exit Function
 End If

 StartWinSock = True
End Function
```

Listing A.3 *Starting Winsock*

Listing A.4 shows my socket creation. It encloses two Winsock routines (socket and bind). While you might conceivably want to call one without the other, I always call them both together.

```
Function CreateSocket(TCPSocket As Long, ByVal TCPPort As Long)

 TCPSocket = socket(PF_INET, SOCK_STREAM, AF_UNSPEC)
 If TCPSocket = INVALID_SOCKET Then
  DebugLastError "Creation of socket"
  CreateSocket = False
  Exit Function
 End If
 sitCallSocket.Family = AF_INET
 sitCallSocket.Port = htons(TCPPort)
```

```
sitCallSocket.Address = 0
sitCallSocket.Zero = " "

Status = bind(TCPSocket, sitCallSocket, Len(sitCallSocket))
If Status = SOCKET_ERROR Then
 DebugLastError "Bind of socket"
 CreateSocket = False
 Exit Function
End If


CreateSocket = True


End Function
```

Listing A.4 *Initializing the socket*

Note that we have to indicate that the family of socket is Internet (AF_INET) and specify which port we want (leaving it "0" if we don't care). We can leave the address (sin_addr) zero too, since Winsock doesn't need to know our own IP address.

Clients will call *ConnectSocket* to connect to the respective servers (Listing A.5). As with binding a socket, we need to indicate Internet family (AF_INTET) and the port, this time of the remote server. We also need to specify the Internet address of the server.

```
Function ConnectSocket(TCPSocket As Long, _
            HostAddress As Long, _
            ByVal TCPPort As Long)
 sitCallSocket.Family = AF_INET
 sitCallSocket.Port = htons(TCPPort)
 sitCallSocket.Address = HostAddress
 sitCallSocket.Zero = " "
 Status = connect(TCPSocket, sitCallSocket,Len(sitCallSocket))
 If Status = SOCKET_ERROR Then
  DebugLastError "Connecting socket"
  ConnectSocket = False
  Exit Function
 End If

 ConnectSocket = True

End Function
```

Listing A.5 *Connecting to remote port*

When sending data to a socket (Listing A.6), I first display it on the Dialog form. Then I call the send function to send it to the remote port. One feature of the send is that it does not necessarily send the whole data in one operation. To get around this I have a loop that checks the length and retries with the remaining data where applicable. I have added a final carriage return—a line feed to the Full before as a service to the caller. When sending ASCII commands these are traditionally terminated with a CRLF (carriage return line feed).

```
Function SendSocket(TCPSocket As Long, FullBuffer As String)
Dim strRemainingBuffer As String
Dim lngRemainingLength As Long

DialogPrint "[ " + Trim(Str(TCPSocket)) + "->]", FullBuffer

strRemainingBuffer = FullBuffer + CRLF

Do
  lngRemainingLength = Len(strRemainingBuffer)
  Status = send(TCPSocket, strRemainingBuffer, _
            lngRemainingLength, 0)
  If Status = SOCKET_ERROR Then
   DebugLastError "Send to socket " + Str(TCPSocket)
   SendSocket = False
   Exit Function
  ElseIf Status = lngRemainingLength Then
   SendSocket = True
   Exit Do
  Else
   strRemainingBuffer = Mid(strRemainingBuffer, Status + 1)
  End If
Loop

End Function
```

Listing A.6 *Sending data through the socket*

Receiving is the opposite of sending (Listing A.7). I call the *recv* from Winsock, truncate any final CRLF, and display the result to the dialog window.

```
Function ReceiveSocket(TCPSocket As Long, SocketResponse As String)
    'Now wait for the response from the server.
 SocketResponse = Space(4096)
 Status = recv(TCPSocket, SocketResponse, 4096, 0)

 SocketResponse = Trim(SocketResponse)
 If Right$(SocketResponse, 2) = Chr$(13) + Chr$(10) Then
  SocketResponse = Left$(SocketResponse, Len(SocketResponse) - 2)
 End If

 If Status = SOCKET_ERROR Then
  DebugLastError "Receive from socket " + Str(TCPSocket)
  ReceiveSocket = False
  Exit Function
 End If

 DialogPrint "[—>" + Trim$(Str$(TCPSocket)) + "] " + _
      CRLF, SocketResponse
 ReceiveSocket = True
End Function
```

Listing A.7 *Receiving from a socket*

To terminate the connection on a particular socket, we release it
with a call to *closesocket* (Listing A.8).

```
Function ReleaseSocket(TCPSocket As Long)
 Status = closesocket(TCPSocket)

 If Status = SOCKET_ERROR Then
  DebugLastError "Close of socket " & Str(TCPSocket)
  ReleaseSocket = False
  Exit Function
 End If

 ReleaseSocket = True
End Function
```

Listing A.8 *Terminating the connection*

Appendix B

Sample Code

In order to illustrate the protocols, I have written a number of applications. Since each one of them consists of multiple modules with numerous routines, you may sometimes find it easier to follow by looking at the content of the routine.

All of this code is available on the Internet (package name PTIM) at various hosts (e.g., www.winsite.com or www.download.com), so I would advise you to get the source and try to crossreference this text with it. For your added convenience, I have also included a listing of all the modules I use. Contact the author at john.rhoton@compaq.com with questions.

Each section in Appendix B represents a topic that corresponds to a subdirectory of the sample code. Within these I have listed the VB projects (left-most column), the modules (single indentation), and the routines/functions (double indentation). In the case of class modules, I also have a fourth column with the properties.

Please note that all code provided is purely intended for illustrative purposes. It is not suitable for production use nor is any part of it supported on any environment.

Common

This directory represents an exception to the format described above. It contains a collection of modules that are used by more than one application. Since it does not contain any applications per se, I have used the left column to indicate an arbitrary categorization of the modules.

General

Win32api.bas
VBWinSockDialog.frm
    btnSave_Click
VBWinSock.BAS
    ConnectSocket
    CreateSocket
    DebugLastError
    DialogPrint
    DialogPrintBinary
    GetIPAddress
    LastSocketError
    ReceiveSocket
    ReceiveSocketBinary
    ReleaseSocket
    SendSocket
    SendSocketBinary
    SocketError
    StartWinsock

RFC 822

RFC822Message.cls
    OpenFile
    Parse
    Compose

AddHeader
SpaceBegin
GetLine
NextLine
Properties:
> Lines
> Headers
> BodyLines

RFC822HeaderLine.cls
Parse
HeaderParameter
Properties:
> Label
> Value

MIME

MIMEMessage.cls
OpenFile
Parse
Compose
AddHeader
AddAttachment
SpaceBegin
GetLine
NextLine
Properties:
> Lines
> Headers
> BodyLines
> Attachments
> PreambleLines
> EpilogueLines

MIMEAttachment.cls
CallAttachment

SaveFile
DecodeBase64
Base64DecodeFoursome
Base64Index
DecodeQuotedPrintable
ReadFile
ReadFilePlainText
EncodeFileQuotedPrintable
EncodeFileBase64
Base64Encode
Base64Table
Properties:
    Filename
    Encoding
    Lines

DNS

DNSMessage.cls
ComposeQuestion
PackIntegerToString
FormatDomain
TransferString
ConvertStringToArray
Parse
GetDomain
GetByte
GetWord
GetLong
Properties:
    ID
    QR
    OPCODE
    AA

TC
RD
RA
Z
RCODE
QDCOUNT
ANCOUNT
NSCOUNT
ARCOUNT
Question
Answer
DNSQuestion.cls
Properties
QName
QType
QClass
DNSResourceRecord.cls
Properties:
RNAME
RTYPE
RCLASS
RTTL
RDATA
MXResourceData.cls
Properties:
Preference
Exchange

ASN

ASN.bas
ASNConstants.bas
ASN1.cls
Compose

Parse
Dump
Properties:
SubItemCount
SubItem
Complete
Tag
Length
TransferString

LDAP

LDAPConstants.bas

Generic Client

Generic Client (GenericClient.vbp)

frmGenericClient (GenericClient.frm)
Form_Load
btnConnect_Click
btnReceive_Click
btnSend_Click
btnQuit_Click
frmVBWinSockDialog (Common: VBWinSockDialog.frm)
Constant (Common: Constant.txt)
modVBWinSock (Common: VBWinSock.bas)

Generic Server

Generic Server (GenericServer.vbp)

frmGenericServer (GenericServer.frm)
Form_Load

btnListen_Click
btnAccept_Click
btnReceive_Click
btnSend_Click
btnQuit_Click
Form_Unload
frmVBWinSockDialog (Common: VBWinSockDialog.frm)
Constant (Common: Constant.txt)
modVBWinSock (Common: VBWinSock.bas)

Generic Asynchronous Server

GenericAsynchronousServer (GenericAsynchronousServer.vbp)

frmGenericAsynchronousServer (GenericAsynchronousServer.frm)
Form_Load
btnListen_Click
txtConnect_MouseUp
txtRequest_DblClick
txtDialog_KeyUp
cboConnection_Click
btnQuit_Click
Form_Unload
frmVBWinSockDialog (Common: VBWinSockDialog.frm)
Constant (Common: Constant.txt)
modVBWinSock (Common: VBWinSock.bas)

Generic Interceptor

GenericInterceptor (GenericInterceptor.vbp)

frmGenericInterceptor (GenericInterceptor.frm)
Form_Load
btnListen_Click

    txtListenClient_MouseDown
    txtReceiveServer_MouseDown
    txtReceiveClient_MouseDown
    PrintLogFile
    btnQuit_Click
    Form_Unload
frmVBWinSockDialog (Common: VBWinSockDialog.frm)
Constant (Common: Constant.txt)
modVBWinSock (Common: VBWinSock.bas)

RFC 822 Composer

ComposeRFC822Message (ComposeRFC822Message.vbp)

frmComposeRFC822Message (ComposeRFC822Message.frm)
    btnBrowse_Click
    btnSave_Click
Constant (Common: Constant.txt)
RFC822HeaderLine (Common: RFC822HeaderLine.cls)
RFC822Message (Common: RFC822Message.cls)

RFC 822 Reader

ReadRFC822Message (ReadRFC822Message.vbp)

frmReadRFC822Message (ReadRFC822Message.frm)
    Form_Load
    Form_Activate
    Form_Unload
modReadRFC822Message (ReadRFC822Message.bas)
    Main
Constant (Common: Constant.txt)
RFC822HeaderLine (Common: RFC822HeaderLine.cls)
RFC822Message (Common: RFC822Message.cls)

MIME Composer

ComposeMIMEMessage (ComposeMIMEMessage.vbp)

> frmComposeMIMEMessage (ComposeMIMEMessage.frm)
>> Form_Load
>> btnSave_Click
> Constant (Common: Constant.txt)
> RFC822HeaderLine (Common: RFC822HeaderLine.cls)
> MIMEMessage (Common: MIMEMessage.cls)
> MIMEAttachment (Common: MIMEAttachment.cls)

MIME Reader

ReadMIMEMessage (ReadMIMEMessage.vbp)

> frmReadMIMEMessage (ReadMIMEMessage.frm)
>> Form_Load
>> Form_Activate
>> Form_Unload
>> lstAttachmentList_DblClick
> modReadMIMEMessage (ReadMIMEMessage.bas)
>> Main
> Constant (Common: Constant.txt)
> RFC822HeaderLine (Common: RFC822HeaderLine.cls)
> MIMEMessage (Common: MIMEMessage.cls)
> MIMEAttachment (Common: MIMEAttachment.cls)

SMTP Client

SendSMTPFile (SendSMTPFile.vbp)

> frmSendSMTPFile (SendSMTPFile.frm)
>> Form_Load
>> btnDisplay_Click

    btnSend_Click
    btnQuit_Click
    Form_Unload
frmReadMIMEMessage (MIME Reader: ReadMIMEMessage.frm)
    modReadMIMEMessage (MIME Reader: ReadMIMEMessage.bas)
    Constant (Common: Constant.txt)
    modVBWinSock (Common: VBWinSock.bas)
    RFC822HeaderLine (Common: RFC822HeaderLine.cls)
    MIMEMessage (Common: MIMEMessage.cls)
    MIMEAttachment (Common: MIMEAttachment.cls)
SendSMTPMessage (SendSMTPMessage.vbp)
    frmSendSMTPMessage (SendSMTPMessage.frm)
        Form_Load
        btnSend_Click
        btnQuit_Click
        Form_Unload
    frmReadMIMEMessage (MIME Reader: ReadMIMEMessage.frm)
    modReadMIMEMessage (MIME Reader: ReadMIMEMessage.bas)
    Constant (Common: Constant.txt)
    modVBWinSock (Common: VBWinSock.bas)
    RFC822HeaderLine (Common: RFC822HeaderLine.cls)
    MIMEMessage (Common: MIMEMessage.cls)
    MIMEAttachment (Common: MIMEAttachment.cls)

SMTP Server

SMTPServer (SMTPServer.vbp)

    frmSMTPServer (SMTPServer.frm)
        Form_Load
        txtConnect_MouseUp
        txtRequest_DblClick
        ReceiveMessage
        RandomName
        cboConnection_Click

btnQuit_Click

Form_Unload

frmVBWinSockDialog (Common: VBWinSockDialog.frm)

Constant (Common: Constant.txt)

modVBWinSock (Common: VBWinSock.bas)

DNS Client

DNSClient (DNSClient.vbp)

frmDNSClient (DNSClient.frm)

Form_Load

btnLookup_Click

btnQuit_Click

Form_Unload

DNSMessage (Common: DNSMessage.cls)

DNSQuestion (Common: DNSQuestion.cls)

DNSResourceRecord (Common: DNSResourceRecord.cls)

MXResourceData (Common: MXResourceData.cls)

frmVBWinSockDialog (Common: VBWinSockDialog.frm)

Constant (Common: Constant.txt)

modVBWinSock (Common: VBWinSock.bas)

SMTP Relay

SMTPServer (SMTPServer.vbp)

frmSMTPServer (SMTPServer.frm)

Form_Load

txtConnect_MouseUp

txtRequest_DblClick

FormatUser

LookupDomain

ConnectNextRelay

RelayMessage
RandomName
cboConnection_Click
btnQuit_Click
Form_Unload
DNSMessage (Common: DNSMessage.cls)
DNSQuestion (Common: DNSQuestion.cls)
DNSResourceRecord (Common: DNSResourceRecord.cls)
MXResourceData (Common: MXResourceData.cls)
frmVBWinSockDialog (Common: VBWinSockDialog.frm)
Constant (Common: Constant.txt)

POP Client

DownloadPOPMessage (DownloadPOPMessage.vbp)

frm DownloadPOPMessage (DownloadPOPMessage.frm)
Form_Load
btnDownload_Click
ExtractMessage
Form_Unload
frmVBWinSockDialog (Common: VBWinSockDialog.frm)
Constant (Common: Constant.txt)
modVBWinSock (Common: VBWinSock.bas)

GetPOPMessage (GetPOPMessage.vbp)

frmGetPOPMessage (GetPOPMessage.frm)
Form_Load
btnConnect_Click
btnExtract_Click
btnShow_Click
btnDelete_Click
btnQuit_Click
Form_Unload

frmReadMIMEMEssages (MIME Reader: ReadMIMEMessages.frm)
frmVBWinSockDialog (Common: VBWinSockDialog.frm)
Constant (Common: Constant.txt)
modVBWinSock (Common: VBWinSock.bas)
RFC822HeaderLine (Common: RFC822HeaderLine.cls)
MIMEMessage (Common: MIMEMessage.cls)
MIMEAttachment (Common: MIMEAttachment.cls)

POP Server

POPServer (POPServer.vbp)

POPServer (POPServer.frm)
    Form_Load
    txtConnect_MouseUp
    txtRequest_DblClick
    LoadUserFiles
    ListMessages
    RetrieveMessage
    DeleteMessage
    cboConnection_Click
    Form_Unload
frmVBWinSockDialog (Common: VBWinSockDialog.frm)
Constant (Common: Constant.txt)
modVBWinSock (Common: VBWinSock.bas)

IMAP Client

ViewIMAPMessages (ViewIMAPMessages.vbp)

frmViewIMAPMessages (ViewIMAPMessages.frm)
    Form_Activate
    Form_Load
    btnConnect_Click
    lstFolderList_DblClick

btnCreateFolder_Click
btnDeleteFolder_Click
btnSubscribeFolder_Click
btnUnsubscribeFolder_Click
chkShowAllFolders_Click
btnExtract_Click
btnShow_Click
btnDelete_Click
btnCopy_Click
ListFolders
btnQuit_Click
Form_Unload
NextIndex
CurrentIndex
GetToken
frmReadMIMEMEssages (MIME Reader: ReadMIMEMessages.frm)
frmVBWinSockDialog (Common: VBWinSockDialog.frm)
Constant (Common: Constant.txt)
modVBWinSock (Common: VBWinSock.bas)
RFC822HeaderLine (Common: RFC822HeaderLine.cls)
MIMEMessage (Common: MIMEMessage.cls)
MIMEAttachment (Common: MIMEAttachment.cls)

IMAP Server

IMAPServer (IMAPServer.vbp)

IMAPServer (IMAPServer.frm)
Form_Load
txtConnect_MouseUp
txtRequest_DblClick
LoadUser
LoadSubfolders
ListFolders
LoadFolder

        FetchMessageRange
        FetchMessage
        GetToken
        DoubleBackslashes
        cboConnection_Click
        Form_Unload
    frmVBWinSockDialog (Common: VBWinSockDialog.frm)
    Constant (Common: Constant.txt)
    modVBWinSock (Common: VBWinSock.bas)

ASN Composer

ASNComposer (ASNComposer.vbp)

    frmASNComposer (ASNComposer.frm)
        Form_Load
        btnAdd_Click
        btnDelete_Click
        btnUpdate_Click
        RefreshForm
        FillArray
        GetDepth
        btnSave_Click
    Constant (Common: Constant.txt)
    ASNConstants (Common: ASNConstants.bas)
    ASN1 (Common: ASN1.cls)

ASN Reader

ASNComposer (ASNComposer.vbp)

    frmASNComposer (ASNComposer.frm)
        btnRead_Click
        RefreshForm
    Constant (Common: Constant.txt)

ASNConstants (Common: ASNConstants.bas)
ASN1 (Common: ASN1.cls)

LDAP Client

LDAPClient (LDAPClient.vbp)

frmLDAPClient (LDAPClient.frm)
    Form_Load
    btnSearch_Click
    SendBindRequest
    SendSearchRequest
    SendUnbindRequest
    ShowMatch
    lstMatches_Click
    Form_Unload
frmVBWinSockDialog (Common: VBWinSockDialog.frm)
Constant (Common: Constant.txt)
modVBWinSock (Common: VBWinSock.bas)
ASNConstants (Common: ASNConstants.bas)
ASN1 (Common: ASN1.cls)
LDAPConstants (LDAPConstants.bas)
LDAPFilter (Common: LDAPFilter.cls)

LDAP Server

LDAPServer (LDAPServer.vbp)

frmLDAPServer (LDAPServer.frm)
    Form_Load
    txtConnect_MouseUp
    txtRequest_DblClick
    ProcessBindRequest
    ProcessSearchRequest

FindAttribute
MatchFilter
MatchAttributes
ComposeResponseEntry
cboConnection_Click
btnQuit_Click
Form_Unload
frmVBWinSockDialog (Common: VBWinSockDialog.frm)
Constant (Common: Constant.txt)
modVBWinSock (Common: VBWinSock.bas)
ASNConstants (Common: ASNConstants.bas)
ASN1 (Common: ASN1.cls)
LDAPConstants (LDAPConstants.bas)
LDAPFilter (Common: LDAPFilter.cls)

Integrated Client

InternetMailClient (InternetMailClient.vbp)

frmSendSMTPMessage (SendSMTPMessage.frm)
Form_Load
btnSend_Click
btnQuit_Click
Form_Unload
frmLDAPClient (LDAPClient.frm)
Form_Load
btnSearch_Click
SendBindRequest
SendSearchRequest
SendUnbindRequest
ShowMatch
lstMatches_Click
Form_Unload
frmViewIMAPMessages (ViewIMAPMessages.frm)
Form_Activate

Form_Load

btnConnect_Click

lstFolderList_DblClick

btnCreateFolder_Click

btnDeleteFolder_Click

btnSubscribeFolder_Click

btnUnsubscribeFolder_Click

chkShowAllFolders_Click

btnExtract_Click

btnShow_Click

btnDelete_Click

btnCopy_Click

ListFolders

btnQuit_Click

Form_Unload

NextIndex

CurrentIndex

GetToken

frmReadMIMEMessage (MIME Reader: ReadMIMEMessage.frm)

Constant (Common: Constant.txt)

modVBWinSock (Common: VBWinSock.bas)

frmVBWinSockDialog (Common: VBWinSockDialog.frm)

RFC822HeaderLine (Common: RFC822HeaderLine.cls)

MIMEMessage (Common: MIMEMessage.cls)

MIMEAttachment (Common: MIMEAttachment.cls)

ASNConstants (Common: ASNConstants.bas)

ASN1 (Common: ASN1.cls)

LDAPConstants (LDAPConstants.bas)

LDAPFilter (Common: LDAPFilter.cls)

Index